Post-Tenure Faculty Review and Renewal III

Post-Tenure Faculty Review and Renewal III

Outcomes and Impact

CHRISTINE M. LICATA
Rochester Institute of Technology/
National Technical Institute for the Deaf

JOSEPH C. MORREALE
Pace University

With special contribution by Estela Mara Bensimon

Published in association with the American
Association for Higher Education

ANKER PUBLISHING COMPANY, INC.
Bolton, Massachusetts

Post-Tenure Faculty Review and Renewal III
Outcomes and Impact

ISBN 1-882982-90-8

Composition by Lyn Rodger, Deerfoot Studios
Cover design by Freedom by Design

Anker Publishing Company, Inc.
563 Main Street
P.O. Box 249
Bolton, MA 01740-0249 USA

www.ankerpub.com

This volume is dedicated to our soul mates and life mates:

Barry R. Culhane
and
Barbara L. McAdorey

Their encouragement, patience, and humor
powered our sails during this
three-year voyage.

About the Authors

CHRISTINE M. LICATA is associate vice president for academic affairs at the National Technical Institute for the Deaf at Rochester Institute of Technology, where she is responsible for curriculum development, program review, faculty affairs, institutional support services, research, and faculty development. From 1998–2004, she served as a senior associate with the American Association for Higher Education (AAHE) in its New Pathways Project "Academic Careers for the Next Century." Responsibilities at AAHE included leadership and direction for all activities related to post-tenure review, including oversight of a post-tenure review mini-grant program where she worked with 35 institutions on the implementation and refinement of post-tenure review practices. She also directed a nine-campus study on the outcomes and impact of post-tenure review on which this volume is based. She has investigated post-tenure evaluation practices since 1984 and authored one of the first national reports on the topic, *Post-Tenure Faculty Evaluation: Threat or Opportunity?* (a 1986 ASHE-ERIC Higher Education Report). During 1998–2001, she worked with the Harvard Project on Faculty Appointments as an adviser and analyst on post-tenure review issues. She is coauthor with Joseph Morreale of *Post-Tenure Review: Policies, Practices, Precautions* (AAHE New Pathways Working Paper No. 12, 1997) and co-edited with Morreale *Post-Tenure Faculty Review and Renewal: Experienced Voices* (AAHE, 2002) and with Betsy E. Brown *Post-Tenure Faculty Review and Renewal II: Reporting Results and Shaping Policy* (AAHE and Anker, 2004). Together with Hans A. Andrews, she has studied post-tenure review policies within community colleges and coauthored *The State of Post-Tenure and Long-Term Faculty Evaluation* (American Association of Community Colleges Research Brief, 2002). She has consulted with more than 100 colleges and universities over the past five years and has written and presented extensively on this topic.

JOSEPH C. MORREALE is provost and vice president for academic affairs at Pace University. He has more than 35 years of experience in higher education and is a full professor with tenure in economics and public administration. He was awarded an American Council on Education Administrative Fellowship (1995–1996) and was a Harvard Administrative Fellow in the Harvard Summer Institute on Educational Management for senior administrators in the summer of 2000. His publications include four books and numerous articles in scholarly journals. Dr. Morreale has been the keynote speaker at a number of conferences and has presented several papers at the national meetings of such organizations as the American Association for Higher Education (AAHE), the Association to

Advance Collegiate Schools of Business (AACSB), the American Council on Education (ACE), and the Coalition of Urban and Metropolitan Universities (CUMU). As an AAHE senior scholar for the past six years, he is recognized nationally for leadership in higher education administration and has published on post-tenure review, faculty development, and senior faculty renewal.

Table of Contents

Note to Our Readers

Our research of eight public four-year institutions and one professional school serves as the primary basis for this volume on the outcomes and impact of post-tenure review. We also used our collective experience in the field as a check and balance for this work. We hope our readers will not rush to judgment or jump to conclusions too quickly in reviewing our results and findings.

We organized our field work, and thus this volume, around two basic premises:

- *Premise 1:* Practitioners want to know if post-tenure review leads to tangible outcomes and, if yes, what factors influence positive outcomes. If no, what factors influence negative outcomes.

- *Premise 2:* Practitioners want more than dry research results. They want different interpretations of data and invigorating ways to think about how to use findings to create more effective programs of post-tenure review.

Assuming these premises hold true for our readers, this volume responds to each. Before you begin this book, we'd like you to anticipate the following.

After you've completed Chapters 1 through 5, you may say to yourself, "Well, there sure don't seem to be many positive outcomes from post-tenure review." You might even want to dismiss the remainder of the book because you think you know how the story ends. We urge you to reconsider that decision. In fact, if you don't make it to Chapters 6, 7, and 8, you'll miss the most useful and thought provoking part of this story—the part that challenges you to consider a different set of questions and actions and helps you write a concluding chapter for your own institution with respect to post-tenure review.

So while Chapters 1 through 5 are filled with important data and local color, all directed at describing the outcomes of post-tenure review and factors contributing to those outcomes, Chapters 6, 7, and 8 focus on ideas, perspectives, and research findings that take aim at a very practical question: Can post-tenure review be designed to create a sustainable process for institutional change and renewal?

We hope you'll read this book to its conclusion. If we are to be successful as research practitioners, our "end" should lead to your "beginning," recognizing as we all do that

> We don't receive wisdom; we must discover it for ourselves after a journey that no one can take for us or spare us.
>
> —Marcel Proust

Preface

For several decades, tenured American faculty have provided the intellectual groundwork on which much of the promise of the oft-touted knowledge-based society has been built internationally. In this country, however, a major cultural strain has developed, resulting in a mixture of admiration for this achievement, resentment, dependence, and disdain for the tenured professor. In the outcomes-based, performance-driven, results-oriented work environment emerging in the larger society, tenure has become an anomaly.

It was in this atmosphere that the focus on post-tenure review became a national concern—off campus and on—and the extensive inquiry resulting in the three-volume series on *Post-Tenure Faculty Review and Renewal* was launched. We are now at the end of a long journey. This third publication in the series brings this ambitious project to completion. The spirited debate over post-tenure review has lost some of its intensity, but by now the review of the work of senior faculty who have been awarded tenure has become an established practice in most colleges and universities and is in the process of being permanently institutionalized. These three volumes will serve for years to come as the most authoritative resource available on the purposes and practices of the review of post-tenured faculty.

The faculty role is now going through a major transition. Alternatives to the traditional tenure-track appointment are being experimented with and widely accepted. A generational shift in the constitution of the faculty is moving ahead with a vengeance. Older, senior professors are retiring in large numbers and are being replaced by faculty members who are not only younger but dramatically more diverse. Technological innovations are transforming the way faculty communicate and think; their teaching and research—the way they go about their everyday lives—are being changed. The walls of the college and university are becoming more permeable; the generation of knowledge is no longer the primary purview of tenured academics. In this rapidly shifting environment, the tenured professor will continue to survive as a fundamental building block of established academic institutions, although on a much more limited basis. For a core set of faculty tenure will continue to be awarded, but in the future—and this is another significant change—tenure will seldom be granted without the expectation of some form of post-tenure review.

This three-volume series on *Post-Tenure Review and Renewal* is the culmination of a much larger initiative launched by the American Association for Higher Education (AAHE). In 1992, AAHE joined the growing national debate about the discrepancy between faculty priorities and institutional mission by establishing the Forum on Faculty Roles and Rewards. In the mid-1990s, tenure and the discussion of alternative career paths for faculty emerged as a major concern and the subject of widespread media attention. In response, the forum initiated a special line of work under the title "New Pathways: Academic Careers for the 21st Century," with the generous support of The Atlantic Philanthropies and an anonymous donor. Fourteen different dimensions of faculty work were selected for examination, leading to the publication of the New Pathways Working Papers. Out of the vigorous debate—and considerable controversy—generated by this work, we chose to target those issues that serve as special leverage points in the academic career, issues having both the potential for contributing to the vitality of individual faculty careers, while also providing institutions with the flexibility needed to respond to the monumental press for adaptive change.

As we moved from inquiry to practice in the more applied phase of the New Pathways Project, we chose to build on the extraordinary work of Christine Licata and Joseph Morreale. Their initial study of post-tenure review (New Pathways Working Paper No. 12) convinced us that despite the enormous changes taking place in the academic career, maintaining the vitality of senior, tenured faculty would remain a critical challenge, and that post-tenure review could be a faculty development opportunity that has been largely ignored. In addition to post-tenure review being a promising response to the incessant call for accountability, Licata and Morreale also underscored its potential for being an occasion for serious career planning within a changing institutional context.

Volume I of this trilogy—subtitled *Experienced Voices*—draws on the rich experience of those leading the way in post-tenure review. Insights gleaned from the efforts to develop, adopt, and implement effective programs at both individual institutions and whole state systems are candidly presented. Lessons learned from departments, chairs, and individual faculty going through the experience are shared. Two of the chapters, "Post-Tenure Review in the Oregon University System" by Shirley Clark, and "Using Post-Tenure Review to Create an Intentional Future" by William M. Plater, will be cited in years to come by those serious about maintaining the vitality of senior academic staff and searching for ways of improving the integration of faculty priorities and institutional mission. Christine Licata and Joseph Morreale, editors of the first volume, draw on their rich experience in bringing these diverse perspectives together, placing the issue within its broader national context.

The second volume in this series, *Post-Tenure Faculty Review and Renewal II: Reporting Results and Shaping Policy*, focuses on how data about post-tenure review are gathered and presented. For those seriously interested in implementing post-tenure review programs, this is not a trivial matter. The editors of this volume, Licata, with her extensive national experience, and Betsy E. Brown, who has worked closely with faculties in two state systems in implementing post-tenure review, are extraordinarily savvy about the way the gathering of data and its presentation can influence policy implementation and understanding. When and how to use quantitative, qualitative, comparative, and anecdotal data can have a profound impact on how both internal and external constituencies understand the meaning and usefulness of post-tenure review. The effectiveness of post-tenure review programs—at both the individual institutional level and through state systems—often pivots on how the questions addressed in this volume are answered.

This culminating third volume focuses on the outcomes and impact of post-tenure review. American higher education has invested substantial time and resources in the review of tenured faculty, and now we have evidence we can use in assessing its significance over time. Having participated in gathering the data on two campuses, I have looked forward to this comprehensive overview—no where else is it available.

This data-based story exposes some misleading stereotypes surrounding the review of senior faculty work. The widespread "faculty bashing" that accompanied—and often drove—the early legislative demand for post-tenure review cannot be substantiated. Most faculty—including the senior tenured faculty—want an ongoing evaluation system of post-tenured professors that is fair, meaningful, acknowledges their achievements, and has consequences. They recognize that holding accountable all academic staff is imperative. A stereotype that faculty often evoke is that the primary purpose of post-tenure review is punitive—externally imposed. That it can be, in fact, an opportunity for faculty to share their accomplishments with colleagues, improve their performance, and integrate their academic work more fully into the lives and needs of their institutions is more often the case.

In this overview, the mistakes that have been made in establishing post-tenure review are not masked, but addressed at length. Strategies for avoiding these pitfalls are presented. The recommendations in Chapter 8 are "must reading" for those developing performance review policies and faculty development programs for future academic staff.

The American professoriate is entering a new era in which accountability will be expected of everyone. New kinds of faculty development programs that encompass effective opportunities for ongoing career planning and advancement will be required. The resources needed to support these efforts will be imperative. This volume will provide enormous assistance in planning for this future.

Christine Licata and Joseph Morreale have brought to this project on post-tenure review an extraordinary commitment and tenacity. They, along with most of their associates in the project, have moved on to assume major positions of academic leadership. What they have learned from this journey through the often rough terrain of post-tenure review will enhance their understanding of faculty and the changing academic career and contribute to their already exceptional talents as academic leaders. I wish them well and thank them for their fine work, professional sensibility, and for being such good colleagues and friends throughout the whole process. Everyone concerned with the future of faculty roles, responsibilities, and rewards will benefit greatly from consulting this record of their journey.

R. Eugene Rice, Ph.D.
Senior Scholar, Antioch Ph.D. Program in Leadership and Change
Former Director of the Forum on Faculty Roles and Rewards and the New Pathways Projects, American Association for Higher Education
February 2005

Acknowledgments

Our work together on post-tenure review began in 1996 when we joined forces to collaborate with the American Association for Higher Education (AAHE) on the New Pathways II initiatives. This has been a fruitful and dynamic union. We are grateful to R. Eugene Rice for recognizing the need to include post-tenure review in the array of New Pathways topics, for being an engaged scholar with us, and for consistently providing us with enthusiastic encouragement. We also thank The Atlantic Philanthropies and an anonymous donor for their generous support of these efforts. Without them, this project could not have taken flight.

We are indebted to our dedicated and talented research team who helped us conduct campus site visits and prepare the campus case study reports. Team members included Estela Mara Bensimon, Professor of Higher Education, Rossier School of Education, University of Southern California; R. Eugene Rice, AAHE Senior Scholar; and Susan B. Foster, Research Professor, Rochester Institute of Technology/National Technical Institute for the Deaf. We also wish to acknowledge the outstanding work of our statistician, Jeffrey A. Jolton, Ph.D., Senior Consultant, Genesee Survey Services, who generated all of our statistical analyses, and the two graduate students from the University of Southern California, Georgia Bauman and Lisa Patriquin, who assisted with analysis of two case studies.

We are grateful to Jane Hamblin, former Director of Publications at AAHE, and Carolyn Dumore, Managing Editor at Anker Publishing Company, for their counsel, advice, and help with the many editing and design details.

A special note of appreciation to Jim and Susan Anker, who saw the value of our work and agreed to copublish with AAHE and market this volume along with the previous two volumes.

Our home campus support staff provided exceptional administrative assistance: Sydney Long, Kelli McIntee-Shaw, and Susan Miller at Rochester Institute of Technology/National Technical Institute for the Deaf and Eleanor Fein at Pace University.

Our CEOs recognized the importance of our work. These leaders, visionaries in their own right, let us know that this scholarship was important and gave us unconditional support for it: Albert J. Simone, President, Rochester Institute of Technology; David A. Caputo, President, Pace University; and Patricia D. Ewers, President Emeritus, Pace University.

We also wish to thank T. Alan Hurwitz, James J. DeCaro, Stanley D. McKenzie, and Marilyn Jaffe-Ruiz for their early and sustained endorsement of our involvement with AAHE's New Pathways Project.

During the course of this research project, we worked with nine institutional liaisons. While we cannot disclose their names, we want to thank them for their engagement with us and for facilitating the large and small details associated with our institutional site visit, survey administration, and summary report. These individuals joined us for two days in Washington, DC, in November 1998 and helped us develop our interview and survey protocols. They were partners with us every step of the way and their counsel kept the project focused on the issues that mattered to practitioners.

We also had the privilege of interviewing tenured faculty members, department chairs, deans, and senior-level administrators—430 in all. These professionals gave generously of their time and were forthright in their responses to our questions. Together with the 1,600 faculty who responded to our survey, these individuals represent the voices that formed the chorus for this research. They generated the opinions about post-tenure review that created the score for this work. In a real sense, these 2,000 individuals are the ghost writers of this volume. We thank them and hope we've represented their views accurately and fairly. Our pen was strongly propelled by the perspectives they shared.

We also want to thank the chief academic officers at our nine case study institutions. These leaders were undaunting in their support of this project. They allowed their institutions' successes and shortcomings with post-tenure review to become public; they wisely knew that the field "needed to know."

Christine M. Licata
Rochester Institute of Technology
National Technical Institute of the Deaf
Rochester, NY

Joseph C. Morreale
Office of Academic Affairs
Pace University
New York, NY

December 2004

Introduction

Regular performance evaluation of tenured faculty, usually referred to as post-tenure review, is now a part of the policy landscape at most public colleges and universities in the United States. This trend is also gaining momentum in private higher education. While such review practices are becoming commonplace, systematic analysis of results and impact has been almost nonexistent. This volume brings together the findings from nine different institutional case studies, focusing on the effectiveness and outcomes of post-tenure review.

Undertaken by an American Association for Higher Education New Pathways II research team, this work represents the only national study to date that uses multiple methods of data collection to understand how campuses of differing size, mission, and culture experience the review process and describe its impact. This book provides the most comprehensive report on the outcomes of post-tenure review within senior-level institutions as reported by campus faculty and administrators.

When taken together with the two previous works, *Post-Tenure Faculty Review and Renewal: Experienced Voices* and *Post-Tenure Faculty Review and Renewal II: Reporting Results and Shaping Policy*, these three volumes offer a far-reaching examination of how post-tenure review policies are conceptualized, developed, implemented, tracked, and assessed. This book and its companion volumes allow practitioners, policymakers, and academic leaders to gain an understanding of the facets and issues associated with successfully conducting programs of post-tenure review.

Accountability and Faculty Performance: The Ties That Bind

> *Whether by trustees who feel compelled to direct faculty work by specifying how much teaching will occur and in what form, or by legislators who provide incentives for increased research productivity, faculty at all types of institutions are seeing their work held up for discussion and evaluation by people other than department chairs and deans.*
>
> —Plater, 2001, p. 57

Faculty across this country have been put on notice. The message is clear. Legislative and governing bodies don't really understand or appreciate why tenure is necessary. They want assurances—no, they want hard evidence—that tenure is not being used as a convenient excuse for keeping nonproductive faculty on the payroll and as a refuge for complacency.

In the early 1990s, attempts to dismantle tenure were unveiled in legislative chambers from Oregon to Massachusetts. While these efforts generally failed, the debate about accountability packed a powerful punch. As a result, a sea change occurred in how colleges and universities assess the performance of tenured faculty.

In exchange for keeping tenure intact, institution after institution developed procedures to review the productivity of tenured faculty and remediate poor performance—procedures fundamentally designed to guarantee that tenure expectations and institutional standards are effectively met. Normally referred to as post-tenure review, such practices are now a routine part of the evaluation culture in this country. In fact, public four-year colleges and universities in as many as thirty-seven states report the establishment of some additional form of review for tenured faculty (Licata & Morreale, 2002). Virtually all two-year community colleges with tenure systems and about half of private four-year institutions have also put such polices in place (Andrews, Licata, & Harris, 2002; Licata & Schuyler, 2002). In the public sector, there is little reported difference in the presence of post-tenure review by various Carnegie classifications (Aper & Fry, 2003). In the private sector, however, comprehensive (master's) institutions lead the way in policy adoption, while research institutions report the least amount of implementation (Aper & Fry, 2003; Licata & Schuyler, 2002).

For most American colleges and universities, what sets post-tenure review apart from longstanding review practices used to make decisions regarding salary and promotion is the expressed intent that post-tenure review go well beyond such traditional procedures. In today's climate, post-tenure review is usually defined as a systematic process aimed specifically at assessing performance and/or nurturing faculty growth and development. Generally, it is an extension of the annual review.

Supporters of post-tenure review assert that it helps preserve tenure, achieves accountability, remedies poor performance, promotes faculty career planning, encourages self-renewal, and ties institutional mission to individual performance (Andrews & Licata, 1991; Bennett & Chater, 1984; Edwards, 1994; Goodman, 1994; Hollander, 1992; Licata, 1998; Licata & Morreale, 1997, 2002; Plater, 2001; Tierney, 1997). Opponents, on the other hand, maintain that traditional evaluation practices are sufficient, that the additional costs in time and oversight are burdensome, and that the process threatens tenure, academic freedom, and collegiality (Alstete, 2000; American Association of University Professors, 1983, 1998; Bennett & Chater, 1984; Edwards, 1997; Tierney, 1997). Controversy almost always surrounds efforts to establish campus post-tenure review policies and attempts to revise existing procedures, particularly if policies are stimulated by external pressure.

Even though post-tenure review practices are now fairly widespread in this country, there has been very little disclosure about actual results or any field-based information describing the impact these policies have on faculty performance and career development.

National interest in measuring outcomes makes uncovering the impact these reviews have on institutions and individual faculty members extremely important. Because most post-tenure review policies are less than 10 years old, answers based on collective experience have been difficult to gather. In fact, the majority of the literature on this topic is confined to supporting or opposing establishment of these reviews (Andrews & Licata, 1991; Bennett & Chater, 1984; Edwards, 1994; Goodman, 1994; Hollander, 1992; Perry, 1983; Portch, Kaufman, & Ross, 1993); discussions about the practical aspects of implementation (Licata, 1999; Licata & Morreale, 2002); and suggested models for tracking and reporting results (Licata & Brown, 2004). Little has been documented concerning the actual results of these reviews on individual and institutional performance.

One educational journalist concluded that opinions about results depend on whom you ask. Reported faculty experiences ran the gamut from claims that the review helped professors get back on track and renew professional interests to condemnations that the review did more harm than good and promoted fluff over substance (Montell, 2002). Another journalist reported that the process as practiced within the nation's eighth largest private institution (Rochester Institute of Technology) was effective in providing positive results and was supported by the faculty and administration (Fogg, 2003). Both of these accounts are based only on a handful of institutions and generalizability is limited. Because empirical evidence is lacking, it is unclear whether post-tenure review is delivering on the promises its advocates advance or is undermining academic traditions as opponents warn.

NATIONAL STUDY: POST-TENURE REVIEW OUTCOMES

Recognizing the need to systematically study the effects of post-tenure review, the American Association for Higher Education (AAHE), through its New Pathways II Project (1998–2001), undertook a two and one-half year study that specifically examined post-tenure review outcomes. This AAHE probe centered on three overarching questions:

- Is post-tenure review working to achieve the institution's stated objectives?

- What impact does post-tenure review have on the professional contributions and careers of faculty?

- Does post-tenure review help advance departmental goals and institutional mission?

Understanding that post-tenure review is controversial, this study was designed to document perceptions and experiences from a cross section of faculty and administrators within differing institutional settings. In order to construct grassroots explanations about the impact and outcomes, our research sprang from the direct experiences of faculty, department chairs, deans, and senior academic officers within the institutions under examination. A qualitative case study approach offered us the depth and scope we believed was necessary to enable beliefs, issues, patterns, and constraints to emerge. Part of this inquiry tried to determine what had already transpired on campuses during policy implementation. Another part tried to ascertain whether post-tenure review does, in fact, impact individuals and their academic units in a particular fashion. Most important, deliberate effort was directed toward examining how effective and beneficial the post-tenure review practices were judged in the eyes of different campus participants.

Methodology in Brief

The methodology used in the study is briefly outlined here. A more detailed discussion is contained in Appendix A. The comprehensive research design called for qualitative and quantitative data to be collected through a series of site visits to nine specifically chosen institutions. This type of approach is widely used when qualitative analysis is desired in order to understand people's level of experience, their perceptions, and the meaning they place on certain processes and events. Selecting this approach was deemed essential because we wanted to conduct empirical inquiry within the context of an institution, its faculty, and its administration. We also considered it critical to be able to gather multiple sources of evidence.

An invitation to participate was extended to 11 institutions in 1997. This solicitation was based on a set of pre-established requirements. The overarching requirement was that each participating institution represent a four-year, public university setting and have had at least five years of experience conducting post-tenure review. Institutions in the public sector were sought principally because the push for policy development in the early to mid-1990s came out of the public domain (for reasons to be discussed in Chapter 2) and experience with these policies was more prevalent in this sector. Other contextual considerations included diversity of mission, variation in size and geographic region, union/non-unionized settings, representation of varying models of post-tenure review, and openness to inquiry and information gathering on campus.

Nine institutions agreed to participate. (See Appendix B for a detailed profile of the nine institutions included in the study.) The mix of institutions selected provided us with different institutional missions (4 research-oriented and 4 teaching-oriented [comprehensive] and a broad range in size of student body (>25,000 students to <5,000), numbers of full-time tenure eligible faculty (>2,000 faculty to <200 faculty), and the type of post-tenure review policy practiced (6 periodic, 1 triggered, and 1 periodic and triggered). A medical school within a private research university was also included because previous work conducted by AAHE New Pathways II scholars suggested that professional schools, particularly medical schools, had significant experience working with accountability mandates affecting employment practices. In fact, of all the institutions studied, the medical school had the longest history and the most experience with post-tenure review. (See Chapter 4 for an in-depth discussion of the medical school and its review practices.)

The bulk of information and data on each campus came from three sources: 1) institutional documents and records, 2) on-site interviews and focus groups with faculty and administrators, and 3) a university-wide survey. Appropriate qualitative techniques were used to analyze transcripts from interviews and focus groups and similarly appropriate quantitative methods were used to analyze the survey results. All institutions and their data were kept strictly confidential. A comprehensive case study report was prepared for each of the nine universities and shared with each institution following the site visit. A cross-case analysis was then undertaken to determine common themes and provide answers to our key research questions.

The use of both quantitative and qualitative data-collection methodologies allowed us to be as inclusive of differing perspectives as possible and to bolster reliability in verifying the recurring themes that emerged. Although we did our best to use multiple sources of data and to be as even-handed as possible, analyzing findings and deriving conclusions from multiple case studies requires considerable interpretation.

This AAHE inquiry is unique because it centers squarely on the "perspectives" of faculty, department chairs, deans, and executive academic administrators from nine four-year institutions. Each of these participants bring differing experiences to bear on questions of post-tenure review impact, change, benefit, and value. This is the only study that uses multiple methods of data collection to understand how campuses of differing size, mission, and culture implement the review process and assess its results.

Further, when considered together with two previous works *(Post-Tenure Faculty Review and Renewal: Experienced Voices* and *Post-Tenure Faculty Review and Renewal: Reporting Results and Shaping Policy)*, these three volumes offer the most far-reaching description available of how post-tenure review policies are conceptualized, developed, implemented, tracked, and evaluated within public institutions. Most notably, this volume addresses questions of policy effectiveness from the point of view of those most closely involved with its implementation and describes the factors that most strongly influence whether a program of post-tenure review is perceived as effective and valuable.

The case studies depict a representative spectrum of successes, failures, challenges, and opportunities inherent in the evaluation cultures of nine institutions. This research tells a fascinating story about nine very different institutional programs of post-tenure review. It also reveals some very important themes common to each institution studied. The sustaining contribution of this work, however, lies in how it informs future decision-making and impacts higher education's accountability agenda. Building on the lessons learned from these nine case studies, we believe practitioners and policymakers will be better able to influence future policy development and assert needed reform in current practice. The real practical value of this body of work, therefore, lies in the future and with those called upon to devise new evaluation models, defend current approaches, debate evaluation outcomes, and apply the lessons learned by these early adopting campuses.

REFERENCES

Alstete, J. W. (2000). *Post-tenure faculty development: Building a system of faculty improvement and appreciation* (ASHE-ERIC Higher Education Report, 27[4]). San Francisco, CA: Jossey-Bass.

American Association of University Professors. (1983). On periodic evaluation of tenured faculty. *Academe, 69*(6), 1A–14A.

American Association of University Professors. (1998). Post-tenure review: An AAUP response. *Academe, 84*(5), 61–67.

Andrews, H. A., & Licata, C. M. (1991). Administrative perceptions of existing evaluation systems. *Journal of Personnel Evaluation in Education, 5*(1), 69–76.

Andrews, H. A., Licata, C. M., & Harris, B. J. (2002). *The state of post-tenure and long-term faculty evaluation* (Research brief). Washington, DC: American Association of Community Colleges.

Aper, J. P., & Fry, J. E. (2003). Post-tenure review at graduate institutions in the United States: Recommendations and realities. *Journal of Higher Education, 74*(3), 241–260.

Bennett, J. B., & Chater, S. S. (1984). Evaluating the performance of tenured faculty members. *Educational Record, 65*(2), 38–41.

Edwards, R. (1994). Toward constructive review of disengaged faculty. *AAHE Bulletin, 48*(2), 6–7, 11–12, 16.

Edwards, R. (1997). Can post-tenure review help us to save the tenure system? *Academe, 83*(3), 26–31.

Fogg, P. (2003, November 14). A happy medium. *Chronicle of Higher Education,* p. A10.

Goodman, M. J. (1994). The review of tenured faculty at a research university: Outcomes and appraisals. *Review of Higher Education, 18*(1), 83–94.

Hollander, P. A. (1992, June 17). Evaluating tenured professors. *Chronicle of Higher Education,* p. A44.

Licata, C. M. (1998). Post-tenure review: At the crossroads of accountability and opportunity. *AAHE Bulletin, 50*(10), 3–6.

Licata, C. M. (1999). Precepts for post-tenure reviews. *Trusteeship, 7*(6), 8–13.

Licata, C. M., & Brown, B. E. (Eds.). (2004). *Post-tenure faculty review and renewal II: Reporting results and shaping policy.* Bolton, MA: Anker.

Licata, C. M., & Morreale, J. C. (1997). *Post-tenure review: Policies, practices, precautions* (New Pathways Working Paper Series No. 12). Washington, DC: American Association for Higher Education.

Licata, C. M., & Morreale, J. C. (Eds.). (2002). *Post-tenure faculty review and renewal: Experienced voices.* Washington, DC: American Association for Higher Education.

Licata, C. M., & Schuyler, P. (2002). *The status of post-tenure review within private four-year institutions* (Briefing report). Washington, DC: American Association for Higher Education.

Montell, G. (2002, October 17). The fallout from post-tenure review. *Chronicle of Higher Education.* Retrieved April 8, 2005, from http://chronicle.com/jobs/2002/10/2002101701c.htm

Perry, S. (1983, September, 21). Formal reviews for tenured professors: Useful spur or Orwellian mistake? *Chronicle of Higher Education,* p. A25.

Plater, W. M. (2001, July/August). A profession at risk: Using post-tenure review to save tenure and create an intentional future for academic community. *Change, 33*(4), 52–57.

Portch, S. R., Kaufman, N. J., & Ross, J. R. (1993, July/August). From frog to prince: From post-tenure review to faculty roles, development, and rewards. *Change, 25*(4), 17.

Tierney, W. G. (1997). Academic community and post-tenure review. *Academe, 83*(3), 23–25.

2

Putting Post-Tenure Review Into Context and Practice

The clamor for accountability has little to do with the strengths or flaws of our system of higher education. It has everything to do with the public's general dissatisfaction with institutions and the broad demand that these institutions be more responsive to the public's needs.

—Graham, Lyman, & Trow, 2000, p. 5

E ven though post-tenure review policies surged during the 1990s, the idea that additional evaluation was warranted was met with suspicion and resistance on many campuses. In the eyes of some, accountability was simply the watchword for external intrusion and the corporatization of the academy. For others, it signified the beginning of an era where public funding was grounded in a culture of evidence—a culture that placed increasing value on that which could be measured. Most faculty understood the importance of demonstrating accountability and complying with established evaluation requirements. Opposition grew largely from the belief that post-tenure review was a veiled threat to tenure and undermined tenure's correlative privileges, including self-governance.

Post-Tenure Review: Not Necessarily New

A highly public profile accompanied the enactment of post-tenure review in states like Texas, Minnesota, Massachusetts, Florida, and Arizona. Not surprisingly, this created the impression that performance review was generally lacking and that post-tenure review was a new idea. Nothing could be farther from the truth. Although the majority of policies were developed after 1995 (Association of American Universities [AAU], 2001; Fry, 2000; Licata & Morreale, 1997), the origin of post-tenure faculty review actually predates the accountability era of the 1990s. Early practices were reported at Coe College in 1973, Earlham College in

1975, St. Lawrence University in 1977, Carleton College in 1980, the California State University System in 1983, and the Oregon University System in 1973 (Licata, 1986).

Notwithstanding, the idea became popularized about 20 years ago through the work of the 57-member National Commission on Higher Education Issues (1982). In its report, the commission described post-tenure faculty evaluation as one of the most pressing issues facing higher education. The commission directed attention to the need for periodic peer review of tenured faculty because it believed that "nothing would undermine the tenure system more completely than its being regarded as a system to protect faculty members from evaluation" (p. 10).

In 1983, the American Council on Education (ACE) and the American Association of University Professors (AAUP) sponsored a Wingspread Conference that examined all facets of post-tenure evaluation. The resulting exchange of opinions prompted the AAUP to issue a highly critical statement on post-tenure review. In its statement, the AAUP affirmed traditional faculty review methods in the academy and concluded that any additional evaluation was costly, unnecessary, and a threat to academic freedom (AAUP, 1985). John Bennett (1998), ACE's event organizer, described his initial enthusiasm for bringing prominent academics together to debate the benefits and shortcomings associated with periodic review of tenured faculty and his eventual disappointment with the general resistance to open and honest self-examination. He concluded that Wingspread represented the "ineffectiveness and protectionism for which the academy is increasingly criticized" (p. vi). He lamented that

> . . . The issue was put to the side and postponed until more than a decade later. Rather than moving assertively and proactively to advance its interests and those of the public, the academy dawdled until the public began to demand that the academy explain itself or surrender its prerogatives. (p. vii)

Widespread adoption of post-tenure review was prompted largely by the actions of policymakers and citizen boards whose concern with the bottom line forced American higher education to "demonstrate that the way faculty [carry out their] work and measure performance makes sense to those outside academe" (Licata & Morreale, 2002, p. 2).

Some institutions, although clearly the minority, did not wait for external pressure but instead undertook such policies based on internally perceived needs and benefits. (AAU, 2001; Henry, 2002; Hornum, 2002; Lees, 2002; Licata & Brown, 2004). The advantage of self-regulation for this group of colleges and universities was that policies were specifically shaped and driven by internal interests rather than external demands. One analyst cites institutional self-initiation as a prerequisite for success because it allows colleges and universities the opportunity and flexibility to design a system that is appropriate to their own institutional mission and goals (Applebaum, 1997, p. 7).

POST-TENURE REVIEW A DECADE LATER: THE ISSUES RECONSIDERED

More than a decade after Wingspread, the AAUP reconsidered the issue of post-tenure review and modified its original position slightly. In a revised statement, the AAUP (1998) recognized the growing prevalence of post-tenure review and continued to argue that summative reviews are particularly objectionable because they substitute "managerial" accountability for professional responsibility. The AAUP cautioned further that such review will alter and diminish due process protections inherent in academic freedom, leaving the door open to the easing of prevailing standards for dismissal by moving that standard from incompetence to unsatisfactory performance. The AAUP acknowledged that faculty performance review can be enhanced and suggested that any additional evaluation systems be specifically directed toward constructive measures for improvement. The association contends that normal collegiate review processes and policy provisions already in place can handle the infrequent situations of underperformance or nonperformance and that additional disciplinary monitoring is redundant.

EARLY IMPLEMENTATION: POLICY AND PRACTICE[1]

Policies today vary considerably in scope, purpose, and frequency. In fact, there are significant differences across institutions when it comes to such things as who is reviewed, who does the reviewing, and what happens as a result of the review. Despite these differences, policies can usually be separated into three basic models: 1) the comprehensive, periodic review of all tenured faculty, usually conducted at five-to-seven-year intervals; 2) the selective review of only those faculty whose performance is below standard as judged by the annual review; or 3) systematic, enhanced review of all faculty on an annual basis. With this latter model, the annual merit review process is typically expanded beyond administrative assessment to include peer review, long-term professional development planning, and provision for appropriate remedial actions when performance is below standard.

Objectives

Differing evaluation objectives drive policies. One objective is summative, where actual consequences from the review are made explicit and can include preparation of a long-term professional development plan, reward/recognition measures, and formulation of an improvement plan when deficiencies are noted. The other focus is formative, which aims at career development and growth and rarely results in immediate personnel action. Regardless of the model and focus, all processes usually build on the annual review and almost all new policies emphasize faculty development as one of the objectives.

Procedural Elements

Despite the variety of intended objectives, most policies incorporate common procedural elements:

- Preparation of documentation by the faculty member under review.

- Assessment and judgment by either a peer committee, the chairperson, or both.

- Performance measured against established criteria and standards at the unit level.

- A development plan (one to three years) drawn up to meet mandated improvement goals, when performance needs improvement.

- Other actions beyond a mandated development plan which correspond to specific policy objectives and the individual evaluation context. These might entail a self-initiated professional development plan supported by resources, incentive or reward for performance, or some other type of reward, recognition, or sanction.

Summative Versus Formative Debate

There continues to be weighty debate in the field about the intended purpose of post-tenure review. Those outside the academy tend to see the post-tenure review process more in consequential terms—as a means to make the academy more outcomes oriented, accountable, adaptable, and responsive to change. Internal stakeholders often hold a conflicted view—believing that post-tenure review is an unnecessary form of oversight rather than a potential way to strengthen performance and continue professional development. An underlying but undocumented fear is that such reviews will be used capriciously by administration to get rid of outspoken or nonconforming faculty. Faculty groups who see value in developmental peer review also remain suspicious about the effect of consequential reviews on tenure norms and traditions.

EARLY IMPLEMENTATION: BEST PRACTICE PRINCIPLES

By the end of the 1990s, guidance and best practice principles were available to institutions engaged in policy formulation and implementation. Early analysis of more than 100 post-tenure review policies and procedures led American Association for Higher Education scholars to establish a recommended conceptual framework for formulating programs of post-tenure review (Licata & Morreale, 1997). This framework outlined a series of operating principles that institutions were encouraged to consider, as shown in Table 2.1.

Table 2.1
Operating Principles

1) Clear definition and articulation of the purpose of the policy—distinguishing between summative or formative; providing academic freedom protection.

2) Development of a plan to measure the effectiveness of the review in accomplishing its stated purpose and determination of what the overall benefit of the review should be for faculty members and the institution.

3) Involvement of faculty, administration, and trustees (when appropriate) in the design and ownership of the process.

4) Careful planning, attention, and follow-through on key operational issues in order to:

Gain campus consensus

- Elicit broad discussion on post-tenure review by inviting external practitioners who are knowledgeable and experienced on the topic of post-tenure review to address the faculty and administration and elicit discussion on the topic.

- Bring all stakeholders into the discussion of post-tenure review early.

- Be open to suggestions from the faculty and demonstrate a willingness to compromise.

- Integrate the concept of post-tenure review into the existing evaluation systems and cycles for promotion, tenure, and salary.

Formulate key policy components

- Dispel the idea that post-tenure review is a retenuring process.

- Keep the faculty at the center of the review system—involving peers in a significant way in the review procedures.

- Make the process simple and focused on past and future faculty contributions to teaching, scholarship, and service.

- Be vigilant about developing processes and procedures that tie directly to the stated purpose of the policy.

- Add funds and resources as needed to support faculty development and other expected results.

Close the loop

- Oversee the actual implementation of the post-tenure review process in each academic unit.
- Make sure there is appropriate follow-up and feedback to the individual faculty under review.
- Remind stakeholders constantly of the purpose and expected benefits of the review.
- Keep careful records of the process and its outcomes.
- Conduct informal evaluation of the process through discussions with deans and chairs.
- Develop a formal assessment process to evaluate the overall effectiveness of post-tenure review. Modify the review based on the assessment.

Note. Adapted from Licata and Morreale, 1997, 2002.

In 1998, the AAUP recommended a set of minimum standards for good practice. These standards offer guidance on key process elements and provide a foundation that institutions can use to ensure that their post-tenure review policy builds on traditional tenure precepts (see Table 2.2).

Table 2.2
Minimum Standards for Good Practice

1) Post-tenure review must ensure the protection of academic freedom as defined in the 1940 *Statement of Principles.*

2) Post-tenure review must not be a reevaluation or revalidation of tenured status as defined in the 1940 *Statement.*

3) The written standards and criteria by which faculty members are evaluated in post-tenure review should be developed and periodically reviewed by the faculty. The faculty should also conduct the actual review process.

4) Post-tenure review should be developmental and supported by institutional resources for professional development or a change of professional direction.

5) Post-tenure review should be flexible enough to acknowledge different expectations in different disciplines and changing expectations at different stages of faculty careers.

6) Except when faculty appeals procedures direct that files be available to aggrieved faculty members, the outcome of evaluations should be confidential, that is,

confined to the appropriate college or university persons or bodies and the faculty member being evaluated, released otherwise only at the discretion or with the consent of the faculty member.

7) If the system of post-tenure review is supplemented, or supplanted, by the option of a formal development plan, that plan cannot be imposed on the faculty member unilaterally, but must be a product of mutual negotiation.

8) A faculty member should have the right to comment in response to evaluations, and to challenge the findings and correct the record by appeal to an elected faculty grievance committee.

9) In the event that recurring evaluations reveal continuing and persistent problems with a faculty member's performance that do not lend themselves to improvement after several efforts, and that call into question his or her ability to function in that position, then other possibilities, such as a mutually agreeable reassignment to other duties or separation, should be explored.

10) The standard for dismissal or other severe sanction remains that of adequate cause, and the mere fact of successive negative reviews does not in any way diminish the obligation of the institution to show such cause in a separate forum before an appropriately constituted hearing body of peers convened for that purpose.

Note. From Post-Tenure Review: An AAUP Response (1998, September/October), *Academe*. For a full description of each standard, along with additional information and guidance, see www.aaup.org/statements/Redbook/rbpostn.htm.

RESEARCH ON COMPLIANCE WITH AAUP STANDARDS: EARLY ANALYSIS

The late 1990s saw early efforts to examine compliance with these AAUP principles on a very limited basis. The Project on Faculty Appointments at Harvard University worked with a representative sample drawn from a population of 1,380 U.S. four-year institutions, stratified by Carnegie classification, to assess the nature and scope of post-tenure review practices. Analysis also compared institutional policy statements to the specific AAUP guidelines which stipulate that post-tenure review policies be both developmental and peer based.

The research team concluded that policies differed significantly from one to another and often had little in common. Findings showed that about 58% of the policies were periodic in design (i.e., all faculty reviewed on established cycle), yet only 25% of these same policies could be characterized as formative or developmental in purpose. Further, while some policies did adhere to all of the AAUP standards, more of them did establish summative goals and allowable sanctions.

Drawing from this analysis, the Harvard team asserted that accountability appeared to be the key policy objective and concluded that "As with so many other aspects of American higher education, post-tenure review policies and practices reveal a wide array of locally determined variations on a basic theme: performance accountability for tenured faculty" (Rule, 2000, p. 198).

Building on this question of how policies comply with AAUP minimum practice standards, Aper and Fry (2003) surveyed the chief academic officer and faculty governance representative in a national sample of graduate institutions (research, doctoral, and master's). Similar to the Harvard findings, the investigators discovered that the purposes for post-tenure, as perceived by their respondents, were mixed. Some described their policies as managerial and others said they were developmental. There was significant disagreement among the faculty and administrator respondents in such areas as whether the main purpose of the review was summative or developmental, whether the process was well-supported in terms of resources, and whether the policy protected academic freedom. Moreover, the results uncovered the failure of most institutions to evaluate the outcomes of post-tenure review. Cost/benefit studies were not conducted (or planned) nor were policies reported to be established on a trial basis as advised by the AAUP.

POST-TENURE REVIEW AND THE COURTS

Even though post-tenure review has a relatively short history, when challenged in the courts, policies have generally prevailed. In a well-publicized case, *Wiest v. State of Kansas* (2003), a tenured faculty member was dismissed for cause because of his failure to satisfactorily respond to a plan for improvement which was put into place after the faculty member received two consecutive years of chronic low achievement ratings from his department peers and department head. The post-tenure review policy at Kansas State University uses the annual review as the primary evaluation method. When a faculty member is assessed in the annual review to have performed below the department's accepted level, improvement is expected in the ensuing year and a plan suggested. When chronic low achievement persists for two consecutive appraisal years or is noted in three annual reviews over a five-year period, dismissal for cause can be invoked. Despite being given the opportunity to improve his performance through a recommended improvement plan, the faculty member refused to take action and was terminated. The courts said that the university acted justifiably and made the necessary case of termination based on professional incompetence.

In a challenge to Colorado State University, *Johnson v. Colorado State Board of Agriculture* (2000), the courts affirmed that the university's post-tenure review policy established in 1997 did not interfere with prior tenure policies, weaken vested rights, or impose new obligations on faculty. The faculty member in this case received two consecutive below-standard evaluations in 1997 and 1998 and claimed that the newly established policy did not apply to him because a five-year waiting period was required. The court ruled in the university's favor and in so doing made it clear that because faculty typically undergo reviews as part of the tenure covenant, a specific requirement for post-tenure review did not undermine tenure or place new expectations on tenured faculty.

In another case, a faculty member at the University of Wisconsin system (*Lubitz v. Wisconsin Personnel Commission,* 2000) had experienced repeated health problems which led to his request for leaves of absence. At the time, the administration expressed concern about his class attendance, participation in expected departmental work, and professional accomplishments. These issues surfaced in his post-tenure review and resulted in the development of a required improvement plan intended to address performance shortcomings. The faculty member's merit points were reduced as a result of the negative review. He brought suit against the university, claiming the results of the review and the ensuing actions by the university were taken in retaliation of his request for a FMLA (Family and Medical Leave Act) leave. The court determined that the university had utilized objective and legitimate evidence from the post-tenure review as the basis for taking action.

Legal scholars Cameron and Lee (2004) derive certain key implications from their examination of these and other recent court rulings involving post-tenure review. Their analysis indicates that:

- A system of post-tenure review can minimize risk of age discrimination.

- Implementation of a post-tenure review system does not impair vested rights or create new obligations.

- Faculty evaluation and dismissal for cause are distinguishable.

- Post-tenure review can provide a framework for selecting faculty members to be eliminated in a financial exigency or other institutional contraction. (p. 4)

CONTEMPORARY ATTITUDINAL STUDIES

Other research undertaken since 1990 has relied almost exclusively on attitudes and perceptions about post-tenure review held by faculty or chief academic officers within a single institution, a group of similar institutions (e.g., selective private liberal arts institutions), or within a limited number of institutions in a state system or particular region. While limited in scope, findings from these early studies shed light on values and beliefs faculty and administrators hold about the affect of post-tenure review on tenure, academic freedom, performance, and professional development. In addition, this early work also identifies contextual factors that influence positive and negative opinions about the process.

A brief summary of key findings from these research studies follows. However, findings from these different studies are not necessarily consistent with one another, particularly those that examine the affect of post-tenure review on faculty performance and development. Another factor that must be taken into consideration when interpreting this early body of research is the national post-tenure review environment in place when individual research studies were conducted. The public's squeeze for accountability in the early 1990s spawned the majority of post-tenure review policies on the books today. One could argue that the research on post-tenure review policies conducted prior to 1995 was grounded in a less demanding national context than those established after 1995. As a result, post-tenure review practices may not have been characterized by the same urgency, suspicion or cogency as those established post-1995. Consider the following findings:

Affect of Post-Tenure Review on Tenure and Academic Freedom

- Faculty do not report that post-tenure review (as practiced in their setting) is a threat to tenure or academic freedom (Fry, 2000; Goodman, 1994; Harris, 1996; Johnson, 1990; Reisman, 1986; Willett, 2000; Wood, 2000)

Affect of Post-Tenure Review on Faculty Performance

- Post-tenure review does not directly improve faculty performance (Ernest, 1999; Johnson, 1990; O'Meara, 2003); has limited impact on performance (O'Meara, 2003): is least effective with low-performing faculty (Reisman, 1986); and has little measurable impact on the institution or holds value for faculty (Wesson & Johnson, 1991; Wood, 2000)

- Post-tenure review provides some motivation to increase research/scholarship (Goodman, 1994; Harris, 1996; Reisman, 1996); the affect on teaching improvement is less clear (O'Meara, 2003; Reisman, 1986)

- Post-tenure review process reduces number of underperforming faculty (University of Hawaii–Manoa, 1997)

- Post-tenure review is a major factor contributing to high faculty productivity (AAU, 2001)

- Process has positive impact on professional growth and improvement (Willett, 2000); leads to improved faculty development (AAU, 2001)

- Post-tenure review influences faculty decisions to retire (Goodman, 1994; O'Meara, 2003); helps advance interpersonal contact with colleagues, improve morale, and provide opportunities for performance feedback (Johnson, 1990).

Factors Influencing Positive Faculty Opinions About Post-Tenure Review

- *Relationship between tenure and post-tenure review:* faculty express a more positive response to post-tenure review when policy is not viewed as a threat to tenure (Wood, 2000)

- *Purpose of review:* faculty view formative post-tenure review more favorably than summative post-tenure review (Fry, 2000; Harris, 1996; Reisman, 1986; Willett, 2000; Wood, 2000)

- *Source of policy introduction:* faculty are more positive when policy is not seen as externally imposed (Johnson, 1990; O'Meara, 2003; Wood, 2000)

- *Incentives and sanctions:* faculty are more receptive to a policy that allows incentives, rewards, and/or sanctions (when needed) (Wood, 2000)

- *Role of faculty union:* faculty are more receptive to policy if union is assistive rather than resistant to development (Wood, 2000)

- *Benefits:* overall benefits outweigh costs involved (Reisman, 1986)

- *Institutional type:* improved teaching and increased research activity are viewed as benefits of post-tenure review in doctoral and comprehensive institutions but not in research institutions (Harris, 1996)

- *Demographic variables:* gender, ethnicity, rank, and discipline do not influence opinions about post-tenure review procedures (Ernest, 1999; Willett, 2000; Wood, 2000)

Reported Problems Associated With Post-Tenure Review

- High costs in time and energy (AAU, 2001; Ernest 1999; Johnson 1990)

- No consequences from review (Wesson & Johnson, 1991)

- Little or no feedback provided following review (Johnson, 1990; O'Meara, 2003; Wesson & Johnson, 1991; Willett, 2000)

- Inflated feedback from peers (O'Meara, 2003)

- No relationship between review and rewards (Andrews & Licata, 1992; Harris, 1996; Licata & Andrews, 1990)

- No consequences imposed for unsatisfactory performance (Andrews & Licata, 1992; University of Hawaii–Manoa, 1997; Wood, 2000)

- Evaluators inadequately trained (Licata & Andrews 1990, 1992)

- Lack of resources to fund faculty development (Fry, 2000; Harris, 1996; University of Hawaii–Manoa, 1997; Wesson & Johnson, 1991)

- Failure to link post-tenure review to existing evaluation policies (Aper & Fry, 2003)

- Institutional cost/benefit analysis not conducted (Fry, 2000)

Documented Administrative Response

- Deans are more positive about post-tenure review outcomes than faculty and chairs (O'Meara, 2003)

- Chief academic officers in public four-year colleges and universities perceive post-tenure review to be achieving its intended purpose (Wilson, 1995)

The value in these findings is that they are the antecedent to important unresolved questions—they help direct attention to where further inquiry is warranted. What is sorely absent from current literature is what some scholars refer to as the "potent next step in the research on post-tenure review . . . [the] degree to which such policies have had systematic, constructive impact beyond symbol management and response to the rhetoric of accountability, cost accounting and personnel management" (Aper & Fry, 2003, p. 258).

The American Association for Higher Education study addresses this call by carrying out a comprehensive examination of the outcomes of post-tenure evaluation as actually experienced and described by the prime institutional players in nine universities across the country.

ENDNOTE

1) Unless otherwise noted, information in this section has been expanded slightly from what was previously reported in Licata and Morreale (2002) and Andrews, Licata, and Harris (2002).

REFERENCES

American Association of University Professors. (1985). *Statement on periodic evaluation of tenured faculty.* Washington, DC. Author.

American Association of University Professors. (1998). Post-tenure review: An AAUP response. *Academe, 84*(5), 61–67.

Andrews, H. A., & Licata, C. M. (1992). Faculty leaders' responses to post-tenure review evaluation practices. *Community/Junior College Quarterly, 16*(1), 47–56.

Andrews, H. A., Licata, C. M., & Harris, B. J. (2002). *The state of post-tenure and long term faculty evaluation* (Research brief). Washington, DC: American Association of Community Colleges.

Aper, J. P., & Fry, J. E. (2003). Post-tenure review at graduate institutions in the United States: Recommendations and realities. *Journal of Higher Education, 74*(3), 241–260.

Applebaum, R. L. (1997). The elephant in the room: Post-tenure review. *Journal for the Association of Communication Administration, 1,* 1–9.

Association of American Universities. (2001). *Post-tenure review.* Washington, DC: Author.

Bennett, J. B. (1998). *Collegial professionalism: The academy, individualism, and the common good.* Phoenix, AZ: American Council on Education/Oryx Press.

Cameron, C. A., & Lee, B. (2004). *Demands for accountability: The implications of review, reorganization, and retrenchment on faculty appointments.* Paper presented at the 25th national conference on Law and Higher Education, Clearwater Beach, FL.

Ernest, I. (1999). *Faculty evaluation of post-tenure review at a research university.* Unpublished doctoral dissertation, Columbia University, New York.

Fry, J. E. (2000). *Post-tenure review: A study of policies and practices at colleges and universities in the United States.* Unpublished doctoral dissertation, University of Tennessee, Knoxville.

Goodman, M. J. (1994). The review of tenured faculty at a research university: Outcomes and appraisals. *Review of Higher Education, 18*(1), 83–94.

Graham, P. A., Lyman, R. W., & Trow, M. (1995). *Accountability of colleges and universities: An essay.* New York, NY: Columbia University.

Harris, B. J. (1996). *The relationship between and among policy variables, type of institution, and perceptions of academic administrators with regard to post-tenure review.* Unpublished doctoral dissertation, University of West Virginia, Morgantown.

Henry, R. J. (2002). Getting out in front: Cumulative review and development for tenured faculty. In C. M. Licata & J. C. Morreale (Eds.), *Post-tenure faculty review and renewal: Experienced voices* (pp. 167–177). Washington, DC: American Association for Higher Education.

Hornum, B. (2002). Transforming post-tenure review into faculty, department head, and departmental renewal. In C. M. Licata & J. C. Morreale (Eds.), *Post-tenure faculty review and renewal: Experienced voices* (pp. 155–163). Washington, DC: American Association for Higher Education.

Johnson, G. (1990). *The innovation process in organizations: A look at post-tenure faculty evaluation.* Unpublished doctoral dissertation, Pennsylvania State University.

Johnson v. Colorado State Board of Agriculture, 15 P.3d 309 (Colo. Ct. of App. 2000).

Lees, N. D. (2002). The evolution of post-tenure review at Indiana University Purdue University Indianapolis. In C. M. Licata & J. C. Morreale (Eds.), *Post-tenure faculty review and renewal: Experienced voices* (pp. 97–110). Washington, DC: American Association for Higher Education.

Licata, C. M. (1986). *Post-tenure faculty evaluation: Threat or opportunity?* (ASHE-ERIC Higher Education Report No. 1). Washington, DC: Association for the Study of Higher Education. (ERIC Document Reproduction Service No. ED270009)

Licata, C. M., & Andrews, H. A. (1990). The status of tenured faculty evaluation in the community college. *Community College Review, 18*(3), 42–50.

Licata, C. M., & Brown, B. E. (Eds.). (2004). *Post-tenure faculty review and renewal II: Reporting results and shaping policy.* Bolton, MA: Anker.

Licata, C. M., & Morreale, J. C. (1997). *Post-tenure review: Policies, practices, precautions* (New Pathways Working Paper Series No. 12). Washington, DC: American Association for Higher Education.

Licata, C. M., & Morreale, J. C. (Eds.). (2002). *Post-tenure faculty review and renewal: Experienced voices.* Washington, DC: American Association for Higher Education.

Lubitz v. Wisconsin Personnel Commission, 619N.W.2d 513 (Wisc. Ct. App. 2000).

National Commission on Higher Education Issues. (1982). *To strengthen quality in higher education.* Washington, DC: American Council on Education. (ERIC Document Reproduction Service No. ED226646)

O'Meara, K. A. (2003). Believing is seeing: The influence of beliefs and expectations on post-tenure review in one state system. *Review of Higher Education, 27*(1), 17–43.

Reisman, B. (1986). Performance evaluation for tenured faculty: Issues and research. *Liberal Education, 72*(1), 73–87.

Rule, C. S. (2000). After the big decision: Post-tenure review analyzed. In C. A. Trower (Ed.), *Policies on faculty appointment: Standard practices and unusual arrangements* (pp. 180–212). Bolton, MA: Anker.

University of Hawaii–Manoa, Office of the Senior Vice President and Executive Vice Chancellor. (1997). *Ten years of post-tenure review at the University of Hawaii–Manoa: 1987–1997.* Honolulu, HI: Author.

Wesson, M., & Johnson, S. (1991). Post-tenure review and faculty revitalization. *Academe, 77*(3), 53–57.

Wiest v. State of Kansas, No. 89-953 (Kan. Ct. App. 2003).

Willett, C. M. (2000). *Post-tenure review: Opinions held by faculty in highly selective, independent, private liberal arts institutions.* Unpublished doctoral dissertation, Seton Hall University, South Orange, New Jersey.

Wilson, S. J. (1995). *Faculty post-tenure review: Perceptions of chief academic officers of public, four-year colleges and universities within the region of the Southern Association of Colleges and Schools.* Unpublished doctoral dissertation, University of Alabama, Tuscaloosa.

Wood, M. S. (2000). *Post-tenure review: The role of academic values and beliefs in shaping faculty response at two research universities.* Unpublished doctoral dissertation, University of Hawaii, Honolulu.

3

Faculty and Administrator Views About Post-Tenure Review Practices: Qualitative Findings

We are using a million dollar solution for a thousand dollar problem.
—Dean, University G

Yeah, I think it is a good idea. I feel it is an obligation in a way that we have for working here. I think that somebody needs to be checking up on people.
—Faculty Member, University B

. . . We sat down, collected materials, wrote a report and it dropped off into oblivion.
—Chairperson, University H

It does seem to motivate some people and it is paying off in major ways with a few.
—Faculty Member, University F

Post-tenure review is a good chance for us to be sure we are all rowing in the same direction.
—Chairperson, University G

These statements reflect the broad range of opinions expressed during our site visit interviews. This chapter thematically summarizes what we saw and what we heard. Whenever possible, we support qualitative findings with quantitative survey data. We have chosen this approach to present a fuller description of the findings. (For a more complete discussion of specific survey data, including significant differences in responses by categories of respondents, institutions, and demographics, see Chapter 5.)

There is an important canon in the art of film criticism that cautions reviewers to remember that it's not only *what* it's about but *how* it's about it that deserves attention. We believe this applies to qualitative research as well. As we began to examine the interview transcripts, we were intent on understanding both what was being reported and how faculty and administrators felt about what they disclosed.

We expect that some readers will find our results surprising; others will label them interesting but not very surprising. And some will classify them as both uninteresting and not surprising. We have no doubt, though, that those who have studied and worked with post-tenure review will denote familiar story lines embedded in the ways people relayed their experiences to us. We challenge readers to focus and reflect on how these findings can help inform new policy development and shape policy reform on a local level.

POLICY SIMILARITIES AND DIFFERENCES

During the 30-month period that began in the autumn of 1999, we interviewed more than 400 faculty members, department chairs, deans, and other senior academic leaders at eight four-year universities and one medical school in the United States. (See Appendix B for institutional profiles.) In order to verify the qualitative findings obtained from these interviews against a broader representation of faculty and administrator perspectives, we also analyzed survey responses collected from another 1,600 faculty within these same institutions. (See Appendix C for the survey instrument.)

Despite differing institutional missions and sizes, the experiences of faculty and administrators were remarkably similar. For example, many responses resembled each other when describing the perceived purpose of post-tenure review and what the review accomplished. Even opinions about what contributed to policy ineffectiveness and what procedural areas needed improvement were not remarkably different across settings. Differences of opinion surfaced principally around issues of overall effectiveness, worth, and benefit.

In general, we found the reactions of faculty and administrators in three settings (University A, University C, and University D) to be principally positive. Four institutions (University B, University E, University G, and University H) were mixed in their assessment of effectiveness, worth, and benefit, and the remaining two institutions were mainly negative in their views (University F and University I).

When taken together, document analysis, interview data, and survey results offer increased definition about overall policy intent and specific outcomes. These findings also offer preliminary answers to the questions that drove this research, principally:

- Is post-tenure review effectively meeting the original institutional purpose?

- Does the process impact faculty performance and professional career development?

- Does the process advance departmental goals and institutional mission?

Data from this study also provide strong evidence about what factors must be present in order to establish a policy that faculty and administrators consider to be highly effective. (See Chapter 6 for a full discussion of these factors.)

It is important to point out that opinions about post-tenure review reflected in this report come from faculty and administrators who characterized themselves as *familiar* with institutional policy and practice. Those interviewed had been through at least one review, and more than 80% of all survey respondents said they considered themselves "generally familiar" with the policy. Not surprisingly, administrators, whom we define for this study as chairs, deans, and senior academic leaders, regarded themselves as *very* familiar with the policy.

WHAT'S IN A NAME?

Even though the faculty and administrators we spoke with in each setting comfortably used the term *post-tenure review* to describe and discuss their practices, the language used in formal policy statements rarely referred to the process as post-tenure review. This was purposeful. We learned that as most institutions crafted policies to govern tenured faculty evaluation, policy framers intentionally tried to convey that the policy was focused on faculty review and development, not on retenuring.

In seven of the nine sites, the label post-tenure review was avoided in favor of what many considered to be a more positive title. Institutions chose the following titles for their policies:

- Cumulative Review and Development Policy (University A)

- Evaluation of Tenured Faculty (University B)

- Periodic Evaluation of Tenured Full Professors (University C)

- Post-Tenure Review (University E)

- Periodic Evaluation of Tenured Faculty (University F)

- Tenured Faculty Review and Development (University G and University H)

- Annual Review Policy (more extensive post-tenure review is an outcome of annual review) (University I)

University D (the medical school) had the oldest policy of any of the institutions studied. Established in 1975, the policy was titled the "Five-Year Tenure Review Policy." By design, this particular policy was a retenuring policy. Because of the nature of this policy and the unique contextual variables present in medical and health center settings, we have chosen to separate out the findings from the medial school and discuss them separately in Chapter 4. Our discussion and analysis in this chapter, therefore, refer only to the eight public universities.

The ways in which each institution moved from policy to practice differed significantly. Processes and procedures were more diverse than uniform. Differences were observed in the following areas.

Review Cycle

One institution utilized the annual review as the vehicle for post-tenure review. One campus reviewed faculty every four years. Another used a four-to-six year cycle. The rest worked around a five-year window.

Documentation Required

Every institution required that a current curriculum vita and evidence of performance/productivity in teaching, scholarship, and service be provided to the reviewers. About half also required a reflective statement on professional development plans and goals. In two institutions, the previous annual reviews constituted the centerpiece of documentation.

Peer Review Body

Peer review committees conducted the review in six institutions. The way in which this review body was established varied widely from the dean appointing committee members in one setting; the use of the promotion/tenure committee in another; the unit's executive committee in another; and independently elected committees in the remaining settings.

Role of the Chairperson

Chairs had a direct role with the review process in all but two institutions. Customarily, the chair received the report from the committee and either added his or her own perspective to the review or wrote an independent assessment which was then forwarded to the dean. In most institutions, if follow up occured, it was the chair that met with the faculty member to discuss the results and to plan needed action. Sometimes the chair of the peer review committee participated in that meeting as well.

Results and Consequences

There was a range of actions taken once a review is completed. A conference (face-to-face meeting) with the chair and/or dean occurred in two settings. In the other institutions, a letter was sent and follow-up meetings were required only when improvement plans were mandated.

Variation existed within institutions in terms of follow up. Some academic units used individual meetings as a way to convey both satisfactory as well as unsatisfactory judgments on performance.

Every institution required an improvement plan be developed when performance is judged as unsatisfactory. These plans were generally one or two years in length. Two institutions allowed up to three years.

QUESTIONS AND ANSWERS

1) IS POST-TENURE REVIEW ACHIEVING ITS INTENDED INSTITUTIONAL PURPOSE?

Before posing this specific question, we carefully probed what institutional participants understood the purpose of post-tenure review to be at their institution. Isolating a single purpose was difficult for many and, for some, impossible.

Multiple Purposes Emerged

Early in our data collection it became apparent that faculty and administrators were making an important distinction about what constituted the *intended* purpose for the policy and what represented the *actual* purpose. For many, this distinction was grounded more in how the policy was actually practiced than in what specific policy language said about it. In fact, when reviewing the language within each of the formal policy statements, it was evident that in one way or another, most policies mentioned three somewhat different and occasionally competing purposes: 1) measurement of faculty performance, 2) promotion of professional development, and 3) assurance that faculty responsibilities to the unit, university, and the taxpayers of the state were adequately met.

The following four policy statements are illustrative of the language we found embedded in most formal policy documents. It should be noted that summative and formative objectives are often coupled within one policy statement:

> *The tenured review policy provides an opportunity to assess faculty development goals and achievements and provide assistance to faculty in ensuring continuous intellectual and professional growth and provides assistance to the unit in ensuring that all faculty members are contributing to the unit's goals and responsibilities.*
>
> —University A

The policy is intended to ensure continuing growth and development in faculty professional skills, encouraging faculty to explore new ways to promote academic excellence, and to identify areas for improvement and provide solutions for problem areas...

The purpose of the review of tenured faculty is to assess periodically each faculty member's activities and performance, in accordance with the mission of the department, college and institution in such a way as to determine that the faculty member is meeting his or her obligations to the university and the State of _____. The review is to be appropriately linked to the merit process and should not involve the creation of unnecessary additional bureaucracy.

—University G

In order to facilitate continuing faculty development, each faculty member shall be subject to comprehensive peer review and evaluation at least once every five years to seven years after the award of tenure. The evaluation may be conducted in conjunction with existing program review procedures or as part of the annual review for salary determination; however, the faculty evaluation must be comprehensive in scope. The faculty member, the dean of the college or school, and other appropriate administrative officers shall be informed by the department chair or the equivalent administrator of the results of the evaluation.

—University E

And, in a unionized setting:

Tenured faculty have earned the right under... [state law] to continued employment by virtue of probationary and tenured service during which both competence and performance have been rigorously reviewed and found to meet high professional standards. Therefore, in light of the special nature of tenured appointments, performance appraisals are formative in that the focus is upon the enhancement of instructional performance.

Periodic evaluation of tenured faculty serves as a means to stimulate the on-going professional development of the faculty and to assure the overall quality of instruction. The review can be used to:

- *Recognize excellence and provide incentives for superior performance in the event of a positive review*

- *Outline the requirement for an interim evaluation in the event of an unsatisfactory evaluation of teaching effectiveness, or a satisfactory*

> *evaluation of teaching effectiveness and unsatisfactory evaluations of both professional development and university/community service*
>
> ~ *Specify the actions to be taken in the event of further unsatisfactory interim evaluations.*
>
> —University F

Given overly broad policy language, most faculty and administrators we interviewed found it difficult to identify only one purpose and almost always described their policies in both summative and developmental ways.

Summative and Formative Language

In spite of various stated policy goals, in only two institutions were faculty, department chairs, and deans in agreement that the main intent was developmental, and the policy was being implemented along those lines. In another institution, there was agreement that the policy was primarily summative and seen as punitive. In every other setting, dual and sometimes multiple purposes were noted. Faculty often commented that it was their impression that the reviews had both internal and external objectives: 1) reviewing performance to see if performance expectations were met, and if not, remedying any deficiencies, and 2) demonstrating accountability to outside constituencies.

The circumstances that created the policies in seven of the nine settings are relevant to the discussion of perceived policy intent. In seven institutions, the political push for accountability earmarked the drive to impose post-tenure review. Despite what was eventually worked out through negotiation as the major policy objective, faculty continued to be influenced by the early rhetoric on the part of the regents, legislators, or governing board.

Summative Objectives

Faculty frequently described their policy as a way to "keep faculty on their toes" or to create the salutary effect of saying "if you're not carrying your load at the current level, you should rethink where you can make the greatest contribution."

Ridding the forest of deadwood was mentioned by many as a key intended purpose, especially by those outside the institution:

> *It [post-tenure review] was the outcome of legislators worrying that we have deadwood on our faculty and so from its very beginning, it is looking for underperformers and not targeting over-performers . . . it was not developed as a positive process . . .*
>
> —Chairperson, University E

This is not to suggest that faculty and administrators talked only about punitive or summative objectives, although summative ends did seem to overshadow discussions about formative goals.

Formative Objectives

In almost every setting, formative policy objectives were mentioned. Faculty members usually characterized development goals in terms of "career reflection," "calibration of professional contributions with department mission and direction," and "career renewal." Frequently, formative policy objectives were described in ways similar to the following:

> *I find it very helpful for me to go back and review what those five years have meant . . . so that somebody else could look at that [reflective narrative] and qualitatively understand what that work was about.*
>
> —Faculty Member, University B

> *The policy is an opportunity for career reassessment . . . a honing in on professional development needs.*
>
> —Faculty Member, University A

> *. . . Projection to future departmental needs was the most valuable part of the discussion.*
>
> —Faculty Member, University H

For various reasons, however, a substantial number of institutional stakeholders did not view their policy as intended solely to serve developmental aims. Further, how well developmental intentions were met was usually considered far from satisfactory. This was a source of concern for some, which led to dissatisfaction with policy implementation.

Key Themes

Accountability

Accountability was a watchword on all eight campuses. A duality in the purposes that accountability served was referred to over and over again. Internal accountability aimed at ensuring that faculty are performing up to tenure standards was frequently noted in parallel with external accountability—proving that tenure doesn't represent a "free ride" for the rest of one's career. Faculty and chairs mentioned the link between accountability and continued productivity:

> *Well, I view it [post-tenure review] as two fold: one for accountability to make sure professors, once they have tenure or promotion . . . continue to be professionally active. And secondly, I think it too serves as a way to motivate*

faculty to keep active. Knowing that a post-tenure review is going to be imminent, or coming up in five years, you continue to be active.
—Faculty Member, University B

The primary purpose is accountability after tenure—to have something in place that says once somebody is tenured, they don't have a blank check for the rest of their lives to do anything they want to.
—Chairperson, University I

The policy is intended to identify faculty whose performance has slipped . . . individuals who have gone to seed. Rather than just being a filter, it would find people that you think are not meeting the expectations and try to inform them and encourage them to come up to standards.
—Faculty Member, University G

None of the public campuses were immune from external oversight and often referred to this in their discussions with us:

It [post-tenure review] is a response to external interests in accountability for the professoriate. Internally there are probably political reasons because the university is in transition from a teaching institution to a research institution, and they have a very large faculty that are, say, non-productive in a research sense. So I am sure that there is some motivation to light a fire under them or get rid of them for that matter!
—Faculty Member, University A

PTR [post-tenure review]helps address public and legislative concerns that tenure is not license to do whatever one wants.
—Faculty Member, University H

Not everyone viewed accountability as a noble force, though. Some viewed it as a pretext to abolishing tenure.

PTR [post-tenure review] is a bone thrown to people who want to eliminate tenure.
—Faculty Member, University G

Making Work More Public
In particular, department chairs who worked with policies that included review by peers pointed out that the peer review component did provide an opportunity for colleagues to gain greater knowledge and appreciation of each other's work and to recognize excellence:

People pay attention to it and are sensitive to not being hopelessly embarrassed . . . it keeps people thinking in terms of how they're going to plan

their next five years so they'll have some things on record that will count as
productivity for the full professor review.

—Chairperson, University C

Symbolic Value

We also noted across the eight institutions that the higher the level of individual administrative responsibility and authority, the broader the viewpoint about what the overall goals and intended outcomes of the review should be. Almost without exception, senior-level administrators (dean and above) in every institution asserted that the policy carried some degree of value and usually talked about that value in developmental, political, or symbolic terms:

> *It works to motivate faculty a bit to look at what they're doing. At this*
> *point if the goal is to remove faculty, it doesn't work for that.... So, if the*
> *goal is to be protective of tenure, it is. If the goal is to be focused on*
> *attempting to provide someone with a developmental plan, it does that.*
> *If the goal is to rid the system of non-performers, it fails miserably.*
>
> —Dean, University B

Cynicism and Concern

Two specific areas of concern came especially from those institutions that struggled with the implementation of post-tenure review. One view was that the stated purposes did not match the actual purposes. This caused faculty cynicism and led no one to take the process seriously. The other concern was that when developmental goals were not perceived as important by the administration or policymakers, the faculty viewed post-tenure review as purely punitive and targeted to get rid of the deadwood:

> *In theory the goal is to bring faculty members who have a low productivity*
> *up to a higher productivity. At the time it went into effect, everybody*
> *viewed it as a Board of Regents policy to prune the deadwood.*
>
> —Faculty Member, University B

> *It is really a kick in the groin, I think, and has made all of us not even*
> *want to do this in the future. If it's not going to have any impact, then*
> *what's the point of doing it at all?*
>
> —Faculty Member, University F

Conclusions

In general, the interviews and surveys revealed that:

- Policies specify multiple purposes—not always mutually reinforcing and sometimes competing.

- Summative objectives clearly outweigh formative goals in terms of how faculty interpret policy as it is actually "practiced."

- Accountability is almost always identified as a critical driver for policy formulation.

- Faculty and administrators seek a greater convergence of purpose with practice including blending more effectively accountability mandates and formative objectives.

2) ARE POST-TENURE REVIEW POLICIES EFFECTIVE?

Broadly speaking, faculty, chairs and deans did not give their policies very high marks in terms of effectiveness in accomplishing the intended policy purpose.

Questionable Effectiveness

Respondents in six of the eight institutions either indicated that their policy was ineffective in achieving its stated purpose or they were on the fence with this question. In only two institutions could the majority interviewed and surveyed offer a positive commentary about their policy effectiveness.

Deans and other senior academic administrators, regardless of the institution, tended to be slightly more positive across the board on the issue of effectiveness than were their faculty and chair counterparts.

Survey responses confirmed these mixed opinions about effectiveness. About 42% of all respondents said their policy was either "not that effective" or "ineffective"; 31% indicated their policy was "very or somewhat effective," and 27% said they were "neutral" or "that it was too soon to know."

Political Effectiveness Noted

Surprisingly, while a large number of faculty lacked conviction that their policies were accomplishing what they were set out to accomplish, many did admit that if the legislature or board of regents was satisfied with the policy and its implementation, then they felt that counted for something. Some even said it counted for everything. Chairs and deans were not always of the same mind on this issue of effectiveness; from time to time, the deans were more inclined to note some measure of effectiveness. (See Chapter 5 for a fuller discussion.)

Reasons for Ineffectiveness: Lack of Outcomes, Follow-Through, and Consequences

Interestingly, there were three major reasons offered over and over again to explain why a particular policy was considered ineffective. The three reasons boiled down to a lack of follow-through after the review was completed. Respondents specifically said:

- The review shows little evidence of positive outcomes.

- The review is not taken seriously because there is no significant follow-up action to the review.

- The review is not taken seriously because there are no sanctions for poor performance.

Lack of Leadership, Resources, and Oversight

When the issue of effectiveness was probed further, respondents often pointed to the lack of leadership and failed actions on the part of chairs, deans, and other senior administrators in following up with faculty after the review to ensure that attention was paid to closing the loop. Depending on the particular institution, this could mean appropriating resources to support an improvement or developmental plan and/or ensuring that proper faculty recognition occurred:

> . . . *It is dependent entirely on the administrative style of the supervisor who in this case is a department chair; the previous one never really addressed it [post-tenure review] in any formal way.*
>
> —Faculty Member, University D

> *I think it's a process that's been in place for 15 years perhaps, but it's had very little effect and I don't think that the reality is that it is taken very seriously.*
>
> —Chairperson, University B

Faculty also drew attention to the importance of serious and conscientious administrative oversight in the process. In turn, chairs, because of their faculty status, looked to their dean for support and often found it wanting:

> *I find that post-tenure review is meaningless because we, as chairs, can't do anything about it. Even though the policy, for example, says that we have to summarize student evaluations, I don't want to summarize those. There is no point to it. Why would I do that if this professor is going to become angry? Do you think that after a recent confrontation [with this professor] I am going to even get into his student evaluations? No, I'll let the dean do it.*
>
> —Chairperson, University F

Some Effectivness Cited

As a rule, chairs were of the opinion that in order for post-tenure review to be effective, the review needed to be positive, constructive, and nonpunitive. Deans, in fact, occasionally pointed to the positive effect that the review had on changes to workload, renewed commitment of faculty, and changes in career paths including retirement. The commentaries that follow reveal the ways in which effectiveness was displayed:

> *I, for one, would like to see post-tenure review continue, but I'd like to see it continue in an improved form where perhaps it would be more forma-tive rather than summative . . . more like collegial mentoring, rather than dismissing a person.*
>
> —Chairperson, University F

> *I have one or two faculty members that went through this process that, for example, were not doing very well in professional development but also were not making any effort in instruction. One of them has at least made the effort to turn around . . . the other one basically doesn't give a damn either way. And now that he has gone through this, he is going to retire in a couple of years, and so there is nothing that I can do. He basically holds everyone ransom. We all have that kind of problem . . . however, it is clear that this person is not going to stick around for the next five-year review. . . . So it does have an effect. It is not immediate.*
>
> —Chairperson, University A

> *I suppose there is the notion that if you have someone who is not produc-tive [then]the signal needs to go out that there is a problem here and that perhaps some change is called for, either by way of retirement or by way of changing one's focus within the department. Perhaps doing more teaching and less research or service.*
>
> —Chairperson, University A

> *The purpose is to develop an opportunity for [the] University to discover if they have any deadwood and to discover whether there is some greenery amidst the deadwood that can be brought to flower by proper nourish-ment. So it's a checkpoint for people who could be missed.*
>
> —Dean, University H

Conclusions

By and large, faculty, chairs, and other academic administrators either seriously questioned the effectiveness of their policy or were on the fence with this issue. The lack of follow-through and consequences was by far the predominant reason cited for this position.

Those able to recount specific examples of effectiveness pointed to the politi-cal capital gained from the review and the belief that the review provided a means by which chairs and deans could help to support shifts in work emphasis, renew professional interests and, accelerate retirement decisions.

3) What Impact Does Post-Tenure Review Have on Faculty Work, Professional Development, and Career Planning?

In those six institutions where post-tenure review was not working as well as faculty and administrators thought it could, the general viewpoint was that there were few tangible results or outcomes related to performance or career development. For two institutions, where it was perceived to be effective, the impact was viewed in more tangible and positive terms.

Impact on Performance: Tangible Outcomes Unclear

Impact requires motion or action of one sort or another. For many we spoke with, the lack of impact was tied to a general evaluation climate that did not lead to impact for the reasons that follow.

Nothing happens. Many faculty and chairs reported that the process was *pro forma*. This led to an opinion, shared by a considerable number in the six institutions, that while in theory post-tenure review is a reasonable idea, in practice the process doesn't carry any material outcomes and rarely leads to significant changes in performance. One faculty member expressed this sentiment in the following way:

> So I think the idea [post-tenure review] is ok—I haven't seen much impact—either in terms of feedback following the review or direct link to next process.
>
> —Faculty Member, University H

We heard many more say nothing happens than say something happens. Not everyone was necessarily disappointed, however, that nothing happened; in fact, some were relieved. Some were also quite satisfied with intangible results:

> It makes no difference to me. I am highly productive with good publications going out and regular grants and contracts coming in.
>
> —Faculty Member, University E

But by far, more expressed frustration about the lack of discernable outcomes or were disappointed with the lack of meaningful follow-through and consequences.

No discernable impact on performance. It is fair to say that, all in all, the interviews did not reveal many examples of specific changes in individual faculty performance caused by a post-tenure review. Often, we heard faculty and chairs express ambivalence about whether tangible outcomes occurred or say that the process was either redundant with the annual review or had the "potential" to be of benefit to them but needed to be improved on one way or the other:

> *It had no tangible benefits. So it took time and there was no change in my teaching or research. I was left with a so-what feeling (but that's what I expected).*
>
> —Faculty Member, University B

> *I've never seen anybody's behavior pattern changed by this.*
>
> —Dean, University G

> *The university needs to be more clear on the outcomes it really wants and convey that to the faculty. We often do not know until the review which are the "dime slots" and which are the "dollar slots."*
>
> —Faculty Member, University E

The ambivalence about tangible outcomes came through loud and clear on the survey as well. While 41% indicated that the process was *not* beneficial to individual faculty work, another 34% were neutral and 23% said the process did hold some benefit.

Frustration. Those who reported that nothing happened often shared resentment because they recognized the process required an investment of time without payback:

> *I'm not sure there's a collective sense about what's done around post-tenure review... what the outcomes are... except it being busywork... and having them tell you some things you already know.*
>
> —Faculty Member, University F

> *It was sort of a non-event because it didn't get me anything... I get most of my praise and strokes and satisfaction outside [the university].*
>
> —Faculty Member, University H

Fear and anxiety. Some faculty discussed the negative consequences of post-tenure review—the fear and anxiety it generated in the faculty:

> *Every time I come up for post-tenure review, it is a dreadful experience. I'm up next year and frankly, I'm already anticipating it. I've found it highly demoralizing in my case.*
>
> —Faculty Member, University F

After post-tenure review, there is a sigh of relief because of concern that the whole thing is punitive.

—Faculty Member, University E

Lack of feedback and follow-through. The reason noted by many for the failure of the process to produce tangible results centered on the lack of any meaningful follow-through and the failure to tie professional development resources to review results:

I haven't had any feedback other than what I get on my teaching evaluations. It [post-tenure review] might just as well not be done. Over the years I've never seen anyone benefit from it or anyone punished for it whatever the case might be.

—Faculty Member, University F

You never get any feedback. You do all of this work and you do not know whether your time was valued, undervalued or devalued.

—Chair, University E

The only time, though, you get feedback on needing improvement is if there is a crescendo of complaints about the quality of teaching. Or, if something is done so outrageous. But, seldom do we give feedback to someone saying you know you can do better. Or you know you could have considered this. . . . It doesn't have to be confrontational but something that kind of reinforces the norms of excellence of the department . . .

—Faculty Member, University G

Lack of consequences: Carrot or stick? Some were quick to point out that there was no muscle attached to the follow-through process either by way of sanctions or rewards:

I don't think there is anything wrong with these types of reviews. I just think there should be some consequences to them. Something should happen after you spend that much energy and effort on something.

—Faculty Member, University C

Put more teeth in it—have sanctions for those who died in office years ago.

—Faculty Member, University H

You can say that the focus is on how I can do better, which is not how it is currently being interpreted . . .

—Faculty Member, University F

Now, for the post-tenure review, what people are going to say is here is one more document and what are they going to do with it? Nothing.

Are they going to fire him? No. Is he going to change? No. So why are we even doing this?

—Faculty Member, University B

Because post-tenure review has affected only 25 of 600 people, it is unclear if it is seen as a Damocles sword hanging over faculty or if they are even dimly aware of its presence.

—Senior Administrator, University I

Lack of resources. The lack of sufficient resources to support faculty development was cited as a reason why a greater impact wasn't realized.

Many, except perhaps senior administrators, pointed to a lack of additional faculty development resources as a contributing factor to the lack of significant tangible results. Senior-level administrators often felt there were ample opportunities and resources available, and that when a case could be made for support, resources could be found. On the other hand, chairs seemed to be saying that discretionary resources should be easier to access.

The issue of outcomes was interesting to probe because key to the discussion was the confusion about whether the review should be tilted in the direction of remediation or development and where support for either outcome can be found. While many senior administrators asserted that any laudable development objective coming from a review would be supported, this belief was not articulated by all constituents:

We've lost the improvement aspect of the policy. You either get a gold star or not. If you don't get a gold star, it is like pulling teeth from that point on . . .

—Senior Administrator, University B

Sometimes there's no outcome on this stuff. I mean, all of us get frustrated because we attend zillions of hours of meetings and we get nothing out of it and it drives us absolutely crazy.

—Dean, University B

I worked very hard with two folks to develop what I hope would have been a productive review. It went into a black hole.

—Faculty Member, University F

I think our group [council of deans] has lacked imagination about what could be possible with this review, but listening to people [other deans] around this table, I understand there are some things we could be doing.

—Dean, University G

Some Tangible Results

There were faculty and administrators in almost every institution who could point to tangible outcomes here and there. In two institutions, it was not a "here and there" but rather a "here and how." Across all the institutions, the two outcomes that were frequently mentioned were increased retirements and increased opportunities, particularly to improve research productivity.

Retirement. One of the outcomes mentioned in every institution and especially by chairs, deans, and senior administrators was a reported increase in the number of retirements by senior faculty:

> *He [the faculty member] was so aghast at the fact that other faculty in the department felt exactly the same that I did that he retired instead of being a negative force and a troublemaker in the department. The post-tenure review told the truth of faculty opinion which they [peers] were unwilling to tell him on a day to day basis in conversation.*
>
> —Chair, University A

New opportunities. The types of tangible results reported included opportunities for a term leave, course release time, financial support for staff and/or equipment, promotion to full professor, special recognition of contributions, successful sabbatical application, research seed money, modifications in teaching workload, and opportunity to engage more deeply in scholarship:

> *... The post-tenure review gave me time to negotiate with the chair and dean what my workload would be for the next whatever years.*
>
> —Faculty Member, University A

Some chairs did report seeing tangible results serving as a real morale boost to the faculty. In one school, reference was made to the really positive impact that the follow-up conference with the dean had for each reviewed faculty member.

Some Intangible Outcomes

Central to the question of results and impact was the distinction some made between tangible and intangible outcomes. Frequently, faculty and chairs referred to the intrinsic or intangible outcomes that the process spawned, such as reaffirmation of quality work and an opportunity for career reflection.

Reflection. For some, the review provided an invitation for self-examination and career introspection:

> *When I knew that I was going to come up for post-tenure review, it actually inspired me to ... say I had better get this publication out or give this gradu-*

ate student a little bit of urging. So for me it was a positive experience, and I can see that it would be a positive experience for people who are doing well.
— Faculty Member, University B

I thought it was just another bureaucratic hurdle that they were going to put into the system when it first started, but I am sold on it now after going through six of them and seeing the faculty that were at the marginal end and at the top end—all of us getting something constructive out of it.
— Faculty Member, University A

Colleague appreciation. Greater knowledge of and appreciation for colleagues' contributions were also cited sometimes by faculty and peer review committee members:

In at least a few cases, I thought it [post-tenure review] was helpful because there were differences in perceptions, and in some cases, the perception on both ends changed; the perception of the individual as to what they are doing as well as the perception of the committee based on the materials they saw changed too.
— Faculty Member, University C

We need to move post-tenure review from the evaluation model to the highlighted model. I think that is a really important consequence. It drives my thinking that says it's worthwhile, because it not only evaluates, but it places work in a context that makes it accessible.
— Peer Review Committee Member, University G

Reaffirmation of performance standards. Chairs saw clarification of performance standards as a worthy outcome in some departments:

. . . If you have people who aren't pulling their weight, not because they're lazy or intellectually incapable of doing it, but for some other reason, then your job is to try and counsel them as to what they should be doing. That's one reason I really like the five-year review and post-tenure review because it forces the chair and dean to do his or her job.
— Chair, University D

Benefit to productive performers. Another view we heard from time to time was that the review offered the most benefit to faculty who are interested in continuous improvement. One faculty member from University C said that "the unexamined academic life is not worth living." Others framed it as encouragement:

It made me encouraged—encouraged me to get more things done, encouraged me to believe that I would actually get the support for everything that I was doing. It provided evaluative recognition and support.

—Faculty Member, University A

. . . It was a time of reflection and going back over what I have and haven't done. And looking through a little bit of self-reflection about what I have enjoyed most and where the successes have been and what can be done to improve. I think it was done in a good way with good faith on everybody's part.

—Faculty Member, University A

I guess one view I have of the whole process is that it's better [at] encouraging people that are generally concerned with their performance, than it is at targeting and punishing individuals that are not performing at the expected level . . . because you don't have very effective ways of dealing with people in the system as it exists.

—Chair, University G

You have got productive people; you have people who may be less productive . . . and you have got the third category of those people that have not been productive and probably will not be productive. If I allocate resources, I want to keep the productive people happy and I want to keep the unproductive ones unhappy. . . . So I direct resources to the productive side of the department, or to that side that is also trying to become productive.

—Chair, University A

Impact on Career Development

When asked about the results of the process on professional/personal career development and planning, more individuals were neutral on this question than had an opinion. It is difficult to interpret what this level of neutrality and ambivalence connotes. It may mean that more time is needed in order to formulate an opinion about the impact on career development or that career development is multifaceted and difficult to unbundle.

At this juncture, our results neither affirm nor disaffirm whether post-tenure review impacts career development and planning. What we know is that when pressed, faculty and administrators don't feel strongly one way or the other on this question.

OTHER RELATED QUESTIONS

4) DOES POST-TENURE REVIEW HELP ADVANCE DEPARTMENTAL GOALS AND INSTITUTIONAL MISSION?

Information gathered from interviews on how post-tenure review affected individual departments and institutions is inconclusive. Survey responses corroborate as almost 50% of all respondents indicated they had not formulated an opinion yet on the question of the overall impact of post-tenure review on the department.

What we are able to derive from this broad-based wait-and-see response is that moving outside the sphere of individual impact is a challenge for many faculty.

Difficult to Discern

Chairs and deans were much more able to discuss the benefits and the shortcomings of post-tenure review at the department level than were faculty. Faculty members either failed to recognize any impact or said they were not in a position to know if any real impact on the department was felt:

> *Difficult to say because I have had no chance to see in terms of what has been reported as targets and what has been accomplished.*
>
> —Faculty Member, University F

Results Kept Confidential

Faculty pointed out that results from reviews are kept confidential and this makes it difficult to know exactly how results affect the department at large. Some chairs said the review provided greater ability to create more flexible faculty workload profiles and was a way to help redirect and rechannel faculty efforts to better meet the overall needs of the department:

> *It does seem to motivate some people and is paying off in major ways for a few.*
>
> —Chair, University H

Promotion

Chairs in some settings agreed that while the process is not a magic bullet, it did help associate professors get over the hump and achieve promotion to full professor. In the words of one associate professor:

> *It was an opportunity to sit down and think about what I want to do and get clarity on it—it was a pleasant surprise.*
>
> —Faculty Member, University H

Retirement

Some chairs also indicated that the review gave them increased ability to spur faculty to be more productive or that the process seemed to assist some faculty make decisions to retire. Some chairs noted that retirements do affect departments and provide opportunities for strategic hiring:

> *My guess is that . . . it [post-tenure review] prompts people who are getting too comfortable to get a little less comfortable . . . so I think it has prompted, I am sure, a few people to think well at age 61 to take the retirement money which is not bad and move out of the way, letting people with more energy and zip to begin to take over. . . . I think some people do feel anxious abut it, and I think that is maybe okay.*
>
> —Faculty Member, University A

Departmental Renewal

One other aspect of impact that came through on several campuses was how the review was used as a means of redirecting and rechanneling faculty efforts and how such action can help departments achieve collective goals:

> *The thing that was really exciting was when we sat down with the faculty and re-channeled from a research agenda to a more teaching agenda; that we were really able to get them excited about teaching . . .*
>
> —Chair, University A

> *I think perhaps people are now being a little more serious about their work; perhaps trying a little harder . . . because I think now there is more accountability than there was before.*
>
> —Faculty Member, University A

> *Yes . . . I know of several instances where the person under evaluation wasn't aware of the area of neglect . . . and they modified their behavior.*
>
> —Faculty Member, University C

A former dean at University C, a setting where post-tenure review had existed for more than 20 years, was quite positive about how the process helped advance unit goals:

> *In addition to the wholly positive reaction of some professors, I can think of one professor who retired as a direct result of the committee's review and required remedial action. I can think of another who, while objecting to the committee's appraisal of his teaching did in fact change his methods of relating to students. A number of others, probably three or so, reviewed their research . . . another significant group of full professors who were returning to teaching roles after a stint as department chair,*

probably 8 of these professors, for them . . . the review stood as a palpable reminder that at some time in the future they would again be reviewed by their peers on the criteria of teaching . . . and there is another large group who took the committee's advice and focused hard on the next piece of writing that they may have postponed for a while . . . there is another very large group of full professors for whom the prospect of the review in the next year served as a spur to retirement.

—Dean, University C

Seriousness of Departmental Implementation

In the minds of many chairs, deans, and other administrators, any positive impact at the department or institution level depended in large measure on how seriously the unit took its evaluation responsibilities. It was apparent that post-tenure review impacted some departments in positive ways and other departments in negative ways:

Some people have taken this quite seriously and others rubber stamp. . . . As a result in a couple of cases, there have been some real substance to the reports, some critical substance for some faculty . . .

—Faculty Member, University G

There have been tremendous changes in our department and there have been so many things going on . . . all of this stuff is good . . . but pinpointing and taking one thing and saying post-tenure review had this effect— there is no way. There is no way to discern it from all of the other things going on.

—Faculty Member, University A

I think the process of post-tenure review supplies evidence to the faculty that it should have, so that when outsiders, who can be anyone, from the governor to the dean, say "I'm not satisfied that your department is pulling the wagon," you can then take out these reviews and say, "Well let's look at the evidence and then talk about what you mean by that."

—Faculty Member, University B

. . . Most of our faculty are performing very well. So I think people would see this as pro forma and perfunctory. . . . But I think if there are cases where departments are having issues with certain faculty and they want them to enhance their teaching or hold up their end of the load, it can be used very effectively.

—Peer Review Committee, University F

> *It does seems to be that prior to the post-tenure review process people felt empowered to complain every year when things didn't go their way in the annual merit review process. Now you have a basis for reflecting back to them that says well look, you now got this report and it said you should be doing this, attending to that. You're not doing this or attending to that, what do you expect?*
>
> —Peer Review Committee, University G

Conclusions

Our interview and survey responses make clear that faculty find it difficult to discuss impact on a broader level than that of the individual. Results of reviews are rarely communicated and generally kept confidential. Only two institutions had initiated any sort of university-wide effort to collect aggregate data on the results from post-tenure review. In every other setting, no comparable type of reporting existed. This may help explain why faculty did not feel equipped to comment on this.

Chairs and deans, on the other hand, were more opinionated on this question and were able to discuss the impact of the review on departmental goal achievement, departmental morale, promotions, retirements, and career renewal.

5) Is Post-Tenure Review Worth It?

When asked whether the post-tenure review process was worth the time and effort required, there was not a majority response in one direction or the other. In fact, survey respondents were almost evenly divided between saying it was worth the effort (36%), feeling it was too soon to know (27%), and stating it wasn't worth the effort (37%). Interview data revealed the same type of three-way split in three institutions. In the other five, two were clearly negative in their assessment of worth, and three were clearly more positive than negative.

Stakeholders across institutions who told us they believed the process was worthwhile generally felt that post-tenure review should be continued. However, these same constituents frequently added specific areas needing modification. The opposite was true in the case of those who saw no worth to the process. These faculty and administrators, although a minority, were usually ready to scrap the process completely. A third group, those on the fence, who needed more time to formulate an opinion or expressed a wait-and-see attitude wanted to reserve judgment until another review cycle occurred.

Some commented that while post-tenure review had not been of benefit to them personally, they realized that it might be a useful process because it helped their institution demonstrate accountability and compliance with external mandates. So while the process didn't carry direct benefit on an individual basis, many were convinced of its symbolic worth.

In at least five of the eight institutions, stakeholders talked about the evolving nature of the process at their own university and noted that while in theory post-tenure review may be a laudable idea, as practiced, it needed improvement. Though the numbers were small, there were faculty and administrators on every campus who were opposed to post-tenure review regardless of the political or symbolic benefit that might accrue from it. Three views were most often voiced:

- Keep post-tenure review as is.

- Retain it, but make modifications.

- Scrap it completely.

Keep Post-Tenure Review in Its Current Form

The reasons for wanting to keep the process in its current form were varied and ranged from feeling personal satisfaction to evoking resignation that it is just the cost of "doing business in today's accountability climate."

Positive personal worth. Those who saw worth in the process sometimes held this opinion because of a positive personal experience either as a member of a review committee or because of their own review experience:

> *Overall the purpose was worthwhile—it gave more understanding of how peers viewed work; it enhanced communication and understanding. It keeps people on their toes and eliminates suspicion of deadwood; and it helps individuals think about his/her role in the department and contributes to strategic mission.*
>
> —Faculty Member, University C

> *Yes, I think it is a good compromise and should be kept at this current level of effort. I don't think it should escalate to make it a lot more onerous. . . . I think to keep it around this level at a dull roar is a good thing, because I think it has some positive effect at least. I'm giving a pat on the back for people to say what they have accomplished over five years and because it does add a little more incentive to the work of the academic enterprise.*
>
> —Faculty Member, University G

> *I think that the overall majority would not consider it [post-tenure review] a bad policy or be in favor of doing away with it. They might differ in terms of how much it helped them out.*
>
> —Chancellor, University C

> *Yeah it is worth it . . . the review is needed because one weak link can't be supported in today's fiscal environment.*
>
> —Faculty Member, University D

Forestalls external intrusion. Chairs often attributed some benefit to the process, even when their faculty didn't. As a group, deans and other senior-level administrators most often said that despite process shortcomings, post-tenure review served a useful purpose on the internal and external levels. The cost/benefit analysis was described in the following way by one chairperson:

> *. . . when you are looking at your benefit and cost, you have got three parties to check: (1) The faculty member who is going through the review—I think the benefits there outweigh the costs, and the principal benefit is that if the faculty member is productive, he gets guidance in terms of what would lead him to being productive. (2) The second entity is the department, and the benefits there, I think, outweigh the costs. The benefit is that the faculty members start to see what the others are doing. A lot of times they don't know what John, two doors down, is doing because it doesn't come up over a lunch conversation. So you start to see some synergism created, a little bit of joint authorship, discussions of different teaching techniques because they see what the other has done. The cost there is obviously the department committee time. (3) And then the third party is the chair, and for me it is beneficial because it keeps my productive faculty happy. It keeps the ones that have to upgrade less anxious than before because they have a sense of what they are doing. And the cost is negligible. . . . But the overriding benefit to me from post-tenure review is that post-tenure review is going to forestall the legislature from trying to eliminate tenure. And if there is no other reason to do it, that is the baseline for me.*
>
> —Chairperson, University A

Accountability enhancer. Many referred to the indirect benefit the policy made in demonstrating accountability and for that reason alone wanted to keep the process in place:

> *It may be worth it [in terms of how much we gained and spent]. Probably wouldn't. If you put it in another sense, though, and that is the amount of accountability and credibility to a public that doesn't understand what we do or doesn't believe we do it right, then you come up with an intangible value that I don't know how you calculate . . .*
>
> —Dean, University G

> *. . . I think if we were to stop doing it, the consequences would be worse.*
> —Senior Administrator, University B

> *More damage can be done by banning tenure than by going through PTR [post-tenure review].*
> —Faculty Member, University H

Useful in "some" circumstances. Because the tangible results from the reviews varied dramatically among departments in every institution, some wanted to keep it only for those "exceptional" circumstances:

> *I am not willing at this point to say this is wonderful or this is terrible. I suspect that it will probably be neither, but, something more in-between. Certainly useful in some cases.*
> —Faculty Member, University H

No pain. Some faculty, chairs, and deans said that because it didn't require an overwhelming amount of effort, the process was worth it:

> *We don't put much effort into it, so it is worth it.*
> —Chairperson, University G

Need time to reap full benefit. In some instances, administrators who reflected on the process in relationship to its potential commented that after faculty have been through it once and realize that demons are not present, they begin to explore how the process can be transformative:

> *. . . What I think we're seeing is people now becoming more reflective about it. We got through this, the first five years, you know. We soft-peddled it purposefully and people have gotten rid of their sea legs and they are feeling more secure. And they know that the administration's not going to use these reviews in arbitrary ways. And now I'm hearing . . . people saying, now, it's time to revisit what we're doing . . . and see if there aren't things that different schools could learn from each other about how they are doing it [post-tenure review] and what their experiences are.*
> —Senior Administrator, University G

Maintain Post-Tenure Review, but Make Changes

Many faculty, chairs, and deans recognized that in theory post-tenure review could serve a useful purpose. What triggered discontent was the lack of attention to follow-through and the lack of clout to make the process worthwhile:

> *Well, in the abstract it does seem to serve a useful purpose to have each person looked at every five years, and I think we all do understand that there are expectations. . . . So I guess my conclusion is that there is value in*

> *the post-tenure process, if it were handled properly. But then more impor-*
> *tant is [to] put some teeth into the process so that if deficiencies are found,*
> *some consequences follow . . . including termination.*
>
> —Faculty Member, University B

The number of recommendations for ways to improve and strengthen the process were significant and are summarized later in this chapter.

Scrap Post-Tenure Review

Faculty and academic administrators who said adamantly post-tenure review was not worth it came principally from two campuses (University E and University I), which were experiencing problems in implementation. These constituents assert-ed that the reviews were not worth the time and effort. Some believed the process increased stress and caused low morale, and some said it duplicated other reviews:

> *I would rather live with a poor performer in the department then trust*
> *administrators to do post-tenure review.*
>
> —Faculty Member, University I

Duplicative of other forms of review. Others felt the process was duplicative of the annual merit review or other informal reviews and, therefore, didn't add any value. Those who voiced this opinion usually pointed out that because concrete outcomes or opportunities from post-tenure review were not defined or prac-ticed, the review lacked substance for career planning and clout for performance modification. These faculty believed the annual review had sufficient reward and consequence levers. Again, faculty who said the review was a complete waste of time pointed to its duplicative nature or misguided implementation:

> *It is superfluous because faculty are already reviewed annually and the*
> *criteria for both appear to be the same. The only difference is the time*
> *period covered.*
>
> —Faculty Member, University E

> *I felt I didn't need it. . . . We have a range—some superstars and some*
> *who aren't adequate—but no one is inadequate or in need of counseling*
> *or a reprimand. I think the informal methods of keeping the tribe mem-*
> *bers in line would work just as well as a formal evaluation procedure.*
>
> —Faculty Member, University F

Waste of time.

> *But for senior faculty it's very hard to change them . . . they feel fairly*
> *secure in what they're doing. They feel that the sanctions are not that*

onerous if they get a bad review. . . . So, I don't really see it as having that much benefit."

—Faculty Member, University B

So you call on your best people. OK. They are taking time away from more important things in my view to do this and I am at a loss as to why this is a good thing."

—Faculty Member, University G

Conclusions

Faculty and administrators on six of the eight campuses saw varying degrees of worth in the process. It ranged from talking about worth on a very personal level, seeing worth because others needed to be prodded, and identifying worth for accountability purposes.

While fewer in number, those pushing for dismantling post-tenure review saw no worth because they felt it was duplicative of other reviews and a waste of time.

One important theme that made its way into this discussion centered on the need to experience more time with the review process in order to determine overall worth.

6) Other Important Observations

Prior to the popularization of post-tenure review, faculty and academic leaders worried that such reviews might have deleterious affects on academic freedom and give unbridled power to administrators to make the reviews prohibitively punitive. Some speculated that the reviews would require an inordinate amount of time, energy, and paperwork. These and other issues were probed in the survey and explored to some degree during the interviews.

Procedures Considered Clear, Fair, and Consistent

In all but one institution, a faculty committee worked in varying degrees with the administration to develop the specific review procedures and review criteria. It is not surprising that regardless of one's opinion about the overall worth of post-tenure review, when questioned about various procedural aspects, faculty, chairs, deans, and senior-level administrators routinely gave positive ratings to the clarity, fairness, and consistency of review procedures and to the criteria used to assess performances. Appeal procedures were also considered adequate.

Documentation Preparation Is Manageable

Likewise, a majority of faculty and chairs concurred that the required documentation was manageable, provided that one kept his or her vita up-to-date. More than 73% of survey responses confirmed this opinion.

Department Chair Role Better Understood Than Dean's Role

The role played by the chairperson in the review is fairly well understood by the majority of faculty in each institution. (See Appendix B for a description of the chair's role in each institution.) The same clarity does not hold true when it comes to the role of the dean. Chairs themselves often do not see their own roles as clear. More than 60% of survey responses indicated clarity about the chair's role, yet only 48% were similarly clear with respect to the role of the dean.

In probing this further, two factors emerged that help explain this. In several settings (University B, University F, and University H), the post-tenure review policy does not formally designate a role for the dean to play in the process. Consequently, faculty were uncertain about what to expect from the dean and what formal responsibilities their dean had in the process. The deans in these same settings confirmed this role ambiguity but for the most part did not feel changes in policy were warranted. In two cases where deans did indeed have a defined role by policy, faculty in particular, and to a lesser degree, chairs, pointed out that their dean did not always fully exercise his or her associated responsibility. This created the impression that the policy was not taken seriously up the line. The lack of role clarity further fueled confusion about the "real" role of the dean in the process and whether the dean ascribed any meaning to the review. In two institutions (University B and University I), the chair conducted the review without any peer committee involvement. In these cases, there was usually no role confusion. A considerable number of these chairs did comment that there was no recourse they could invoke, nor any real resources to tap into, so their power to give meaning to the process was very limited. In general, even chairs who worked with peer committees labeled their responsibilities as more of an "enforcer" than a "developer."

We were unable to find any definitive connection or correlation between the perceived effectiveness of post-tenure review, the length of service as a chair or dean, and the perceived clarity that the chair or dean expressed with respect to his or her role in the process. One might speculate that the shorter the term as an administrator, the less motivation to worry about overall policy impact. Interestingly, in the two universities where faculty had the strongest positive views about post-tenure review, the role of the dean and chair were reversed. In University A, the department chair was the nexus for actions following the review; in University C, the dean assumed that role and the chair had no formal role in developing the follow-up action plans with the faculty member.

Follow-Through and Meaningful Consequences Are Lacking

Interview and survey data clearly uncover a pervasive dissatisfaction on the part of campus stakeholders about the lack of meaningful follow-through. Dissatisfaction was voiced time and time again about the inadequacy of follow-up procedures or the lack of follow-through by those entrusted to ensure that rewards, development opportunities, and sanctions are available for use in the review process. More than 53% of survey respondents said there wasn't an adequate range of rewards and development opportunities available.

For many, this lack of follow-through seemed to beg the question, "What value does post-tenure review add to existent review practices?" While some (clearly the minority) believe nothing substantial should happen if the review is designed to be a developmental tool, others expressed the desire to see intentional follow-through by the appropriate administrator occur consistently and be coupled with the ability to provide development resources and opportunities. This combination was cited by many as what makes for a meaningful process.

Further, engagement by the chair and/or dean in the process was cited as critical in order to facilitate the establishment of a follow-up plan and essential in order to encourage and support development for all faculty.

There was disagreement about whether adequate resources existed to support such plans, however. The majority of deans and senior-level administrators said resources existed but needed to be requested, reallocated, or combined in ways to respond to review results.

Peers Play a Significant Role in Review Process

In six of the eight institutions studied, peers played a major role in the review itself. Peer review committees of various sizes and with different modes of selection review tenured colleagues. The majority of faculty that we spoke with who served as peer reviewers and a majority of the survey respondents (83%) indicated they felt either fully or somewhat qualified for the responsibilities that peer review involved. Likewise, from their direct experience, these same individuals felt that peer committees are capable of rendering fair and objective assessments and helpful recommendations.

Peer Review Makes Faculty Work Public

As previously noted from the interview narratives and corroborated by the survey, regardless of whether the review actually leads to positive follow-through, an overwhelming majority (>75%) of peer reviewers were able to separate their concerns about the follow-through and allowed that their involvement in the review increased both their knowledge of their colleagues' work and increased their appreciation of that work.

Pre-Tenure Review Practices and Tenure Review Procedures Not Affected by Post-Tenure Review

In the institutions studied, constituents were unable to cite any specific affect that post-tenure had on either the pre-tenure or tenure process. Rarely were these processes even raised in discussions, and survey respondents indicated in a majority voice that no discernable affect on either process was noticed. Well over 60% of survey responses indicated no affect. This finding was unexpected for two reasons. First, many faculties in their deliberations about possible negative repercussions from enforcing post-tenure review asserted that the review would either lead to more rigor or less rigor in the tenure review processes. Neither seems to have happened, at least based on the group of institutions studied here. Also surprising is the fact that the presence of post-tenure review did not seem to have influenced, at least, in the first cycle of implementation, an intentional reexamination of pre-tenure and tenure review practices in order to more closely align and link them together in terms of criteria and results.

Tenure, Academic Freedom, Professional Autonomy, Collegiality, and Professionalism Not Negatively Affected

Rarely during the interviews did individuals assert that post-tenure review was eroding core values such as academic freedom, professional autonomy, collegiality, and professionalism. Survey results instantiate this as well. Close to 60% of respondents said that these values were not impacted in a negative way by the post-tenure review process, although close to 20% indicated it was too soon to know what the impact was. Again these findings do not support the underlying fears expressed initially by many faculty groups (including the American Association of University Professors) that post-tenure review would undermine tenure and its corollary academic values. Very rarely did faculty recount instances of colleagues using the process (peer review) to punish another for not "getting along or going along."

Benefit Directed Mainly at Accountability—Other Benefits Unclear

When invited to discuss or list core benefits derived from post-tenure review, those cited were almost always directed at external stakeholders and characterized as "increasing faculty accountability." More faculty and administrators affirmed that the review helped "establish a culture and expectation for continuous growth and development" than said it didn't.

Conspicuously absent from the discussion about benefit was any strong or consistent suggestion of the review as an effective stimulus for greater efforts by faculty in teaching, research, service, or faculty planning to meet departmental priorities.

Resources Tagged as Problematic

Discussions about problems frequently converged on the lack of sufficient development resources, usually defined as funds to support both self-initiated faculty development plans and those that are required as a result of the review. Following fairly closely behind and identified mostly from the survey is the issue of excessive time and paperwork required. Both were seen as minor and less problematic than insufficient development funds. During the interviews, time and paperwork were considered more of a nuisance for some but not of an intolerable nature. One other shortcoming identified in the narratives and the survey was the lack of positive change in the performance of individuals over the long term. This problem squares with perspectives discussed earlier which point to a belief that post-tenure review does not lead to wide-scale changes in individual performance.

There were other problems identified which have already been discussed. These include the lack of substantive feedback and follow though; failure of process to make reward and recognition outcomes explicit; lack of viable ways to sanction and remediate unsatisfactory performance; and lack of any regular communication about the post-tenure review process and, in particular, about what the results have been for the institution.

7) Can the Process Be Improved?

Almost everyone interviewed offered suggestions for ways to improve policies. In fact, slightly over one-half of all survey respondents indicated changes were needed. Four improvement themes were consistent across institutional settings. These suggestions for improvement are closely coupled with faculty frustrations and dashed hopes identified earlier in this chapter.

Strengthen Review Outcome: Provide Timely Follow-Through and Feedback

If there was one complaint that every constituent group aimed its arrows at, it was the lack of a meaningful finale to the review. Time and time again, faculty, chairs, and members of peer review committees expressed frustration or disappointment about what appeared to them to be an empty process. The emptiness related to two factors: 1) lack of follow-through/feedback, and 2) missed or insufficient professional development opportunities. The issue of feedback and outcomes converged on the amount, the kind, and from whom the feedback was received.

No feedback. In six of the institutions, faculty complained that they didn't receive much meaningful feedback on their reviews. Some didn't care, but more did than didn't.

Feedback from dean or chair. Faculty suggested that formal feedback (either in writing, in person, or both) should come from their dean because this gives a positive indication that the dean values the process and is interested in assisting in career renewal. Further, the person who provides the feedback needs to have enough clout to make things happen.

Strengthen outcomes to follow feedback. Not surprising, feedback was characterized as only half of the desired equation; specific outcomes and consequences make up the second half. Faculty and chairs alike want the process to carry real meaning. The specific outcomes sought varied by institutional context, but common among all was that "something" happens following the review. The form that "something" takes was not necessarily the same across each institution but the range included recognition in the form of a monetary or a symbolic reward, access to funds or other opportunities in support of a developmental goal, a green light in terms of readiness for promotion, or allowing sanctions for unsatisfactory performance.

Increase and Improve Communication Across Institution About Purpose, Process, and Outcomes of Review

In the seven institutions studied that had a periodic review process, all "players" were not on the same page in their understanding of what was required or expected in the process. Further, many said that understanding how a developmental approach could/should be maintained was important to them but rarely discussed. Some department chairs and deans shaped the developmental framework better than others. Some consistently found ways to encourage prospective planning. Some simply didn't know how to do this or didn't consider that part of their role. One campus met with some success in using its program improvement process as the means to tie some resources to the post-tenure review.

Improve Certain Procedural Aspects of Review

A range of procedural improvements were suggested—many of which took aim at the following process components.

Uniformly and consistently carry out the process across the entire university. In at least three settings, our focus group discussions with deans and chairs uncovered some uncomfortable realizations. For example, in one setting, the conversation made it clear that some units had suspended post-tenure review; some departments and colleges were confused about what event triggered an intensive review. In another situation the weighting that student ratings played in the process was unclear.

Incorporate a professional career planning component into the process. Even the institutions that adopted a more developmental review culture were not always able to boast of having succeeded at integrating career planning into the process. Sometimes this occurred because chairs weren't interested in encouraging this particular goal. On other occasions, the process had lost its developmental intent because resources and other support were simply not available. There were at least two campuses where a development plan was only established when improvement was needed, thus giving the impression that development was punitive rather than valued.

Explore more creative ways for shifting allocations of faculty efforts and contribution. There was interest expressed in almost every institutional setting that the reviews should recognize the changing interests of mid- and late-career faculty and tie departmental needs to the roles faculty carry out within their departments. We saw this successfully accomplished in only two campuses.

Increase and better coordinate available professional development funds and resources. From our discussions with deans and other senior academic administrators, it was not clear whether there really was a bona fide lack of funds and opportunities that might be channeled to support the outcomes of this process. Or whether there was just a lack of coordination or communication among senior officers, deans, and chairs about the amount of resources available and where such resources reside. With the exception of one university, deans generally indicated that they had discretionary funds to work with. The presence and availability of those funds to support faculty career development and performance improvement were not always readily communicated, though.

Other faculty development resources (e.g., center for teaching effectiveness, research seed money, leave of absence opportunities, special funds for teaching innovation proposals, etc.), available in several of the universities, appeared to be plentiful. The challenge was that existing services and opportunities were not advertised or packaged in a coherent fashion that made it easy for faculty and chairs to tap into when a review concluded.

The next chapter examines these same questions within a private medical school setting. Despite the difference in policy, purpose, and approach, the themes that emerged from the eight public universities find considerable replication in the opinions expressed at a large medical school and academic health center.

4

A Medical School Version of Post-Tenure Review

The professions are replete with examples of changes to traditional employment practices. No sector is static. In recent days especially, everyone has been compelled to re-examine (and in some cases reengineer) its traditional employment policies to be more responsive to external and internal constituents, to increase financial and market flexibility, and to increase organizational agility.

—Trower, 1998, p. 1

Nowhere in American higher education has accountability been more pronounced than in medical schools and academic medical centers. Volatile fiscal conditions have plagued this environment, forcing changes in contractual arrangements and rewards systems for faculty. Because of these market-based challenges, medical schools have long been recognized as mavericks in developing innovative approaches to faculty employment issues. Including a medical school in the mix of institutional contexts we studied was important to our understanding of the variety of post-tenure review approaches possible and the particular results experienced. We were interested in seeing whether practices in this sector were dramatically different or significantly more effective than in mainstream higher education. Medical schools have led the way in adopting quality assurance practices related to performance and productivity. This suggested to us that valuable insights might be gained from examining this environment and discerning the effectiveness of performance reviews within this type of setting. This particular medical school is of interest because it has a five-year tenure review system (i.e., retenuring every five years), which is unique within the broader context of higher education—where the more traditional definition and application of tenure and post-tenure review are almost ubiquitous. One commentator in the field described the medical school milieu in the following way:

> Forty years ago, about 54 percent of the funding for medical education came from the federal government and only 17 percent from

clinical subsidies, tuition and the like. Today those numbers are reversed with government support representing less than 20 percent and the income from practice plans climbing about 58 percent. (Eisenberg, 1999, p. 28)

Curiously, during this same period, the number of basic science and clinical faculty hired grew from about 11,000 to 89,000. The ratio today of basic science faculty to clinical faculty is about 5½:1 (Andreoli, 1999, p. 33). This growth is staggering and contributes to the fiscal crisis currently facing medical schools. The funding base to support medical faculty has eroded because managed care, HMOs, and Medicare have reduced fees and payments for clinical services. As a result, "fiscal consideration in a competitive market drives the decisions, not the academic, clinical or research goals of departments" (Eisenberg, 1999, p. 28).

Because of the economic conditions and risks facing academic medicine, the rationale underlying tenure for medical school faculty and the relationship of tenure to salary have undergone stiff examination. New contractual arrangements have emerged that give medical schools increased flexibility to remain competitive and able to fill changing research or clinical staffing needs. These arrangements include term contracts, rolling contracts, and clinical appointments that do not carry a promise of tenure.

Embedded in these new approaches are varying ways in which salary is determined as well. The trend today is moving away from guaranteeing the entire salary. Instead, formulas are used which lay out what portion is guaranteed and what is expected to be generated through grants, awards, or clinical revenues. Frequently, the formulaic shorthand used is $X + Y + Z$, where X is the guaranteed salary, Y is income generated by the faculty member, and Z represents a bonus of some type. Another variation is to use median salaries associated with a subspecialty and rank. The faculty member is only guaranteed a specific percentage of the median salary. Compensation plans such as these require tenured faculty to share the risk with the university, which includes dwindling grants and shrinking clinical income.

Some in the field worry about the implications this market-driven solution holds for the rest of higher education, principally because it redefines one of the protections of tenure—economic security (see Medical Schools in the Era of Managed Care, 1999; Tierney, 1999; Trower, 1998).

Jordan J. Cohen, president of the American Association of Medical Colleges, believes that new realities in conceptualizing medical education are needed.

The existence of tenure in medical schools represents a linkage to the broader academic culture of the university, with its traditional devotion to a free exchange of ideas without threat of economic penalty.

Yet, medical schools, because of their increased involvement in the real word of health care delivery, also are linked to the corporate culture, with its brutal devotion to productivity without guarantees of economic security. The clash of these cultures is reaching deafening proportions and will challenge the most adroit academic administrators. If medical schools are to succeed, they must avoid the Scylla of an ivory-tower disregard of new competitive realities and the Charybdis of a corporate sellout of academic values. (Cohen, 1995, p. 294)

Cohen asserts further that these new realities must include required periodic evaluation to ensure appropriate productivity and a call for shifting faculty skills because of changing needs in the areas of clinical programs and educational research.

University D: History and Organization

University D is a private university with a School of Medicine that was established in 1902. The Medical Center's growth over the past 25 years has expanded the nature and scope of the school. This School of Medicine is one of 125 academic medical centers in the United States. As such, programs of the medical school and the affiliated hospital are interwoven to provide medical education, patient care, and bio-medical research and community service. Personnel at the Medical Center number about 9,000, and nearly 2,400 students—medical students, nursing students, nurse anesthesia students, bio-medical graduate students, house officers, physician assistant students, and allied health students—receive training annually through the center's teaching programs.

The work of the School of Medicine is divided among 29 academic departments. Each department includes an appropriate number of professors, associate and assistant professors, and instructors. Clinical departments also utilize the services of volunteer faculty, drawn from the state's privately practicing physicians and surgeons.

The control of the School of Medicine is vested in the Board of Trustees of University D. The senior vice president for health affairs and the dean are responsible for the operation of the School of Medicine through the president of the university.

Strategic Directions
The evolution of the Medical Center and the School of Medicine are ongoing. University D's strategic plan drives goals and objectives for faculty productivity and market position, including, among others, a specific intent that the medical center must

... be among the best nationally and maintain its traditional values and cultures. The Medical School should continue its migration to a level of institutional academic accomplishment that places it into the top ten percent of such institutions in the country.

The fiscal climate within this academic health center is changing, due in large part to changes in the health care industry described earlier. The strategic plan draws particular attention to what is referred to as a "new era":

The Medical Center is entering a new era and faces more change in a shorter period of time than at any point in its history. National health care reform is imposing tremendous stress on "status quo" methods of practice and historic methods of financial success. Cost-based funding of hospital services is a fond memory and "fees for service" are now heavily discounted, if not disappearing, as a method of professional reimbursement. These facts and changes in federal funding of medical and graduate medical education have mandated paradigm shifts in behavior and funding with Academic Health Centers (AHC). Revenue (sources) to both the academic and clinical enterprises of the AHC will be constrained. A premium will be placed on funding those AHCs, which can demonstrate "value," as defined by their funding source. Those AHCs which have not created timelines of change are facing shortened life expectations without hope of success or even survival ...

As a result of this fiscal environment, the medical school uses a budgeting model which it calls mission-based budgeting. As outlined in a 1999 presentation to the faculty by the dean of the School of Medicine, this budgeting model sets the framework for how faculty efforts are allocated and rewarded:

- *The economic environment for all U.S. medical schools places great emphasis on the ability to strategically focus constrained resources.*

- *The allocation of resources dedicated to undergraduate teaching should be based on the strategic needs of the curriculum.*

- *The research mission requires institutional support even at the highest level of success. In order to provide the resources to enhance a research mission, a consistent methodology for allocating basic research dollars to departments is necessary.*

- *The annual budget for each department is based on the institutional need for teaching and administrative effort and on a defined percentage of research effort.*

Faculty Responsibilities and Performance Review

The medical school has 701 full-time faculty, of which 468 are tenure eligible and 94 are currently tenured. Tenured faculty fall primarily into two appointment classifications: clinical faculty and basic science faculty. Tenure-eligible faculty are required to meet school criteria for tenure and promotion at the appointed rank.

Tenure within the medical school is applied differently than tenure within the remainder of University D. The seven-year "up and out" rule for tenure applies only to faculty within the greater university. Within the medical school, this is not the case. In fact, tenure is not a condition for continued employment, and today only about one-third of the tenure-eligible faculty (at rank of associate or full professor) currently hold tenure. One can be promoted in rank without tenure. As defined in the medical school faculty handbook,

> *Tenure, although limited to _five-year_ terms, implies continuation of employment until retirement and the right to participate fully in the activities of the department, provided that the faculty member continues to demonstrate productivity in the appropriate areas of patient care, research, teaching, service and other school functions, at a level comparable to that demonstrated by peers within the same department or section.*

Post-Tenure Review

Unlike the other settings studied, the medical school affiliated with University D has a post-tenure review process that technically is a five-year retenuring process. (This is not true for the other schools and colleges associated with University D.) In practice, continuation of tenured medical school faculty employment (renewal) is implied provided that the faculty member continues to demonstrate productivity in the areas of stated effort distribution. This productivity is assessed compared to that demonstrated by peers in the same department or section. Four different appointment pathways exist for medical school faculty.

Teaching	Majority effort in teaching activities
Research	Majority effort in research
Clinical/research	Majority effort in clinical and research activities
Administrative/service	Majority effort in administrative and/or service activities that would not be considered as primary clinical, teaching, or research activities

An *annual review* of all faculty is conducted by the chairperson for the purposes of salary adjustments, reappointment of nontenured faculty, promotion, and tenure. A *five-year review* is prepared by the department chair. A detailed written performance report from the department chair is sent to the dean. The five-year tenure review is intended to be summative in assessing performance and formative in allowing a two-year time period for remediation/improvement, if warranted. If deficiencies in performance are not remedied, resignation is expected.

Review Results

University D's School of Medicine has not formally tracked the results of its five-year tenure review system. In conversation with the dean and associate dean, both recalled only a couple of cases over the past 25 years when tenure had been formally revoked. Phased retirement has occurred in a few cases, and individuals have chosen to leave the institution on occasion as well. By and large, however, the process has not resulted in large-scale tenure revocation and the dean commented that 95% of the recent reviews have been positive.

CASE STUDY AND FINDINGS

One-on-one interviews were conducted with 21 tenured faculty members at University D. Included in this group were faculty from the majority of the departments that comprise the medical school. All had experienced at least one five-year review cycle and many had gone through at least two.

Senior-level administrators were interviewed individually. Three focus groups totaling 14 department chairs were also conducted. The department chairs in these focus groups represented a majority of the departments that comprise the school.

The survey used with the other eight institutions was modified and sent to all tenured faculty members and all academic administrators. The response to the survey was very high (65% response rate).

Purpose and Goals of Post-Tenure Review: Accountability Tool

Study participants identified the objective of the five-year review to be primarily an accountability tool; that is, to assess performance to see if expectations are met. Participants in the interviews and focus groups discussed several goals for post-tenure review. The most frequently cited purpose was accountability. Faculty and department chairs said the purposes of post-tenure review were to assess faculty performance and assist with improvement, keep productivity on target, and align contributions with mission. Several common sub-themes emerged on the purposes and goals of post-tenure review, such as its developmental aspect and its policing against deadwood function.

Participants also noted differences between the value and need for tenure within an academic health center as contrasted with their perspectives about the usefulness of a five-year review process. In general, participants (especially clinical faculty) were not strong advocates of tenure within the medical school model but did support the need for performance review. Basic science faculty, on the other hand, tended to place much more value on tenure.

Survey results suggest that while the majority of faculty and administrators indicated some level of familiarity with the policy, administrators were much better informed about the school's five-year tenure review policy than faculty. Additionally, over half of the respondents indicated that they thought the policy had a primary purpose: to review performance to assess if performance expectations are being met (77%). Administrators, as a group, tended to note career development as a goal much more frequently than faculty did.

Policy Effectiveness: Uncertain About Effectiveness

There seems to be no general agreement among faculty and administrators in this medical school about the effectiveness of the policy. Responses suggest that the policy's effectiveness in achieving its intended purpose was unclear. For faculty, this is due in part to the lack of information about the policy and its practice. Faculty interviewed were unable to discuss effectiveness because they did not have information about the outcomes from the review. Faculty were almost unanimous in their opinion that the five-year review was invisible, occurring many times without their knowledge and not considered a major evaluation "event." Department chairs were more cognizant about the reviews but were split in terms of whether they believed the process effectively achieved its purpose. Administrators were inclined to be slightly more positive about policy effectiveness and were able to discuss direct results to some degree because they are involved in all departmental reviews.

The results of the survey also supported the same type of ambivalence and lack of information about results. About one-third of respondents viewed the policy as either "somewhat" or "very effective." Another third were either "neutral" or held "no opinion," and 18% said it wasn't that effective. The reasons given for the policy's ineffectiveness corresponded to those identified by interviewees; for example, "no information is released so I don't know how policy is being implemented" (45%) and "review is not taken seriously because there is no significant follow-up action to the review" (45%).

It is important to note, however, that on this question of effectiveness, basic science faculty respondents were more positively opinionated about effectiveness and less neutral than clinical faculty respondents. This was the only area of significant difference between clinical and basic science faculty respondents on survey items.

Tangible Results: Little Reported Impact

Other than the anecdotal results mentioned by a small number of faculty, the interviews and survey did not reveal many review results that demonstrated tangible impact on performance or career development. The overall perception was that there were few tangible results from the post-tenure review process. Very few faculty received feedback from their chair or dean. Most of the results mentioned were of an intrinsic nature; for example, a "silent vote of confidence in my work" or a "no news is good news" philosophy. Faculty talked in anecdotal ways about summative review results that they knew about principally through the rumor mill. Chairs, on the other hand, voiced a concern about the absence of tangible developmental results and reflected mostly on difficult situations in which the review helped faculty redirect energies, reach retirement status, or leave the school.

By almost a 2:1 ratio, survey data showed that more respondents were neutral about how beneficial the process was to faculty work than said it was either beneficial or not beneficial. Survey data also showed that more respondents were neutral (44.4%) on whether the process is beneficial to professional/personal career development than think it is either beneficial or not beneficial. While administrators on the survey were more likely to view post-tenure review as beneficial than faculty, this difference was not evident in the interview data.

Impact on Department: Unable to Discern

Study participants as a group were unable to comment on the impact of the review process on the department. In general, participants were more inclined to focus on the theoretical purpose for the five-year tenure review. Most did not identify any negative effect on collegiality or productivity and talked in general terms about the benefit of the process in working to ensure a highly productive faculty. Chairs saw the annual review, on the other hand, as having more impact because everyone—tenured or not—participated in it.

Survey responses revealed that 50% of respondents held neutral opinions about the impact of the review on the department. The transparent nature of the review and lack of follow-up were cited again as reasons for inability to determine impact.

Worth the Time and Effort?

Surprisingly, administrators and faculty felt that the five-year tenure review was worthwhile primarily because of the accountability and productivity thrust. The review requires little effort, and this may contribute to the tendency to be positive or neutral about the usefulness of the process. A common, almost unanimous, theme that surfaced from faculty was that it serves a useful purpose for "some" faculty and that, in principle, it was good for the medical school as a whole. Similarly, the majority of chairs were also positive about the worth of the process.

They referred to it as one more leverage point or "tool" that they had to ensure productivity. The senior administrators voiced similar support.

The survey revealed that about 40% said the process was worth the effort, but almost as many were unsure or thought it was too soon to know. Only 15% said it was not worth the effort. Administrators were significantly more positive than faculty.

Procedures and Processes: Minor Difficulties

The faculty and administrators interviewed were not overly critical of the procedures and processes. Likewise, the results of the survey did not discover any great dissatisfaction with the procedures and processes. Interview participants identified a few problems with the procedures and processes, the most frequently being lack of information about the review itself (when it was occurring, etc.), varying interpretations about the procedures, and the lack of any substantial feedback following the review. Although not exactly a complaint, some said the review did not emphasize teaching effectiveness. Another weakness noted was the lack of any uniform definition about review standards and criteria.

Survey respondents were generally more favorable in their assessment about the clarity of the chairperson's role in the process, manageability of documentation, and clarity about the outcome of the process than they were about all of the other aspects. Faculty and administrator responses to procedural and process components differed significantly in a few areas. Administrators responded more positively than faculty that review criteria were clear, applied fairly, and that the dean's role in the process was understood. There was overall agreement that the process is not widely known and understood. Further, more faculty responded negatively or with uncertainty as to whether the procedures and criteria are clear and whether any follow-up to the review occurs.

Benefits of Post-Tenure Review: Few Noted

Participants did not identify any major benefits of the five-year tenure review process. Faculty and chairs asserted that the process signals increased accountability and provides one opportunity, but clearly not the only opportunity, for strategic mission, individual direction, and productivity to intersect. As a group, administrators are more positive about specific benefits attributed to the process than are faculty.

The only ongoing benefit that faculty consistently associated with the post-tenure review policy was that it provides a structured opportunity to reflect on their work, assess performance, and affirm tenure status. The chairs recognized that the process has potential benefits for the department in facilitating allocation of effort and redirecting energies, if need be.

Survey results substantiated that there were no areas seen as a major benefit by a majority of the respondents. Only three areas were seen as holding some level of benefit: increasing faculty accountability, sustaining senior faculty vitality, and establishing a culture and expectation for continuous growth and development.

Problems

The five-year tenure review policy did not appear to be plagued with major problems. The survey revealed several areas construed as problematic in a minor way. These include insufficient funds to support self-initiated faculty development plans and insufficient funds to support required faculty development plans. A majority of respondents did not feel that the policy eroded collegiality or faculty professionalism.

Improvements

Interviewees and survey respondents offered many suggestions for ways to improve the process. In general, these recommendations fell into a few well-defined categories for action.

- Increasing emphasis on providing more information and understanding about the review itself and the function of the tenure review committee.

- Strengthening follow-through and feedback following the review.

- Providing process enhancements, especially addressing the need for consistent review criteria, more uniformity in annual review processes; addition of retrospective and prospective planning element in five-year review; and consideration of using external peers as reviewers.

When queried about whether internal peers should have a role in the five-year review process, a majority (55%) indicated they thought they should. Internal peers do not currently play a defined role in the review process.

OTHER IMPORTANT OBSERVATIONS

The purpose of this study was to assess the impact of the five-year tenure review process on faculty and departments. Curiously, these findings closely parallel the findings from the eight public universities discussed earlier. This suggests that even though the contextual dimensions between the medical school and the other settings studied differ greatly, process impact and outcomes were not that dissimilar. In fact, the recommendations for improvement were almost identical among all nine institutions.

During our site visit, however, we found ourselves repeatedly engaged by participants in discussions about tenure, accountability measures facing health care, and the changing culture within medical schools. We summarize those discussions here because they represent a line in the sand between University D and the other case-study institutions. The issues discussed below are important to those who work in medical school environments and may also be of interest to faculty within a university that has a medical school. These issues impact the faculty evaluation culture within medial schools and, to some degree, their host institutions.

The Medical School: A Clash in Cultures

Our interviews pointed to a longstanding ethos within the medical school at University D, one that many referred to as caring, supportive, humane, and principled. Yet faculty and administrators recognized that financial constraints within the health care industry as well as managed care regulations have exerted pressure on the medical school to be more corporate and bottom-line focused. While there is an overall appreciation for current fiscal realities, there is also a longing to maintain the kinder, gentler climate. There is a fear that these new realities are shifting the culture and pointing it toward a "show me the money" environment. Many feared that the future would be based solely on a balance sheet mentality and, in such an environment, tenure would become meaningless.

Tenure Within the Medical School: Almost a "Non-Issue"

Tenure as it is currently defined within University D is almost a non-issue, especially for clinical faculty. It holds more meaning for basic science faculty. Many clinical faculty reported that they "don't personally care if they are tenured or not"; that "tenure was never a critical part of the reason why they went into academic medicine"; that having tenure "has had no effect on performance"; and that "tenure just isn't a pressing issue." Many faculty did emphasize, though, that the situation is different for basic science faculty who do not have as many employment options as those on the clinical track. As one interviewee put it:

> *Tenure to a real clinician doesn't mean much; to a basic scientist, it means his/her future.*

Likewise, department chairs recognized that the value of tenure to a Ph.D. faculty member is amplified because of the financial requirements of basic scientists. One chair speculated that:

> *I think [tenure] means more to my Ph.D. faculty member than it would to me. He's not really ever talked about that, but I think it does. He knows what our agreement is—he came here with a performance expectation*

> *and he knows that if he were to lose all of his funding that we would support him for a two-year period, no questions asked. But beyond that, he would be at risk. So, I think that would be an issue. . . . If he had tenure, I guess theoretically he could be at a position where he takes five years instead of the two years that we agreed to.*

Even so, confusion within all ranks and among all faculty existed with respect to what tenure really guarantees and what is "up for grabs" even with tenured status.

Certain themes surfaced time and time again as faculty reflected on what tenure represented within the medical school context. These included the understanding that tenure meant:

- A position guarantee (not salary guarantee) for 5 years

- An honorific title/recognition of sustained contribution

- An investment by the institution in human capital

- A safety net for career "bumps"; added protection while getting back on track

- A bargaining chip for career moves

- A "last-to-go" status in financial exigency situation

Post-Tenure Review: "An Invisible Hand"

Like tenure, post-tenure review in this particular medical school is almost a nonevent. Even though by policy it is a retenuring process, most faculty do not appear to be threatened by this notion, and many are unaware that the five-year review even occurs. Some describe it as a transparent process—almost an invisible hand—that is activated only when needed, which is rare. There were, however, two very different perspectives on this. Many saw the need for the review and didn't want to give it up but wanted it to become more well defined, routine, and connected to the annual review process:

> *I feel that the five-year tenure review process provides a means for the department to deal with faculty who equate "tenure" with "retirement." No institution can afford "deadwood" on their staffs. In my opinion, the five-year review process provides a means to correct a situation where a tenured faculty member stops making an effort to be productive. At our institution, only the most extreme abusers of tenure have been denied renewal of their tenure, to the best of my knowledge. I think the low visibility and simple approaches of the past for reviewing tenure at our institution are appropriate as they are and have not been abused by the school.*

An opposite view was suggested by a few:

> *I think I have been reviewed two times. Very little effort is involved but there is no benefit or feedback that I am aware of. It is like a vague threat held over one's head. I have no idea what criteria are used or what would cause one to lose tenure. I imagine that grants = tenure, no grants = ?? There is no benefit to the faculty that I have ever seen. The only negative factor is that it promotes a general feeling of unease or cynicism.*

In general, the ways in which the review is regarded by faculty ranged from the opinion that:

- It answers the question: Am I on target? Near target? Need to adjust my target or establish new target?

- The review is intentionally invisible if you're on target and so in this way "no news is good news."

- It promotes a culture that tenure does not constitute a hiding place for anyone.

- The process provides administration with a tool and strategy to redirect energies, mentor, develop, and promote faculty.

- The review is "all about money" and "what have you done for me lately."

- The review is a sieve with big holes—consequences are difficult to eventuate both in terms of reward and remediation.

CONCLUSIONS AND IMPLICATIONS

Most medical schools with post-tenure review policies have come by these policies in much the same way that the rest of higher education has—through mandates for accountability. Calls for such types of performance monitoring are far from new to the medical school setting. In fact, medical schools have been forced because of marketplace dynamics to increase revenue stream and productivity benchmarks. Because of this, the clash between the business culture and the academic culture was felt in academic medicine long before it appeared on the scene throughout the rest of higher education. While some might argue that findings in this sector have little applicability to mainstream higher education or that a case study of one medical school limits the generalizability of these particular findings to other medical school environments, we believe that general evaluation principles and trends found in the medical school culture do have relevance to the rest of higher education. Even though the majority of medical school post-tenure review processes today follow the periodic review model and are not patterned as a retenuring process, University D sheds light on important faculty dynamics prevalent in medical education settings.

Evaluation Principles

Some general evaluation principles emerged from this study. First, it is important to recognize that performance review and productivity benchmarking are reasonable expectations of tenured faculty. Faculty generally acknowledged this and, along with department chairs, often commented that post-tenure review serves a useful purpose for some faculty and, in principle, it was good for the medical school as a whole. Only one faculty member interviewed said the review was not necessary. In the words of one physician:

> *I think that as the Medical School wrestles with ways to develop its faculty properly, in the next 10, 15, or 20 years, when the health care area is going to be very complicated, and we have this tension between academic mission, clinical mission, educational mission, it is really important to give fairly clear feedback, and that that feedback needs to be consistent, and that that process is never a problem.*

Second, follow-through and actionable feedback after a performance review are critical to program effectiveness and individual valuing. Closely connected to follow-through is the need to make the evaluation more prospective in nature, focusing on career planning and professional renewal. One faculty member said it this way:

> *I remember at one point the annual review certainly had an impact on me. . . . The annual conversation is a good opportunity for the faculty to express concerns about what they need to further their careers as well as for the chairman to say what he thinks needs to be done to make one a better faculty member in this school.*

Third, institutions need some type of lever to help restart faculty careers. One faculty chair recalled:

> *You can see individuals who basically want to put in a little time, get off and running, and there are others who need something else, who have a hunger. So you need to know how to feed the hungry and how to help somebody create some hunger.*

Shift in Culture

This study affirmed that the culture in medical schools and in academic medical centers is shifting dramatically due to a management philosophy that focuses on keeping the balance sheet in the black. This culture transformation affects faculty contractual arrangements, tenure benefits, performance benchmarks, and even salary guarantees.

Accountability in the professions. The underpinnings of post-tenure review are implicitly part of this culture. It is not unrealistic to speculate that post-tenure review in this setting (assuming tenure continues to be viable for medical schools) will remain strong and sustainable because the medical school culture nurtures accountability and demands results in larger measure than mainstream higher education. We would argue that because of the medical school culture, post-tenure review may be a better fit in this type of a "professions" setting (and possibly in other professional settings such as nursing, dentistry, law, and social work) than in other academic disciplines. One faculty member said it best:

> *It is the change in culture and what is expected because of health care industry emphasis on costs that has [the] greatest impact on productivity. We have almost a whole new faculty. We have had people quit. And, that is what I am talking about, the changes that have occurred. But, you know, the new environment demands productivity. And it means revenue productivity. You just can't go spend four days in a lab anymore and expect to work one day in the clinic and live O.K. It doesn't work that way anymore.*

Tenure viability. Another trend that deserves watching is whether tenure will continue to be viable within academic medicine and clinical settings. What is well entrenched in medical schools is a system of employment tracks and appointment pathways. If the clinical faculty in our study are typical, tenure is not a riveting concern. It is a concern for basic science faculty, however, and this may be where the waters part in the future. One faculty member summed up the future of tenure with these thoughts:

> *… the concept of extending tenure to many faculty is a handicap to a chairperson's management and to the leadership of the institution (i.e., the dean and vice president for Health Affairs), since such entitlements become obstructions to the array of professionals that seem necessary for the institution's success.*

The real market value of tenure in a medical school has not been put to the test in the minds of many faculty in our study. Others questioned honestly whether tenure belongs or is needed in a medical school at all, particularly for clinical faculty:

> *I think in a medical school setting, it is a very different environment than the traditional academic setting in a lot of universities. There are many similarities, but there are also many differences. It is a much more fast paced, probably more corporate environment where it is more important that people are productive. If they're not productive, there is a lot of*

money involved institutionally. Medical school salary support is highly dependent on productivity, either with research or with patient care. Usually, tenured faculty are relatively expensive faculty. If that faculty is not being productive from a financial perspective, in addition to an academic perspective, they are somewhat at risk, and probably should be. So I don't feel that in the academic and medical environment, that tenure is very useful. Protecting academic freedom is much more important for the more traditional liberal arts and those sorts of areas, I think. Academic freedom is rarely an issue in health care, and I think it has to be protected, but the issue comes up so rarely, that I don't know that having a very expensive system where you have people tenured for life really justifies that. I think if there is an issue of academic freedom, that issue needs to be addressed on an ad hoc basis, not because you're protected by tenure.

CLOSING COMMENT

The School of Medicine at University D is an example of the varying dimensions surrounding faculty appointment, review, and tenure in a professional school setting. It is particularly informative because the impressions and opinions about tenured faculty evaluation generated by what some might term non-mainstream medical center faculty mirror closely many of the views expressed by the more traditional faculty we interviewed in four-year public settings. It may well be that the direction in which academic appointments in higher education are headed will resemble the medical school model. As public institutions continue to be increasingly tuition driven and less dependent on state support, academic employees may find themselves working under contractual arrangements that relate productivity to revenue streams.

Some readers may be shocked by the way in which tenure and its corollary privileges were perceived and valued by many University D medical school clinical faculty. An explanation for this may be that medical schools have been more concerned with finding effective ways to deal with the fiscal constraints and the complex reimbursement schemes wrought by managed care than with the life of the academy. Some pundits suggest that preoccupation with such things is not short lived and may eclipse or even further redefine tenure within medical schools. One scholar asserts that medical faculty are particularly vulnerable because

> . . . The term academic community has almost become an oxymoron. Academics reside in different disciplinary configurations and often seem unable to communicate across interests. Nowhere is this more true than in medical schools, where many faculty members are

involved only tangentially in traditional activities of university life. The pitched battles an arts and sciences faculty might have over the undergraduate curriculum, for example, may seem remote to a professor whose time is spent in teaching hospitals. (Tierney, 1999, p. 41)

The future of tenure and faculty employment in professional schools can, and probably will, have a direct influence on what happens in the rest of higher education.

For years now fiscal restraints coupled with needs for experienced practitioners who are interested in teaching but not as concerned with tenure guarantees have led professional schools (architecture, medicine, law, nursing) to use alternative faculty employment arrangements. Full-time contractual employment without tenure has grown in these settings. In pointing out ways in which such employment relationships can be designed to either attract or demean incumbents, Breneman (1997) argues that a wage premium should be placed on such tracks so that incumbents are adequately compensated for the cost of foregoing tenure. Employment at American University, Purdue University's Schools of Pharmacy, Nursing, and Health Sciences, and the University of Virginia Medical School allows six different faculty tracks to exist. Each track is linked in varying ways to teaching, research, and service. Each track also carries different contractual guarantees: "Three of the tracks (academic investigator, clinician investigator and clinician educator) require tenure for long-term employment. Three tracks (clinical, research and instructional faculty) do not have tenure as an option" (Gappa, 1996, p. 21).

While widespread adoption of these unconventional approaches to staffing have been slow to be implemented in the rest of higher education, a remarkable shift in faculty staffing patterns is emerging. For example, more than one-half of all new full-time faculty members at four-year institutions are not on the tenure track, and the numbers of adjuncts continue to rise. Recently, some private institutions have been receptive to the idea of examining whether one tenure track fits all.

A case in point: A new category of academic appointment is on the drawing board at Duke University and New York University. Duke has hired what they call professors of practice. About 10% of Duke's arts and science faculty carry this title and focus solely on teaching. There are no research requirements, and faculty are not eligible for tenure but receive renewable (three- to ten-year) contracts. Salaries are reported to be comparable to those faculty on tenure track, and all other fringe benefits apply except guaranteed sabbaticals (Fogg, 2004). Another 10% of Duke's faculty are hired as research professors. Like professors of practice, these appointments don't carry tenure, and faculty are assessed on their research activities and productivity. Most salaries are directly paid by outside grants and contracts (Fogg, 2004).

Following suit, the president of New York University has proposed a similar idea where teaching professors and global professors (faculty from abroad) would have renewable thee- to six-year contracts and no rights to tenure. One interesting aspect of this proposal is the individualized nature of each appointment: "... [the president] expects to tailor relationships to the idiosyncrasies of the discipline ... there will be no attempt to impose a uniform set of standards and rights, although NYU would create floors for benefits like salary" (Fogg, 2004, p. A14).

Only time will tell whether these employment arrangements find their way into mainstream public sector institutions. The laissez-faire attitude toward tenure expressed by many faculty at University D's School of Medicine may well represent a new generation of faculty who are attracted to places like Duke University, not-for-profit institutions like Phoenix University, and other professional schools where tenure is not part of the employment package.

REFERENCES

Andreoli, T. E. (1999). The undermining of academic medicine. *Academe, 85*(6), 32–37.

Breneman, D. (1997). *Alternatives to tenure for the next generation of academics* (New Pathways Project Inquiry No. 14). Washington, DC: American Association for Higher Education.

Cohen, J. (1995). Academic medicine's tenuous hold on tenure. *Academic Medicine, 70*(4), 294.

Eisenberg, L. (1999). Marketplace medicine: Rx for disaster. *Academe, 85*(6), 26–29.

Fogg, P. (2004, April 16). For these professors, 'practice' is perfect. *Chronicle of Higher Education,* p. A12.

Gappa, J. M. (1996). *Off the tenure track: Six models for full-time, nontenurable appointments* (New Pathways Working Paper Series No. 10). Washington, DC: American Association for Higher Education..

Medical schools in the era of managed care: An interview with Arnold Relman. (1999). *Academe, 85*(6), 16–23.

Tierney, W. G. (1999). The end of medical tenure as we know it. *Academe, 85*(6), 38–42.

Trower, C. A. (1998). *Employment practices in the professions: Fresh ideas from inside and outside the academy* (New Pathways Working Paper Series No. 13). Washington, DC: American Association for Higher Education.

5

Similarities and Differences Across Institutions: Quantitative Findings

The preceding chapters have described the combined findings from interview and survey data collected across eight universities and one medical school. In this chapter, we focus exclusively on an analysis of survey data. In many ways the survey results reinforce the qualitative findings, but they also provide the opportunity to examine whether significant findings of differences occur within specific respondent categories. The latter include analysis by role (deans, chairs, and faculty), institutional type, policy type, and gender.

This chapter is quantitative in nature and may seem repetitive of findings previously discussed. We have organized it, however, so that those interested mainly in general trends and significant differences among categories of respondents can focus on the discussion found in the section on survey findings and the section on interesting differences of opinion. Those interested in a more detailed presentation of all survey results will want to cover the entire chapter.

SURVEY FINDINGS OF TENURED FACULTY AND ADMINISTRATORS

A survey was sent to all tenured faculty members and academic administrators at each institution. Survey items specifically targeted questions related to policy effectiveness, impact on performance and professional development, benefits and problems, usefulness of peer review, assessment of overall worth in relationship to time involved, and suggestions for improvement.

Across all of the universities, 4,671 surveys were distributed, and 1,677 were returned. This represents a response rate of 35.9%[1]. For survey research with this sample size, this is considered a moderate response rate. Still, one must exercise caution in generalizing from these results alone. The focus here should be on the trends and patterns revealed rather than on the absolute numbers obtained. Appendix C contains a copy of core survey questions.

The survey respondents are characterized as follows: approximately 75% faculty and 25% administrators; approximately 70% male and 30% female; 60% between 49–59 years of age; 70% full professors. In addition, almost half were at their institutions 20 years or more.

Survey responses were analyzed using descriptive statistics, including frequency distributions, measures of central tendency, cross tabulation, analysis of variance, and correlation matrices.

GENERAL TRENDS AND DIFFERENCES

- Across all institutions, administrators (particularly chairs and deans) tended to be more positive about the post-tenure review process and the policy than faculty.

- Research institutions tended to view the post-tenure review policy more favorably than respondents from teaching institutions or from the medical school.

- At institutions where a periodic review approach was used, respondents were significantly more positive and satisfied with the process than at institutions using any other type of approach. In general, the blended approach (periodic and triggered) commanded the least positive views.

- Female respondents were significantly less positive than males about three specific areas: the fairness of procedures and criteria, understanding of the process and the roles in the process, and the issue of insufficient resources.

SUMMARY OF MAJOR FINDINGS

General Familiarity
There was general familiarity with the institutional post-tenure review process across the respondents. Administrators tended to be more familiar with the policy than were faculty.

Policy Goals/Purpose
There was general agreement that the policy had multiple goals. The purposes most frequently cited were to review performance relative to performance expectations and to assess individual performance so as to remedy deficiencies. Faculty and administrators differed in their views—administrators pointing more frequently to assessing career development and increasing instructional

effectiveness. Females were more likely to note unevenness in the application of criteria and standards as a problem. This difference appears to be related to existing differentials in the treatment of males versus females in higher education that still persist. Many women academics still perceive a difference in their roles and rewards when compared to their male colleagues. As a whole, female professors are still in the minority in higher education.

Policy Effectiveness
There was almost an even split between those who thought the policy was effective and those who thought that it was not effective. Administrators were much more positive than faculty. Males were more favorable than females.

Impact on Faculty Within Department
The general view here was one of neutrality. Of those who expressed a more definitive view, more were positive than negative. Administrators were somewhat more positive than faculty.

Impact on Individual Faculty Member
Whether we looked at benefit to faculty work or to professional/career planning, responses were separated into three opinion groups. The largest plurality was with those who were neutral about the policy's impact; an almost equal number felt that it was not beneficial, and a small group felt that it was beneficial. Administrators tended to see more impact on self-reflection, follow-up, and clear outcomes.

Worth the Time and Effort?
The respondents' views again separated evenly into three opinion categories: the review was worth it, the review was not worth it, and those who said they were not really sure. Again, administrators were much more positive than faculty.

Benefits
Respondents generally held that two benefits were achieved: an increase in faculty accountability and establishment of a culture for continuous growth and development. Administrators were more positive than faculty in their opinion that the review prompted increased teaching effectiveness as well as increased research contributions.

Problems
Four areas were indicated as problematic: excessive time required to prepare and perform the review, excessive paperwork, insufficient funds for faculty development, and no positive change resulting from the review. There were varying degrees of importance attached to these by administrators and faculty.

Peers Review Members and Peer Review Committees

Peer review committees were considered objective and able to render helpful recommendations. Most members of such committees felt prepared for the role and said that the procedures were clear and were performed in a fair and objective manner. Yet there was some disagreement about whether or not peer committee members were sufficiently trained for their role.

Chair's and Dean's Role

Respondents generally understood the chair's role but were very divided in their understanding of the dean's role. The chairs and deans were much clearer than faculty about their administrative roles in the review process.

Erosion of Faculty Values

Respondents, in general, did not view erosion of faculty values (autonomy, professionalism, collegiality, risk taking) as a problem. Even a majority of faculty did not see any problem here. The administrators were even more positive about this.

SURVEY OF TENURED FACULTY AND ADMINISTRATORS: MORE DETAILED RESULTS

Analysis of Survey Responses

Survey responses were analyzed using descriptive statistics, including frequency distributions, measures of central tendency, cross tabulations, and correlation matrices. We also considered the differences in responses between faculty and administrators on specific questions of interest and we examined some other categories to see if significant differentiation[2] existed. This analysis was performed with much care and using general state-of-the-art statistical methodology.

Demographic Characteristics of Survey Respondents

Most faculty survey respondents were full professors, male, between the ages of 46–59, and with less than 10 years in their current rank and tenure and 20 years or more of overall service at the institution. Most administrators held the position of chairperson.

Faculty and administrators. There were 1,230 faculty and 447 administrators who responded to the survey. Proportionately, this amounted to a distribution comprised of 73% faculty and 27% administrators. This distribution varied across institutions and ranged from a high of 77:23 in one institution to a low of 60:40 at another. In all cases, the majority of the respondents were tenured faculty members.

Gender. The majority of respondents were male (72%). Female respondents totaled 28%. Across the nine universities, this gender (male to female) distribution ranged from a high of 95:5 to a low of 65:35. In fall 2001, the overall relationship of male to female professors with tenure was 71:29 in the United States. Our results mirror the national picture.

Age. The majority of respondents were between 46–59 years of age, making up almost three-fifths of the respondent population. This was expected given the tenured faculty age profiles at the institutions studied and the age distribution for tenured faculty within higher education in general. This particular age range also varied widely across the institutions. At one institution 83% of faculty fell into the 45–59 bracket; in another only 29% did so.

Years of Age	%
Less than 30	1%
31–45	19%
46–59	59%
60 or older	21%

Rank. The majority were full professors, making up seven-tenths of respondents. In each of the universities, full professors made up the majority of respondents, but in absolute percentages the range of full professors varied from 52% to 90%. In fall 2001, full professors accounted for 56% of the professoriate on a national level, so our sample is skewed toward more full professors.

Rank	%
Professor	70%
Associate	24%
Assistant	3%
Other	3%

Time in rank. Slightly over one-half of respondents have held their rank for 10 years or less. This time in rank also ranged from a low of 33% to a high of 65%.

Time in Current Rank	%
10 years or less	57%
11–19 years	23%
20 years or more	20%

Length of tenure. Four out of every ten respondents held tenure for ten years or less, and one-third held tenure for twenty years or more. Only two universities had a plurality of faculty outside the ten years or less range. In these two cases, the majority fell within the 11-19 year range.

Length of Tenure	%
10 years or less	41%
11–19 years	27%
20 years or more	32%

Time at institution. Almost half of the respondents had been at their institution 20 years or more. This statistic held true at seven of the nine institutions. In one of the two remaining institutions, the distribution was more dominated by those between 11–19 years. In the other institution, there was an even distribution, with one-third for each group.

Time at Institution	%
10 years or less	23%
11–19 years	29%
20 years or more	48%

Administrative profile. Of those holding an administrative role, almost one-half were department chairs, and one-fifth were deans, associate deans, or assistant deans. Another one-third held other administrative positions. In seven of the nine universities, chairs were the dominant group among the administrators. At two institutions the "other" administrator category was of greater proportion.

Administrative Profile	%
Chairperson	50%
Dean, associate dean, or assistant dean	20%
Other	30%

SUMMARY OF RESPONSES

Familiarity With Institutional Periodic Review Process

Respondents were generally familiar with the post-tenure review policies at their institutions. Approximately 85% indicated some level of familiarity; 48% said they were very familiar and 36% were somewhat familiar. This result was consistent across the eight institutions in the study, with at least 80% of the respondents at each campus denoting some familiarity with the policy. At the medical school, this response much lower: only 62% indicated familiarity. We speculate that it is possible because the policy in the medical school was activated by the chair only when needed, and many were unaware that it even occurred.

The expressed level of familiarity with policy did differ significantly between faculty and administrators, however. Administrators as a group responded more often than faculty that they were very familiar with the policy.

Policy Goals/Purpose

A majority (62%) of respondents indicated that they thought the policy had multiple purposes rather than only one objective. This was generally consistent across all institutions. The purposes cited most frequently appear below.

There were significant differences between faculty and administrators on this question. Administrators chose two purposes with much more frequency than faculty: to assess career development goals and to increase instructional effectiveness and responsiveness.

Policy Purposes	%
Review performance in order to assess if performance expectations are being met	67%
Assess individual performance in order to remedy deficiencies	50%
Increase accountability to outside constituents	40%
Assess career development goals and establish plans for continued growth and redirection	39%

Policy Effectiveness

When asked how effective the post-tenure review process was in achieving its purpose, slightly more respondents reported that the process was not that effective or ineffective (42%) than considered the process to be effective or somewhat effective (31%). The remaining responses registered neutrality (16%), too soon to know (4.6%), or no opinion (6.3%).

On this question, there were no significant differences in the way faculty and administrators responded, although administrators were slightly more positive than faculty. This can be seen in Figure 5.1 which breaks down aggregate responses by respondent group.

Figure 5.1
The Effectiveness of the Post-Tenure Review Process

Question 3: How Effective Is Policy in Achieving Primary Purpose?

	Respondents (%)		Faculty (%)		Administrators (%)	
Very Effective	4.4	} 31.3	4.3	} 28.9	4.9	} 37.1
Somewhat Effective	26.9		24.6		32.2	
Neutral	16.0		16.7		13.3	
Not That Effective	25.0	} 41.7	25.2	} 42.5	25.1	} 41.1
Very Ineffective	16.7		17.3		16.	
Too Soon to Know	4.6		5.1		3.6	
No Opinion	6.3		6.7		4.9	
	100.0		100.0		100.0	

Reasons Given for Ineffectiveness

The following are the most cited reasons for policy ineffectiveness. As with the question of effectiveness, there were no significant differences between faculty and administration in the reasons given for policy ineffectiveness.

Reasons for Policy Ineffectiveness	%
Review has shown little evidence of positive outcomes so far	52%
Review is not taken seriously because there is no significant follow-up action to the review	51%
Review is not taken seriously because there are no sanctions for poor performance	46%

Impact on Performance and/or Development: Faculty Within Department

Based on their direct experience with post-tenure review, more respondents (48%) expressed neutrality about its impact on the performance or development of fellow department faculty than rendered a positive or negative opinion. About one-quarter of the respondents (23%) said that it had a positive impact and less than one-fifth (17%) felt that it had a negative impact. Twelve percent expressed no opinion. These results were generally true of all of the institutions studied. However, two institutions had a much more positive view of post-tenure review, with at least a plurality stating that it had a positive impact. At one other institution, the plurality was negative and at the other six institutions, the plurality denoted neutrality.

When responses were analyzed by respondent category, the results show that there are no significant differences in how faculty and administrators responded to this question, although, again, administrators were slightly more positive than faculty (see Figure 5.2).

Figure 5.2
Impact of Post-Tenure Review on Faculty

Question 6: What Is the Impact of Post-Tenure Review on the Performance and/or Development of Department Faculty Members?

	Total Respondents (%)		Faculty (%)		Administrators (%)	
Highly Positive	2.0	} 22.5	2.0	} 20.5	1.8	} 28.5
Somewhat Positive	20.5		18.5		26.7	
Neutral	48.4		48.9		46.6	
Somewhat Negative	12.8	} 17.4	13.5	} 18.3	11.4	} 15.3
Highly Negative	4.6		4.8		3.9	
Too Soon to Know	5.7		5.3		6.6	
No Opinion	6.0		7.1		3.0	
	100.0		100.0		100.0	

Benefit to Faculty Work

A very small percentage (2.3%) of respondents indicated that their own review resulted in an assessment that their work was in need of improvement and that a professional development plan was required. Virtually all others (88.3%) reported being assessed as meeting or exceeding expectations, and another 9.4% answered "other" on the survey.

Responses to this question were divided between those who thought the process was not beneficial (41%) and those who were neutral as to its benefits (34%). Almost one-quarter (23.2%) said the process held some benefit for them.

Further analysis also showed that there was a somewhat significant (at .05 level) difference in the benefit to faculty reported by administrators and faculty. Administrators viewed the process as slightly more beneficial than did faculty.

Benefit to Professional/Personal Career Development Planning

Approximately 40% of respondents expressed neutrality about the benefit of post-tenure review on career development planning; 36.5% reported that the review was clearly not beneficial, and 21% said it was beneficial. Figure 5.3 displays all responses. There were no significant differences between the way faculty or administrators answered this question.

Figure 5.3

Benefit of Post-Tenure Review on Career Development Planning

Question 13: How Beneficial Is the Process to
Professional/Personal Career Development and Planning?

	Total Respondents (%)	
Very Beneficial	2.0	
Mostly Beneficial	10.0	21.1
Slightly Beneficial	9.1	
Neutral	40.1	
Clearly Not Beneficial	36.3	
Too Soon to Assess	0.8	
No Opinion	1.7	

We have been asked if we noticed any differences in responses among academic disciplines on the issue of career development planning. Unfortunately, our data was not that finely tuned. This could be an interesting direction for future research.

Worth the Time and Effort?

There was no clear trend in the opinions expressed about whether the process was worth the effort. Respondents were fairly evenly divided: 36% said it was worth the effort and 37% said the costs outweighed the benefits. Over one-quarter (27%) were unsure.

Benefits

There was only one area ("increases faculty accountability") where close to a majority of respondents (48%) indicated that it held some benefit. One additional potential outcome ("establishes a culture for continuous growth and development") was chosen where more respondents (42%) indicated some benefit than indicated no benefit. Other benefits mentioned by about one-third of the respondents were "forestalls further external interference," "increases effort in research," "acts as a safeguard to tenure," "sustains senior faculty vitality," and "increases public confidence in higher education."

Problems

The majority of respondents indicated three areas to be problematic (either rating it as a major or minor problem).

Problems	%
Excessive time and excessive paperwork	55%
Insufficient funds for faculty development plans (either self-initiated or required)	45%
No positive change in performance resulting from the review	40%

Peer Review Committee

Faculty and administrators were asked to comment on their experience as a member of a peer review committee. Three-quarters of those surveyed said that a peer review committee played a major role in the post-tenure review process. Fifty-eight percent had served on a peer review committee. The majority (56%) felt generally prepared for the role and another one-quarter (27%) said that they felt somewhat prepared. The majority also said that the peer review procedures were clear and performed in a fair and objective manner. Eight out of ten noted further that their participation on a peer review committee increased their knowledge and their appreciation of colleagues' work to some degree.

When queried about whether peer review committees are capable of rendering objective/helpful recommendations, the majority of respondents (60%) agreed that they were. Respondents were less certain whether the outcome of the review resulted in positive faculty actions. More than one-third (37%) said that it had not done so while one-quarter (25%) said that it had and another one-fifth (21%) said that it had somewhat.

Chair's and Dean's Role

When asked if the chair's role and the dean's role in the process was understood, there was not a majority opinion expressed. Forty percent of the respondents said the chair's role was understood, 23% said it was somewhat understood, and 21% said it was not. When asked if the dean's role in the process was understood, there was an even split between those who answered in the affirmative and those who answered in the negative (28% in each group). Twenty-one percent answered that the dean's role was somewhat understood, and another 21% indicated they had insufficient experience to make that determination.

Training of Committee Members, Chairs, and Department Heads

Respondents were queried on the training given to peer committee members, chairs, and department heads and whether any problems existed. Responses indicated that there is less than overwhelming certainty about and confidence in the training provided to all key stakeholders in the process. When asked whether peer committee members were trained appropriately, 17% answered yes, but 22% answered no. Another 20% answered that the training given was somewhat appropriate. When asked if insufficient training of peer committee members was a problem, one-third said that it was not a problem, but another 37% noted some degree of dissatisfaction; 22% said that it was a minor problem, and 15% said that it was a major problem. When asked the same question about the chair/heads of departments, approximately the same divided responses were given: 35% said no problem, but 37% said this was problematic; 21% named it as a minor problem, and 16% said that it was a major problem.

Need for Improvement

Respondents were invited to share their opinion about whether policy improvements were needed. The majority (51%) indicated that improvements could be made to the post-tenure review procedures to make the process more beneficial, effective, and/or constructive. About 30% indicated they were uncertain whether improvements were necessary, and 19% indicated they did not think improvements were warranted.

INTERESTING DIFFERENCES OF OPINION

Significant differences in responses among specific groups (as measured at a 99% significance level) are discussed in the next section.

Faculty, Chairs, and Deans

Chairs play a pivotal role in carrying out evaluation and development procedures in institutions. Post-tenure review extends and expands these responsibilities, particularly for addressing performance, productivity, and vitality issues. Many academic leaders admit that "taking faculty evaluation seriously and performing this responsibility well is not an easy assignment by any means, especially because most chairs are not selected or elected because of their evaluation expertise" (Licata, 2000, p. 108). Some characterize this expanded role as one of a "professional guide, career advisor, judge, and diplomat . . . [and assert that] for some chairs, these roles can be new and uncomfortable" (Barr, Lees, & Brown, 2000, p. 10).

Our analysis of the survey responses across the nine institutions suggests that department chairs often are unclear about the actions they are empowered to take in the post-tenure review process and/or are frustrated by a perceived lack of power to do anything and by a less than supportive developmental culture on their campus. Many department chairs have significantly different opinions than their faculty about certain aspects of their institutional practice, and they sometimes disagree with the viewpoints expressed by deans.

Initially, interview narratives called attention to some general differences in the opinions expressed by deans, chairs, and faculty especially as they related to certain topics. These differences were further substantiated by survey data. We evaluated differences among 225 chairs, 90 deans, and 1,230 faculty members.

In general, chairs and deans tended to be more positive than faculty about the real or potential value of having a post-tenure review process in place. This trend, however, varies in relationship to the following specific review components.

Faculty Effectiveness

As described in Chapter 3, the jury is still out for most institutions in our study on whether post-tenure review is effective in achieving its intended purpose. Chairs and deans view the effectiveness of post-tenure review more positively than faculty—but not by very much. Chairs are evenly split between saying it is effective (39%) and saying it is not effective (38%). Interestingly, faculty and deans tilt the scale in the other direction and are more inclined to say that it is not effective (42%).

Impact on Faculty Performance and Development

Of those offering an opinion on this question, chairs and deans are significantly more optimistic than faculty that post-tenure review has a positive impact. However, about 50% of faculty, chairs, and deans are either neutral or say that it is too soon to know if post-tenure review has an impact on faculty performance and development.

Worth the Time and Effort?

One-half of the deans and almost one-half of the chairs (46%) indicate that post-tenure review is worth the time and effort, whereas only one-third of the faculty feel this way.

Outcomes of Review

Chairs and deans are also more positive about the actual outcomes that occur from post-tenure reviews. In three specific areas there is a significantly more positive response voiced by deans and chairs than by faculty that post-tenure review leads to self-reflection, follow-up, and clear outcomes. About one-quarter of the deans and chairs are in agreement with these outcomes while only 17% of faculty are so inclined.

Benefits of Post-Tenure Review

Faculty, chairs, and deans all indicate there is no discernable benefit of post-tenure review for actually stimulating increased faculty effort in teaching, research, or service. For each type of faculty performance activity, at least four out of ten faculty and chairs answered "no benefit." In relative terms, chairs tend to see more positive benefit than faculty when it comes to impact on teaching (32% versus 24%, respectively). The most pronounced impact seen by both chairs and faculty is on research (39% versus 32%, respectively). The lowest impact seen by chairs and faculty is on service (24% versus 19%, respectively).

Chairs and deans feel more strongly than faculty about certain other benefits flowing from post-tenure review. For example, the majority of chairs and deans (53% and 51%, respectively) feel that post-tenure review increases faculty accountability. Similarly, the majority of chairs and deans (53% each) note that the review helps to establish a developmental culture. Only about 40% of the faculty share these same opinions.

Problems With Post-Tenure Review

Chairs, deans, and faculty all note specific problems associated with post-tenure review. Generally speaking, a majority of all groups see as problematic to some degree the excessive time and paperwork required and insufficient funds to support both required and self-initiated faculty development projects.

Chairs felt more strongly than both deans and faculty that time and paperwork were a problem. On the other hand, deans felt more strongly than chairs and chairs more strongly than faculty that insufficient funds to support faculty development was problematic.

Fairness of Procedures

Another significant area of difference between faculty and deans and chairs is the issue of the fairness of procedures and their implementation. One-third of faculty feel favorably about fairness of application and consistency of procedures. Only 25% feel the review criteria were applied fairly and consistently. Chairs are much more positive about all of these (from one-half to two-thirds) while deans often fall between the two groups.

Understanding Roles and Process

Faculty are much less clear about understanding the role of the chair and the dean in the post-tenure review process (only one-quarter to one-third were clear about the roles) than are the chairs and deans themselves. Moreover, the faculty are less sanguine about the review criteria (only one-quarter felt the criteria at their institution were clear).

Chairs and deans are much more clear in their understanding of their roles (45%) and of the review criteria (40%). This difference suggests a real communication issue in the post-tenure review process.

Erosion of Faculty Values

There was a significant difference in the views of faculty and administrators about the impact of post-tenure review on the erosion of faculty values. A series of questions were asked pertaining to erosion of faculty professionalism, confidence in tenure, risk taking, controversial scholarly inquiry, collegiality, devaluation of senior faculty, and invasion of professional autonomy. The majority in each group did not see faculty values eroding because of post-tenure review. In most instances, 50% or more of the faculty did not view erosion of faculty values as a problem. Chairs and deans were even more positive, with two-thirds to three-quarters saying that this was not a problem. In the case of the faculty, the percentage was between 50% and 60%.

DIFFERENCES AMONG INSTITUTIONAL TYPES

Three types of institutions were represented in our study: research, teaching, and one professional school. Analysis was done to see if there were significant differences in responses among the three types of institutions. Carnegie Classification categories and institutional mission statements were used to divide the institutions by type. Using this breakdown, there were four research universities, four teaching universities/colleges, and one medical school.

In general terms, research institutions tend to view the post-tenure review policy more favorably than the other two types of institutions. We can only speculate why this is the case. One explanation might be that traditionally, peer review has been a hallmark of the research university culture. Perhaps faculty within these institutions are more attuned and comfortable with a culture where peers are empowered to judge each other's work. One might also reason that because of the significant internal and external funding that supports research institutions, accountability mandates have been part of the fabric of these institutions for a longer period of time. Therefore, faculty within research institutions have had more experience with external review mechanisms and have seen that review processes do not need to impinge on cherished academic values and traditions, particularly as applied to risk taking and pursuing controversial areas of inquiry.

Effectiveness

When taken together, there was no significant difference among the three types of institutions about the effectiveness of post-tenure review. However, when viewed individually we find a clear breakdown: A majority of respondents from two institutions (one research and one teaching) indicate that post-tenure review is effective; one institution (medical school) has a plurality of respondents who agree; and one institution (research) was evenly split. Likewise, four had a majority saying post-tenure review was ineffective (one research and three teaching) and one (research) had a plurality of respondents who agree. (See Table 5.1 for institutional responses.)

Table 5.1

Effectiveness of Post-Tenure Review Process

	Very/Somewhat Effective	*Not That Effective/Very Ineffective*	*Difference (Effective/Ineffective)*
Universities			
C (Teaching)	56%	27%	+29
A (Research)	52%	26%	+26
D (Medical)	33%	18%	+15
G (Research)	33%	32%	+1
I (Research)	27%	41%	−14
H (Teaching)	33%	50%	−17
F (Teaching)	28%	55%	−27
B (Research)	24%	54%	−30
E (Teaching)	16%	66%	−50
Overall	31%	42%	−11

Worth the Time and Effort?

There was no discernable significant difference among the three types of institutions on the question of whether post-tenure review was worth the effort. However, we see significant differences when viewed individually. A majority of respondents from two institutions (one research and one teaching) indicate that post-tenure review was indeed worth it. One institution (medical school) has a plurality of respondents who agree; and one institution (research) was evenly split. Four had a majority saying post-tenure review was not worth it (one research and three teaching) and one (research) had a plurality say so. (See Table 5.2 for institutional responses.)

Table 5.2
Was Post-Tenure Review Worth the Time and Effort?

	Yes	*No*	*Difference (Yes – No)*
Universities			
C (Teaching)	61%	18%	+43
A (Research)	61%	22%	+39
D (Medical)	40%	15%	+25
G (Research)	37%	37%	0
B (Research)	33%	35%	–2
I (Research)	31%	42%	–11
F (Teaching)	32%	48%	–16
E (Teaching)	28%	56%	–28
H (Teaching)	22%	50%	–28
Overall	36%	37%	–1

What is seen in these two tables is a clear separation between those universities that have a positive view of post-tenure review and those that have a much more negative view. This distinction leads us to contrast the results for the two sets of institutions to see if we can find any critical factors that explain the differences. These factors are discussed fully in Chapter 6.

Understanding Roles and Process

The significant difference seen in the understanding of the role of chairs and deans and the procedure was between the research/teaching institutions and the medical school. The medical school reported much less positive results for the questions about the role and process. For example, whereas about 30% of the faculty and administrators surveyed at the research or teaching institutions answered that the procedures were clear, only 13% of the medical school faculty and administrators surveyed responded in the affirmative. Such significant differences are seen for the dean's role, review criteria, and other procedural aspects. Only in the case of judging the preparation of the peer review committee members were the surveyed members of the medical school much more significantly positive than other institutional respondents.

Peer Review

Research institution members were more likely (60%) than were teaching institution members (48%) to say that the peer review process was performed in a fair and objective manner and that the peer committees were capable of rendering objective and helpful recommendations. Two reasons could be given for this difference. One is that research institutions expect colleagues to seek research grants which are based on the peer review process. Teaching institutions place much more emphasis on teaching where peer review occurs less frequently. Moreover, evaluation of teaching is based on much less objective criteria and is more difficult to measure.

Also, teaching institution faculty and administrators are less likely (one-quarter) than are research or medical institution members (one-third) to say that insufficient training for peers and for chairs is not a problem of the post-tenure review process.

Administrative Burden and Excessive Time and Paperwork

Administrative burden, excessive time, or excessive paperwork seem to be a much greater problem to faculty and administrators in research institutions than in teaching institutions. Only 15% of teaching institution faculty members rated these as problematic, while 23% did so at research institutions. Almost 50% of medical school respondents indicated these were not problems.

Erosion of Faculty Values

Erosion of collegiality was deemed significantly greater in teaching institutions than in research or medical institutions. In the latter two, more than half of the survey respondents said it was not a problem, yet only 40% of teaching institution respondents replied in this same way.

Differences in Policies

There were four different types of policies represented in the study: triggered, periodic, a blend of both, and retenuring review. Six of the institutions studied used periodic review, only one used triggered, one used blended (periodic and triggered), and one used a retenuring process (medical school).

In general, those institutions using the periodic review approach were significantly more positive and satisfied with the process than respondents using the other three types of policies. This result was not surprising because the periodic approach usually includes a career development thrust and establishes an even playing field, negating the perceived punitive nature of a policy that kicks in for faculty who have been identified with performance issues.

Overall Value of the Post-Tenure Review Process

There was no significant difference in the views about overall value across the institutions with differing policy models. Nonetheless, the one institution using a blended process reported the least favorable results. Only 16% of that institution's respondents answered that the post-tenure review process was effective while almost twice as many of the respondents at the other types of institutions said that it was effective.

Worth the Time and Effort?

When asked if the post-tenure review process was worth the time and effort, there was no majority opinion expressed with any policy group. However, the results for the institution with the blended policy were the lowest, with 28% saying the process was worth the time and effort. This clearly was not that different from the other three types of policies (31%–40%).

Understanding Roles and Process

There was a significant difference in the degree to which process and roles were understood by policy type. Institutional respondents with a periodic review score much higher in understanding the department chair's role, the procedures, and the review criteria.

Fairness of Procedures

There was a significant difference between the periodic and blended policy institutions and the triggered institutions on the question of fairness. The faculty and staff surveyed at the triggered institutions were much less positive about fairness of procedures, application of procedures, and consistency in following review criteria and procedures. One reason for this may be the fact that peer involvement was minimal in institutions with triggered policies. By and large, administrators assumed greater roles in rendering judgments. Another plausible explanation for this difference is that triggered policies seemed to be far less well understood and the results rarely discussed.

Administrative Burden

A significant difference was seen in the amount of administrative burden reported by respondents with different types of policy. The survey results from the medical school with a retenuring process showed the least burden while the blended policy institution indicated the most burden. Periodic policy responses were between these two extremes. (No data was provided for the triggered institution.)

GENDER DIFFERENCES

We were interested to see if there were significant differences between male and female responses to questions about post-tenure review. In general, female respondents were less positive than males about specific aspects of the post-tenure review process, particularly their views about fairness of procedures, understanding the process and roles, and insufficient resources.

It is difficult to speculate why this difference emerged because the interviews did not identify issues of gender bias or issues related to the old boy network when it came to process and procedures. We suspect that the prevalence of a male-dominated peer system may be at the base of these differences. Females were in the minority within every institution and, for the most part, within their academic unit.

Male-dominated departments and the nonlinear career trajectory of female faculty (starting later, stepping out for child raising, balancing family with career) may coalesce to isolate female faculty and marginalize them from departmental decision-making.

Effectiveness/Worth the Time and Effort?

There was no discernable significant difference in the views of males and females about the effectiveness or worth of the post-tenure review process. However, males were significantly more favorable than females in their views of fairness of procedures, understanding of process and roles, and insufficient resources.

Fairness of Procedures

Most all items within the Fairness of Procedures category are significantly different by gender. Females are less favorable than are males in ratings of procedures being followed in a fair fashion, procedures being followed in a consistent fashion, and review criteria being followed in a consistent fashion. Furthermore, males are more likely than are females to say unevenness in the application of criteria and standards is a not a problem.

Understanding Roles and Process

Within the Understanding Processes and Roles category a significant difference by gender is found, where females are less favorable than are males in beliefs that the process is widely known and understood. Four near significant results suggest that females are less positive than are males in understanding the department chair's role in the process, believing that the procedures are clear, and that peer review committee members are trained appropriately. Males are more likely than are females to say they are familiar with their institution's post-tenure review policy.

Insufficient Resources

Three items within the Insufficient Resources category show a significant difference. In general, males are more likely to say issues of insufficient funds to support required faculty development plans and training of chairs/department heads and peers are not a problem, whereas females are more likely to perceive these areas as being a minor or major problem.

ENDNOTES

1) The response rate varied by institution, ranging from 28% to 66%. See Figure 4 in Appendix B for details.

2) Analysis of differences was accomplished by performing the standard *t*-distribution test for differences between means with the appropriate degrees of freedom. In order to extract differences of import, we typically used a 1% significance, two-tailed test for the analysis. For the most part, we report here only on those differences that were found to be significant at this critical level.

REFERENCES

Barr, S. H., Lees, N. D., & Brown, B. E. (2000, Fall). Preparing chairs for expanded roles in post-tenure review: New perspectives for chairs. *The Department Chair, 11*(2), 9–10.

Licata, C. M. (2000). Post-tenure review. In A. F. Lucas & Associates, *Leading academic change: Essential roles for department chairs* (pp. 107–137). San Francisco, CA: Jossey-Bass.

6

Bridging Results to Practice

*If your research doesn't result in practice, your research is no good;
and if your practice is not based on research, your practice is no
good.*

—Bedell, 1988, p. 138

BROAD IMPLICATIONS

Before we synthesize our results and return to the questions that initially drove
this study, it is important to note several broad implications that can be derived
from our work.

Post-Tenure Review Works Moderately Well for Some Campuses and Not as Well for Others

In specific terms, we know that a plurality of faculty, department chairs, and
deans at three universities attributed worth and benefit to their process while a
plurality at four other universities attributed little overall value to the process. At
the remaining two campuses, opinions were evenly split between positive and
negative opinions about value.

Impetus for Establishing the Review Seems to Matter

On the same three campuses where faculty and administrators were more satisfied
than dissatisfied with their review practices and results, the policy originated from
the inside out and not the other way around. There was considerable involvement
of faculty in formulating the policy at these three institutions, whereas direct faculty buy-in at the other sites seemed lacking.

Political Benefit Is Universally Recognized

The majority of faculty, department chairs, and deans in each of the nine institutions recognized the political advantages to having a program of post-tenure
review on the books. Even though the value and benefit of such reviews to individual faculty was seriously questioned on at least four campuses, there was not any
movement underfoot to abolish post-tenure review at any of the nine campuses.

Ritualistic Compliance Is Commonplace

Given the recognition we saw with respect to the political benefit of having post-tenure review on the books, it is not surprising that ritualistic compliance was far reaching. Actionable feedback and meaningful follow-through after the review were sorely lacking in six of the nine settings. What was surprising were the repeated requests expressed by faculty and administrators that their institutions strengthen follow-through procedures and convert ritualistic compliance into substantive practice. Suggestions for what and how to make this happen were plentiful.

Periodic Review With Strong Developmental Focus Is the Most Successful Approach

Acceptance and support for post-tenure review is more evident when faculty see that a developmental focus is visibly emphasized and supported and that the review procedures are implemented on a periodic cycle for all faculty. In the three institutions where a plurality of faculty expressed a positive view about their policies, these characteristics were in place.

HAVE WE ANSWERED OUR ORIGINAL QUESTIONS?

Our data provide some preliminary answers and reveal some provocative trends.

1) IS POST-TENURE REVIEW ACHIEVING ITS INTENDED INSTITUTIONAL PURPOSE?

What emerged with clarity from this study is recognition that faculty and administrators view post-tenure review as having multiple purposes. Post-tenure review was frequently described as a practice established to: 1) review performance in order to assess if performance expectations are being met, 2) assess individual performance in order to remedy deficiencies, 3) increase accountability to outside constituents, and 4) assess career development goals and establish plans for continued growth and redirection.

It also became apparent that there was an important distinction made by many between what constituted the *intended* purpose for the policy and what represented the *actual* purpose. This distinction was grounded more in how the policy was practiced or perceived than in what specific policy language suggested. Faculty in most of the institutions studied indicated that summative ends seemed to overshadow formative goals. Only in two universities were faculty, department chairs, and deans in agreement that the main policy intent was developmental and that the policy was actually being implemented along those lines.

Accountability was a clear goal on all nine campuses. This involved both internal and external forms of accountability aimed at ensuring that faculty were performing up to standards and that external criticism about faculty productivity was quelled.

Those institutions that struggled with the implementation of post-tenure review voiced specific concern that because the stated purposes did not match the actual purposes, faculty cynicism hampered serious implementation. The other prevailing concern was that when developmental goals were not perceived as important by the administration or policymakers, the faculty then viewed post-tenure review as purely punitive and targeted to get rid of the deadwood.

As a group, administrators tended to have a more positive view than faculty about the use of post-tenure review for developmental purposes. Across the institutions, the higher the level of individual responsibility and authority, the broader the view about what the overall goals and intended outcomes of the review were and the greater the experience with faculty performance improvement plans.

Our results correlate with other studies on the purpose of post-tenure review and its acceptance by faculty. Other researchers have found that formative post-tenure review is viewed much more favorably by faculty than summative post-tenure review (Fry, 2000; Harris, 1996; Reisman, 1986; Willett, 2000; Wood, 2000). O'Meara (2003) found that deans are more positive about outcomes from post-tenure review than faculty and chairs. Wilson (1995) reported that chief academic officers in public four-year colleges and universities maintain that post-tenure review is achieving its intended purpose.

2) Are Post-Tenure Review Policies Effective?

On the question of effectiveness, the vote is inclusive—slightly more reported that the process was not that effective or was ineffective than considered the process to be effective or somewhat effective. Administrators in general were more positive than faculty on this question but not at a level of significance.

Surprisingly, while a large number of faculty lacked conviction that their policies were accomplishing what they set out to accomplish, many did admit that if the legislature or board of regents was satisfied with the policy and its implementation, then they felt that counted for something. Some even said it counted for everything. Chairs and deans were not always of the same mind on this issue of effectiveness. Some deans were more inclined than their chairs to note some measure of effectiveness.

Three major reasons were offered over and over again to explain why a particular policy was considered ineffective. The three reasons boiled down to a lack of follow-through after the review was completed.

- The review shows little evidence of positive outcomes.

- The review is not taken seriously because there is no significant follow-up action to the review

- The review is not taken seriously because there are no sanctions for poor performance.

When the issue of effectiveness was probed further, respondents often pointed to the lack of leadership and failed actions on the part of chairs, deans, and other senior administrators in following up with faculty after the review was completed to ensure that attention was paid to closing the loop. Depending on the particular institution, this might mean appropriating resources to support an improvement or developmental plan and/or ensuring that proper faculty recognition occurred.

Faculty also drew attention to the importance of serious and conscientious administrative oversight in the process. In turn, chairs, because of their faculty status, looked to their dean for support and often found it wanting.

As a rule, chairs were of the opinion that in order for post-tenure review to be effective, the review needed to be positive, constructive, and nonpunitive. Deans occasionally pointed to the positive effect that the review had on changes to workload, renewed commitment of faculty, and changes in career paths including retirement.

3) What Impact Does Post-Tenure Review Have on Faculty Work, Professional Development, and Career Planning?

Likewise, when it comes to the issue of impact on faculty work, professional development, and career planning, opinions were mixed. The majority of respondents were neutral on questions related to policy effect. Only results from two institutions showed clear positive impact on faculty performance or development. There was no real difference in points of view expressed by faculty or administrators on this question.

It is important to keep in mind that assessment of impact, regardless of what is being discussed, has immediate and long-term dimensions. The neutrality expressed here often came from an understanding on the part of faculty and administrators that measuring impact required time and reflective analysis. Even though each institution had at least five years of experience with post-tenure review, no one within any of the institutions was responsible for gauging overall impact. Only one university had looked at this question of impact from a continuous process improvement perspective to try to get a handle on whether there were recognizable "markings" related to impact.

Despite the overall sense of neutrality or "not ready yet to venture an opinion" attitude, there were some subtext impact messages that came through.

Impact on Faculty Performance and Development: Hard to Isolate

All in all, it is fair to say that the interviews did not reveal many examples of specific changes in individual faculty performance resulting from a post-tenure review. Often, we heard faculty and chairs express ambivalence about whether tangible outcomes occurred or say that the process was either redundant with the annual review or had the "potential" to be of benefit to them but needed to be improved in one way or another.

This result matches previous reported findings by researchers: post-tenure review does not directly improve faculty performance (Ernest, 1999; Johnson, 1990; O'Meara, 2003); is least effective with low-performing faculty (Reisman, 1986); and has little measurable impact on the institution or value to faculty (Wesson & Johnson, 1991; Wood 2000).

The reasons given for why the process failed to produce tangible results converged on the lack of any meaningful follow-through and the failure to tie professional development resources to review results. Some were quick to point out that there was no muscle attached to the follow-through process either by way of sanctions or rewards.

Many, except perhaps senior administrators, referred to a lack of additional development resources as a contributing factor to the lack of significant tangible results. Senior administrators often felt there were ample opportunities and resources available, and that when a case could be made for support, resources could be found. Deans and chairs seemed to say that discretionary resources should be easier to access.

The key to the discussion of outcomes was the confusion about whether the review should be funneled in the direction of remediation or development and where support for this comes from. While many senior administrators asserted that any reasonable development objective coming from a review would be supported, this belief was not shared by all constituents.

Tangible Outcomes: What Are They?

Faculty and administrators in almost every institution could point to a tangible outcome here and there. In two institutions, it was not a "here and there" but rather a "here and how."

The types of tangible results reported included opportunities for professional leave, course release time, financial support for staff and/or equipment, promotion to full professor, special recognition of contributions, successful sabbatical application, research seed money, modifications in teaching workload, and the opportunity to engage more deeply in scholarship. These tangible results mirror previous studies which pointed out that the post-tenure review process reduces the number of underperforming faculty (University of Hawaii–Manoa, 1997); has positive impact on professional growth and improvement (Willett, 2000); leads to improved faculty development (Association of American Universities, 2001); and provides some motivation to increase research and scholarship (Goodman, 1994; Harris, 1996; Reisman, 1986).

One outcome that was mentioned by chairs, deans, and senior-level administrators was an increase in the number of senior faculty retirements. Goodman (1994) and O'Meara (2003) found the same outcomes in their studies.

Chairs occasionally reported seeing tangible results serving as a morale boost to the faculty. In one school, reference was made to the positive impact that the follow-up conference with the dean had for each reviewed faculty member. This mirrors Johnson's (1990) work, which found that post-tenure review helps advance interpersonal contact with colleagues and improve morale and opportunities for performance feedback.

Intangible Outcomes: What Are They?

Vital to the question of results and impact was the distinction some made between tangible and intangible outcomes. Frequently, faculty and chairs referred to the intrinsic or intangible outcomes that the process spawned, such as reaffirmation of quality work and an opportunity for career reflection.

For some, the review provided an invitation for self-examination and career introspection. Greater knowledge of and appreciation for colleagues' contributions was also cited occasionally by faculty and peer review committee members. Chairs saw clarification of performance standards as a worthy outcome for some departments. Another view we heard periodically was that the review offered the most benefit to faculty who are interested in continuous improvement.

Impact on Career Development: Inconclusive

Similar to impact on performance, when asked about the result of the process on professional/personal career development and planning, more individuals were neutral on this question than had an opinion. It is difficult to interpret what this level of neutrality and ambivalence connotes. It may mean that more time is needed in order to formulate an opinion about the impact on career development or that career development is multifaceted, longitudinal, and difficult to unbundle and discuss at a discrete point in time. Because most institutions studied had only been through one complete review cycle, it is plausible that perspective on this question needs to be grounded in at least one more cycle of reviews.

At this juncture, our results don't affirm or disaffirm whether post-tenure review impacts career development and planning. What we know is that when pressed, faculty and administrators don't feel strongly one way or the other on this question.

4) Does Post-Tenure Review Help Advance Departmental Goals and Institutional Mission?

Information gathered from interviews on how post-tenure review affected individual departments and institutions is inconclusive. Survey responses corroborate this as well because almost 50% of all respondents indicated they had not formulated an opinion yet on the question of the overall impact of post-tenure review on the department. What we are able to derive from this broad-based wait-and-see response is that moving from the sphere of the individual to the department as a whole is difficult for many to assess.

Chairs and deans were better able to discuss the benefits and the shortcomings of post-tenure review at the department level than were faculty. Some chairs said the review created more flexible faculty workload profiles and helped redirect and rechannel faculty efforts to better meet the overall needs of the department. Faculty members either failed to recognize any impact or said they were not in a position to know if any real impact on the department was felt.

Faculty pointed out that results from reviews are kept confidential and this makes it difficult to know exactly how results affect the department at large. Only two institutions made any effort to aggregate results for faculty, chairs, or more public consumption. The first institution waited almost 10 years to collect and share data, and even then the data didn't make its way to the faculty in any coordinated fashion. The second institution did report review outcomes over the first three-year period and used outcomes data as a basis for discussing the impact of the policy and future policy potential with faculty, chairs, and deans. A third institution discussed results with the regents, when requested, but did not move that discussion down into the university in any meaningful way. Every other campus made no attempt to report or discuss the results of post-tenure review with internal constituents.

Another aspect of impact that came through on several campuses was how the review was used as a means of redirecting and rechanneling faculty efforts and how such action can help departments achieve collective goals.

In the minds of many chairs, deans, and other administrators, any positive impact at the department or institution level depended in large measure on how seriously the unit took its evaluation responsibilities. It was apparent that post-tenure review impacted some departments in positive ways, other departments in negative ways, and some departments not at all. It was also clear that academic departmental leadership was important to any positive impact.

5) Is Post-Tenure Review Worth It?

This line of inquiry was perhaps the most interesting and the most perplexing. The majority of faculty and academic administrators did not want to see post-tenure review discontinued but wanted, instead, to see it improved. When asked whether the post-tenure review process was worth the time and effort required, there was not a strong response in one direction or the other. Survey respondents were almost evenly divided between saying it was worth the effort (36%), feeling it was too soon to know (27%), and stating it wasn't worth the effort (37%). The interview analysis revealed the same type of three-way split in four institutions. In the other five, two were clearly positive in their assessment of worth, and three were clearly more positive than negative.

Stakeholders across institutions who told us they believed the process was worthwhile generally also felt that post-tenure review should be continued. However, these same constituents frequently added specific areas needing modification. The opposite was true in the case of those who saw no worth to the process. These faculty and administrators were usually ready to scrap it completely. A third group, those on the fence, needed more time to formulate an opinion and expressed a wait-and-see attitude.

Some commented that while the review had not been of benefit to them personally, they realized that it might be useful to keep it because it helped their institution demonstrate accountability and compliance with external mandates. What this group was saying is that while the process didn't carry direct benefit on an individual basis, they were convinced of its symbolic worth.

In at least five of the nine institutions, stakeholders talked about the evolving nature of the process within their own setting and noted that while in theory post-tenure review may be a laudable idea, as practiced, it needed improvement. Additionally, some faculty and administrators on every campus, although not a compelling number, were opposed to post-tenure review regardless of the political or symbolic benefit that might accrue from it.

Chairs and deans were much more positive than faculty. One-half of the deans surveyed and almost one-half of the chairs indicated that it was worth the effort, whereas only one-third of the faculty felt this way.

Where Do These Findings Lead?

From the beginning, our key goals for this study were to expand current understanding about post-tenure review processes and to improve institutional practice. In order to improve practice, it is necessary to know what contributes to effective policy implementation. Given the very general themes that emerged, we probed further to see if there were any factors or conditions that might work in tandem to create a positive opinion about the overall value and effectiveness of post-tenure review. We found that such factors could be identified. By using advanced statistical analysis (factor analysis and structural equation modeling) to drill down the survey data, a model emerged that produced very high predictive power. Because of its predictive strength, we believe this model offers important "intelligence" about what is essential if post-tenure review is to have an impact and be favorably regarded by faculty and academic administrators. The following is a description of what the model reveals and the implications that stem from it. A description of the methodology used to construct this model can be found in Appendix D.

A Model for Effective Post-Tenure Review

The model (see Figure 6.1) depicts those factors which converge as key drivers of predicting overall value. What is particularly compelling about this model is the strength of its predictive power. It carries a prediction coefficient of .93. Perfect prediction would be 1.00. In layman's terms, this means that 93% of the time the model explains the factors that must be present for faculty, department chairs, and deans to give their post-tenure review policy high marks on value. Some factors are more powerful than others in predicting overall value. Because of this, when applying the model, practitioners should pay particular attention to those that we refer to as major drivers because those factors strongly influence the value and benefit of post-tenure. Figure 6.1 displays the six major and minor factors that emerged from the model.

Major Drivers: What Are They?

The most influential factor in predicting if post-tenure review has overall value is whether the policy stimulates faculty to make changes in their performance, effort, professional emphasis, and/or vitality. This is not surprising: If the process doesn't lead to change, why have it? The power of this factor demands attention. It is almost twice that of the next strongest driver which is whether the review results in actual outcomes for a faculty member (path value of .41 versus .24).

Figure 6.1
Initial Model of Overall Value

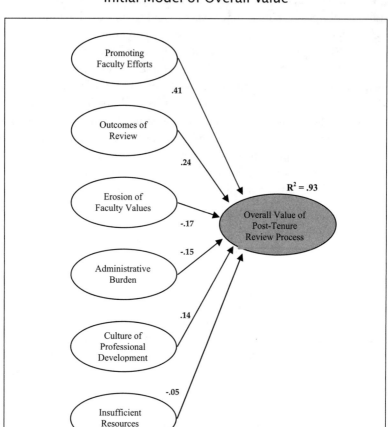

What this suggests is that post-tenure review programs that are perceived as stimulating and promoting change in faculty effort or performance are more likely to lead to opinions that the post-tenure review program itself has value (e.g., if the process is beneficial to faculty members, it is effective in achieving its purpose and is worth time and effort).

The next most influential factor is having a post-tenure review program that provides real outcomes and ensures that the outcomes are clearly understood. According to the model, institutions that are looking to maximize the perceived value of their post-tenure review programs will make the most gain toward this goal by taking steps that ensure their programs directly stimulate change in faculty effort and result in clearly understood outcomes (which may include both rewards and consequences). This supports well what we heard in the interviews and with the improvement recommendations offered. Repeatedly, complaints took aim at the fact that "nothing happens" in terms of stimulating change in behavior and that the lack of meaningful outcomes was a primary reason for ineffectiveness.

Moderate Drivers

Three aspects of the model function as more moderate drivers of perceptions of overall value. These are erosion of faculty values, administrative burden, and the public nature of faculty work. These three areas appear to be about half as influential as ensuring there are real outcomes from the review.

Erosion of faculty values and administrative burden both display a negative relationship. This means that the less erosion and burden that exist, the greater the perceived value of the process. Given the characteristics of the academic culture, it makes sense that post-tenure review programs that minimize the erosion of faculty professionalism, tenure, and autonomy would increase the perceived value of the program. Conversely, programs that show higher levels of erosion would produce more negative views of the program's value. From a cost-benefit perspective, it is logical that programs which purposively keep the amount of paperwork and time required to a manageable level (i.e., decrease administrative burden) are more likely to increase the perceived value of the process.

The third driver in this category, the public nature of faculty work, has a positive relationship. This suggests that review programs that as part of their design include ways to increase awareness and appreciation of a colleague's work are more likely to be seen as carrying greater value. This might include such things as establishing peer review as apart of the process or a department convening a specific meeting for the faculty member under review to share highlights of his or her last five years in teaching and/or research. It might mean that a dean uses a positive five-year review report as the impetus to recognize specific faculty for sustained achievement or that a school or college establishes a senior faculty seminar series that highlights interdisciplinary research contributions or innovative teaching strategies. Peer review committees constitute another important facet of making one's work more public. We often heard faculty who served on peer review committees say, "Professor X has been in our department for 30 years and has an office right down the hall from me, but I never really knew the scope of his research or appreciated the breadth of his contributions." Making one's work public can help dispel colleague suspicion that a faculty member is coasting.

Institutions capitalizing on this idea will want to ensure that peer review plays a significant role in their process and that other strategies of using the review as a means to make more public the contributions of faculty are explored and adopted.

Minor Drivers

There is a minor influence on overall value exerted by insufficient resources (which also shows a negative relationship). Fundamentally, this means that institutions lacking sufficient funds for training of reviewers and support for the development plans can effect a slight impact on overall value by making sure that such resources do exist. One might think of it this way: Having sufficient resources is a fine-tuning element to enhance perceived value of the program. In other words, once more critical areas such as stimulating faculty efforts, providing outcomes of the review, and reducing administrative burden have been achieved, a final enhancement may come from assuring that sufficient funding is available. This factor clearly has more leverage when the other conditions affecting value have been adequately met and will not by itself beget effectiveness. It might also be reasonably presumed that if the other elements in the model are in place, then sufficient resources are being provided—although this presumption needs further testing.

EXPANDING THE MODEL: ADDITIONAL REQUIREMENTS

There is a secondary driving force in the model that helps shed additional light on how an institution might enhance or improve the primary drivers just discussed. It is what we refer to as an expanded model (see Figure 6.2), and it parses out what is behind the drivers described earlier. What is striking about this secondary screen or thrust in the expanded model is the strong force that it carries on all of the other contextual, outcome, and process factors already discussed. The secondary driving force is what we refer to as a culture of professional development. What this tells us is that in order for programs of post-tenure review to carry benefit, they must be grounded or contextualized within an environment that promotes professional development. As a practical matter, this translates to ensuring that a positive evaluation atmosphere is in place—one that provides support for new professional directions, increases opportunities for mid- and late-career transition planning, and establishes an expectation for continuous growth and development. This culture is also important in creating an environment that increases understanding/awareness of colleagues' work (i.e., public nature of one's contributions).

A culture of professional development is less influential with respect to the negative drivers, however (i.e., erosion of faculty values, administrative burden, and insufficient resources). It can have some influence on these areas, but it is

Figure 6.2
Extended Model of Overall Value

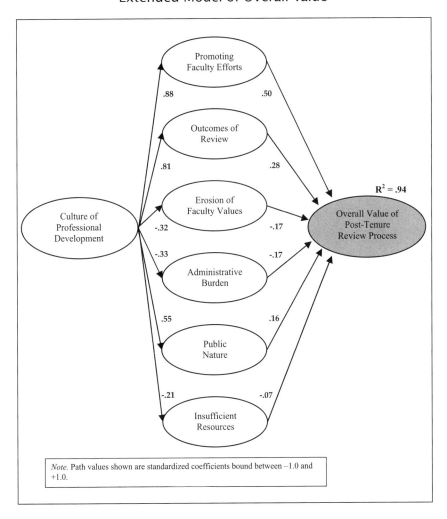

Note. Path values shown are standardized coefficients bound between −1.0 and +1.0.

likely they are more directly affected by other issues such as budgets, skills of the program administrators, and individual differences influencing perceptions.

Implications

The benefit of using this expanded model is that it can help institutional leaders identify and prioritize what policy or procedural dimensions are lacking and/or need to be strengthened in order to improve the value of post-tenure review practices. At a very basic level, if institutions hope to have an effective policy, they must establish and nurture an evaluation culture that supports professional development. Second, institutions must purposefully design evaluation programs to directly enhance and support faculty efforts, making sure that expected outcomes are clearly defined and actually happen. Without these contextual markers in place, it is unlikely that perceptions about the value of the program will be positive. This model reminds us that institutions that place real importance on faculty development and do more than simply talk the talk are likely to have significantly more success with their post-tenure review programs than those that don't.

Once a professional development infrastructure is in place, the model also suggests that removing obstacles such as burdensome paperwork and any threats to tenure or academic freedom can help promote the worth of the program. The same can be said for using the program in a positive way to share and inform others about a colleague's work—usually but not exclusively through peer review.

Some attention should be paid to the financial resources available to support the program. When discussing resources, it is important to understand that unless the post-tenure review process is nested within a culture that places a priority on providing faculty with support for career planning, renewal, and redirection, any amount of tinkering at the fringes with resource allocation and with those other things described here as moderate and minor drivers will not give the program the punch it needs to be effective and valuable in the eyes of faculty and administrators. Throwing resources in a haphazard and uncoordinated way at a program of post-tenure review is not sufficient to guarantee effective policy implementation.

Remember that while this model is based on survey responses, it mirrors the interview commentary on effectiveness discussed in Chapter 3. Recalling that discussion reiterates the point that three of the five most frequently suggested recommendations to make the process more effective zeroed in on different aspects of a professional development culture—namely, the need to incorporate a professional career planning component into the process; explore creative ways for shifting allocations for faculty efforts; and increased and better coordinated professional development funds and resources.

DISCUSSION

The model described here is derived directly from the survey responses of faculty, chairs, and deans across the nine case-study institutions. It provides empirical evidence about what must be in place for a program of post-tenure review to be considered valuable and effective. It matches with strong precision what the qualitative findings showed. In so doing, it provides overall stability and continuity to the study. Additionally, the model further affirms, and in some cases disaffirms, previous speculation about specific dimensions or components that carry the most compelling influence on predicting overall value.

Commentary in the literature regarding post-tenure review up to now has equated value with a review that is exclusively developmental and peer driven (American Association of University Professors [AAUP], 1998); a policy that protects tenure and academic freedom (AAUP, 1998); an evaluation supported by additional resources for professional development (Wesson & Johnson, 1991), and a practice earmarked by follow-through and clear outcomes (Andrews & Licata, 1992; Andrews, Licata, & Harris, 2002).

Without question, this model recognizes the role that all of these variables play in producing value. Yet this model suggests that there are two factors that provide the strongest influence on whether an institution's post-tenure review program will be viewed by faculty and administrators as valuable: 1) whether outcomes from the review, including feedback and follow-through, occur, and 2) whether the review stimulates faculty and chairs to discuss how professional efforts can be shifted, increased, replaced, or modified in order to achieve increased contribution in some performance area or areas.

Equally important is how an institution ensures that these two aspects are in place. This only occurs when a culture of professional development surrounds the evaluation environment. The defining features of a professional development culture are the presence of:

• Opportunities to support new professional directions.

• Increases in opportunities for mid- and late-career transition planning.

• Establishment of ongoing expectations for continuous growth and development.

These findings should not strike anyone as particularly unusual. Career development scholars studying faculty career stages have emphasized for years the need for this type of cultural presence (Baldwin, 1979, 1990; Clark & Corcoran, 1985; Furniss, 1981; Rice & Finklestein, 1993). A study of faculty vitality and productivity by Bland and Bergquist (1997) acknowledges that most institutions offer a "hodgepodge" of individual and organizational development strategies lacking cohesive and comprehensive rationale. Further, because of the importance of the interplay between institutional vitality and individual vitality, they concluded that productive academic organizations must provide effective leadership and a supportive environment which connects the individual's goals, motivation, and interests to the organization's goals, culture, and policy. In order to achieve this, academic evaluation programs must be part of a professional development program: ". . . if evaluation is coupled with a professional development program, or even more specifically, a professional plan, then it holds the potential that senior faculty will receive it in a positive manner" (Bland & Bergquist, 1997, p. 114).

Sorcinelli (2000) reminds us that one issue that has consistently captured the interest and concern of department chairs is the need for institutional acceptance and support for a "more integrated faculty career in which faculty can contribute where they are more interested, talented, and productive and be recognized and rewarded for their efforts" (p.16). Some see this integration accomplished through a coordinated corporate-like effort involving institutional, collegial, and individual action (Corcoran & Clark, 1985). Calling for a new academic compact, institutions in the Associated New American Colleges propose that,

> While other strategies should be implemented to assure institutional agility and viability, a focus on faculty development that allows for more flexible and effective roles is paramount for colleges and universities . . . [as is] a dedication on the part of both institution and faculty to developmental processes at each state of the faculty career . . . (Terenzio, 2002, p. 58)

Programs of post-tenure review, if they are squarely focused in the developmental direction, can also serve as a platform by which individualized work plans, faculty development, and differentiated workloads are given meaning and made viable. With this in mind, practitioners should use this model as a touchstone and identify opportunities to strengthen post-tenure review practices within their collegiate environment. Leveraging our findings can lead to discussions about how feedback processes can be improved and what rewards and consequences can and should be expected. Faculty and chairs can also use these findings to lobby deans and provosts to improve and enhance the developmental culture on their campuses. A good place to start such a campaign is by communicating clearly about faculty development opportunities already available and identifying where the gaps lie. Using a department's mission and strategic priorities as the portal from which to begin planning, chairs can discuss longer-term contributions that each faculty member can make and how the various faculty career stages can complement departmental and institutional expectations. Based on our model, the key is for chairs and deans to connect career planning to professional development opportunities. It is this connection that then moves these conversations to action. Such occasions to change performance are better spawned on a small scale by academic leaders who see the opportunity that a post-tenure review conversation can offer.

This model offers catalytic guidance for colleges and universities in any policy stage. Experienced institutions, and those already well along in policy implementation, can use this model as an impetus to assess whether institutional practices align themselves in a positive fashion with essential components identified in the model. Institutions in early stages of policy formulation can capitalize on the direction this model offers by proactively putting in place those factors that are most important to overall policy effectiveness. We discuss this in more detail in Chapter 8.

REFERENCES

American Association of University Professors. (1998). Post-tenure review: An AAUP response. *Academe, 84*(5), 61–67.

Andrews, H. A., & Licata, C. M. (1992). Faculty leaders' responses to post-tenure review evaluation practices. *Community/Junior College Quarterly, 16*(1), 47–56.

Andrews, H. A., Licata, C. M., & Harris, B. J. (2002). *The state of post-tenure and long term faculty evaluation* (Research brief). Washington, DC: American Association of Community Colleges.

Association of American Universities. (2001). *Post-tenure review.* Washington, DC: Author.

Baldwin, R. G. (1979). Adult and career development: What are the implications for faculty? *Current Issues in Higher Education, 2,* 13–20.

Baldwin, R. G. (1990). Faculty career stages and implications for faculty development. In J. H. Schuster & D. W. Wheeler (Eds.), *Enhancing faculty careers: Strategies for development and renewal* (pp. 20–40). San Francisco, CA: Jossey-Bass.

Bedell, B. (1988). Making ideas work: Ralph Bedell and the NDEA Institutes. *Journal of Counseling and Development, 67*(2), 9–16.

Bland, C. J., & Bergquist, W. H. (1997). *The vitality of senior faculty members: Snow on the roof—fire in the furnace* (ASHE-ERIC Higher Education Report, 25[7]). Washington, DC: George Washington University, School of Education and Human Development.

Clark, S. M., & Corcoran, M. (1985). Individual and organizational contributions to faculty vitality: An institutional case study. In S. M. Clark & D. R. Lewis (Eds.), *Faculty vitality and productivity: Critical perspectives for higher education* (pp. 112–138). New York, NY: Teachers College Press.

Corcoran, M., & Clark, S. M. (1985). The stuck professor: Insights into an aspect of the faculty vitality issue. In C. Watson (Ed.), *The professorate: Occupation in crisis* (pp. 57–81). Toronto, Canada: Ontario Institute for Studies in Education.

Ernest, I. (1999). *Faculty evaluation of post-tenure review at a research university.* Unpublished doctoral dissertation, Columbia University, New York.

Fry, J. E. (2000). *Post-tenure review: A study of policies and practices at colleges and universities in the United States.* Unpublished doctoral dissertation, University of Tennessee, Knoxville.

Furniss, W. T. (1981). *Reshaping faculty careers.* Washington, DC: American Council on Education.

Goodman, M. J. (1994). The review of tenured faculty at a research university: Outcomes and appraisals. *Review of Higher Education, 18*(1), 83–94.

Harris, B. J. (1996). *The relationship between and among policy variables, type of institution, and perceptions of academic administrators with regard to post-tenure review.* Unpublished doctoral dissertation, University of West Virginia, Morgantown.

Johnson, G. (1990). *The innovation process in organizations: A look at post-tenure faculty evaluation.* Unpublished doctoral dissertation, Pennsylvania State University.

O'Meara, K. A. (2003). Believing is seeing: The influence of beliefs and expectations on post-tenure review in one state system. *Review of Higher Education, 27*(1), 17–43.

Reisman, B. (1986). Performance evaluation for tenured faculty: Issues and research. *Liberal Education, 72*(1), 73–87.

Rice, R., & Finkelstein, M. (1993). The senior faculty as teachers. In M. Finkelstein & M. Lacelle-Petersen (Eds.), *New directions for teaching and learning: No. 55. Developing senior faculty as teachers* (pp. 7–19). San Francisco, CA: Jossey-Bass.

Sorcinelli, M. D. (2000, Winter). Department chairs and deans: A longitudinal look at issues that dominate their lives. *The Department Chair, 10*(3), 15–16.

Terenzio, M. (2002). Professional development across the faculty career: An engine for implementing a new faculty-institutional compact. In L. A. McMillin & W. G. Berberet (Eds.), *A new academic compact: Revisioning the relationship between faculty and their institutions* (pp. 29–60). Bolton, MA: Anker.

University of Hawaii–Manoa, Office of the Senior Vice President and Executive Vice Chancellor. (1997). *Ten years of post-tenure review at the University of Hawaii–Manoa: 1987–1997.* Honolulu, HI: Author.

Wesson, M., & Johnson, S. (1991). Post-tenure review and faculty revitalization. *Academe, 77*(3), 53–57.

Willett, C. M. (2000). *Post-tenure review: Opinions held by faculty in highly selective, independent, private liberal arts institutions.* Unpublished doctoral dissertation, Seton Hall University, South Orange, New Jersey.

Wilson, S. J. (1995). *Faculty post-tenure review: Perceptions of chief academic officers of public four-year colleges and universities within the region of the Southern Association of Colleges and Schools.* Unpublished doctoral dissertation, University of Alabama, Tuscaloosa.

Wood, M. S. (2000). *Post-tenure review: The role of academic values and beliefs in shaping faculty response at two research universities.* Unpublished doctoral dissertation, University of Hawaii, Honolulu.

7

Is Post-Tenure Review a Lever for Organizational Change?

Estela Mara Bensimon

ORGANIZATIONAL CHANGE

Although not directly stated, the discussion that surrounded the development and adoption of post-tenure review policies indicated that advocates viewed post-tenure review as a lever for bringing about changes in the activities, behaviors, and values of faculty members. It was hoped that post-tenure review would increase awareness about the need to align faculty work with institutional priorities, that the processes of post-tenure review would increase collegiality and even reinvigorate faculty who felt stuck.

In essence, there was a movement to change aspects of the academic culture that were perceived as being detrimental to the overall quality and purposes of higher education, and post-tenure review was one way in which institutional and systemic change could be initiated. This chapter considers the following question: In what ways has post-tenure review served as a lever for change in the nine institutions that participated in the American Association for Higher Education's project? The answer to this question is not clear-cut. Faculty members and administrators attributed two specific behavioral changes to post-tenure review: 1) It pressured faculty members who were no longer productive to retire in order to avoid post-tenure review altogether or to avoid being reevaluated after their performance was found to be unsatisfactory, and 2) it increased emphasis on the production of traditional research.

Faculty Retirements

The most salient change linked to post-tenure review was the retirement of faculty whose academic careers were viewed as having slowed or stagnated. At one university, the deans estimated that approximately 10% of faculty under review eventually exercised early-retirement options. Individuals who mentioned this outcome felt that had it not been for post-tenure review these faculty members might have coasted along for several more years.

The most effective and direct way of bringing about change in an organization is through strategic recruitment; thus the decision to retire provided institutions with an unexpected opportunity. Surprisingly, however, the faculty and administrators we interviewed did not elaborate on how these retirements made other changes possible, and there was no indication that institutions or departments considered these retirements in relation to other goals. For example, none of the individuals we interviewed mentioned that retirements had enabled the institution to be more proactive about increasing the racial diversity of their faculty, even though this was one of the expected benefits of attrition among tenured faculty. If decision-makers viewed these retirements as strategic opportunities, it was not clear from their comments if the two were linked or considered an outcome of post-tenure review per se.

Research Productivity

In addition to encouraging faculty to retire, the evaluation processes involved in post-tenure review have reinforced the importance of research productivity, even though this was not the intended effect. In most institutions, post-tenure review requires faculty members to prepare a dossier in which they document their activities in accordance with the traditional division of academic labor into teaching, research/scholarship, and service. We suspect that post-tenure review reinforces research-oriented productivity because these activities result in concrete and quantifiable products. It is much easier for faculty members to demonstrate their industriousness by producing a list with the number of papers presented at conferences, articles and books published, and the dollar amount received in funded research. This is true for research universities as well as comprehensive four-year colleges where teaching is the predominant activity. It is also easier for those who are responsible for doing the evaluation to count products than to review the content of, say, syllabi. The availability of indicators of quality in scholarship, such as differentiated rankings for journals and publishers and different levels of prestige associated with national versus local conferences, allows for easier judgments about the status a faculty member has in her or his field. Essentially, the products and prestige accrued from research are easy to document.

On the other hand, the documentation of teaching productivity is not well developed and the metrics that one might use, such as the number of students or courses taught over a period of time or the results of student evaluations, do not carry the same credibility or legitimacy as the quantifiable products of research.

It is not unusual for the majority of faculty members to invest innumerable hours preparing to teach a course, tutor and mentor individual students, review students' written work and make extensive comments, and learn how to incorporate new technology (e.g., Blackboard) into the classroom. Even though these teaching activities represent the heart of academic work in the great majority of institutions of higher education, the labor associated with them tends to be overlooked because it cannot be compressed into a single metric. For the most part, we did not find that post-tenure review was managed in a way that invited reflection about the practices that take up the greatest amount of time for the majority of faculty.

For many stakeholders the turn toward post-tenure review was in reaction to reports about the decline and neglect of undergraduate teaching. The expectation that post-tenure review would bring about greater balance between research and teaching was a prominent topic in discussions leading up to its adoption, but based on our interviews and survey results, post-tenure review seems to be having the opposite effect. Repeatedly, we heard from faculty, chairs, and academic administrators that one of the changes brought on by post-tenure review was the reemergence of research as an expectation. One chair told us that

> at one time making conference presentations was considered to be appropriate, but now in our school things are a little different. Now we're looking for higher amounts of publications. So PTR [post-tenure review] gave me, as a chair, an opportunity to communicate with that person and explain that some of the presentations need to be turned into articles.

In the same manner that we did not find that retirements were seen as an opportunity for more strategic and targeted hiring, we also did not find that the evaluation processes for post-tenure review took into account the relevance of research and scholarship vis-a-vis institutional or departmental goals. That is, the criteria for evaluating research were generic and in no way linked to the institution's mission or to specific goals or to advance particular values. In fact, when we asked directly about the connection between post-tenure review and an institution's strategic plans or a department's priorities, we were told that there was little or no connection. At one institution the president said that post-tenure review was not intended to try to reorient faculty members to the strategic plan, rather,

> It [post-tenure review] was an attempt to bring out the best in the individual, not to try to force them into any cubbyhole.

There were some chairs who saw beyond the mechanics of getting post-tenure review done. One chair thought the process led to a "better understanding of university goals on the part of faculty." Chairs from one particular college referred to the follow-up conference between the faculty member and the dean as providing "a more direct pipeline to the dean" and an opportunity for a "constructive conversation." We want to note that follow-up conversations such as the one mentioned by this chair were very rare, since most deans and most chairs did not hold them. Another chair viewed the strategic value of post-tenure review as a proactive approach: "a focus, an organizational approach to doing this [longer-term development] than just dealing with things as they come up."

Upper-level administrators were much more likely than faculty or chairs to view post-tenure review as a conduit for institutional change. Most of the impact that administrators saw this process as having on faculty was anecdotal or based on informal observations. For example, in one university a group of deans felt that post-tenure review resulted in the reallocation of faculty effort among teaching, research, and service. Some particularly noted that their one-on-one discussion with faculty members led to real improvements in faculty and real benefits to the department. The specific examples of impact cited by these deans included changes in workload emphases, renewed commitment by faculty to research and service, redirected and realigned activities, and exercising options of early retirement either before or after the review. At the same institution, the provost cited three significant outcomes that he attributed, at least in part, to the post-tenure review policy: "Increased scholarship productivity; improved conversations about career directions and departmental need and increased respectability." However, these impressions were not supported by the results of the institution-wide surveys.

Overall, there is little indication in the data from the interviews and the campus surveys that post-tenure review has been the catalyst for far-reaching changes. We did not find evidence, either in the interviews or in the survey results, that post-tenure review had major impact or has changed the status, quality, or quantity of teaching, that it has changed faculty behaviors, or that the criteria used for post-tenure review has facilitated a better alignment between the work of faculty and institutional goals. Even the retirements prompted by post-tenure review, which represent the best possible outcome one might wish for, were not seized as a strategic opportunity. Then again, post-tenure review may never have had as its central purpose fundamental organizational change.

We recognize that post-tenure review's seemingly limited impact as a lever for institutional change may have to do with its relative newness. However, there were four institutions that had been doing post-tenure review for a decade or longer and, other than retirements, no other significant changes were attributed to post-tenure review by campus leaders, faculty, or chairs. We also recognize that the limited impact of post-tenure review as a lever for organizational change may be an artifact of the individuals we interviewed or of the questions we asked; however, if post-tenure review is a lever for organizational change it would have been more apparent in the results of the institution-wide surveys which covered a broad spectrum of institutional roles. But the survey results tended to support our conclusion that post-tenure review has not stimulated the kinds of changes anticipated by supporters. It is also worth noting that post-tenure review has not produced the threats to tenure, academic freedom, and collegiality that were anticipated by its opponents.

It is possible that one reason for the limited impact of post-tenure review as a lever for institutional change is its conceptualization as an instrument of behavior modification. In the next section, we discuss the reasons why the behavioral model of post-tenure review is *not* an effective lever for organizational change.

THE BEHAVIORAL POST-TENURE REVIEW MODEL

In order to understand why post-tenure review has not led to behavior modification, we must first ask:

- What are the underlying assumptions in post-tenure review about how the practices of individuals or groups of individuals change?

- In what ways might these assumptions be suitable or unsuitable for such post-tenure review aims as revitalizing faculty, practicing teaching as a type of scholarship, and instilling commitment to collective values?

We suggest that the dominant ways in which post-tenure review are being implemented reflect the assumptions that are characteristic of behavioral models of human motivation and social control. Behavioral models are based on the presumption that individuals are averse to effort and are moved to act based on self-interest. From this perspective, the best means of managing behavior is through incentives, rewards, and surveillance (Pfeffer, 1997). Post-tenure review is a form of surveillance in that its purpose is to ensure that the work of tenured faculty undergoes a formal process of scrutiny or inspection. It came about from the perception among some stakeholders that tenure is a disincentive to productivity and that there needs to be a way to motivate faculty members to invest their talent and time on behalf of institutional priorities. The idea that the guarantee of life employment—tenure—may diminish an individual's motivation to be productive is consistent with the central notion of behavioral models, which is that individuals act in certain ways in order to receive rewards or avoid punishment. Presumably, tenured faculty will continue being productive in order to avoid the embarrassment or the loss of status that would be set off by a negative review. As two professors commented:

> *My guess is that ... [post-tenure review] prompts people who are getting too comfortable to get a little less comfortable. ... So I think one result*

that it has had is that it has prompted, I am sure, a few people to think, well, I might be better at age 61 to take the retirement money, which is not bad, and moving out of the way and letting people with more energy and zip to begin to take over. So don't misunderstand. I don't think it is a deadwood clearing operation. But I think that some people do feel anxious about it, and I think that is maybe OK.

There is a large group of faculty that are, say, non-productive in a research sense. So I am sure that there is some motivation to light a fire under them or get rid of them for that matter.

Our point is not that supporters of post-tenure review perceive faculty to be lazy and in need of close supervision, but rather that these are the assumptions implicit in behavioral models of social control such as post-tenure review. Critics of behavioral models in general and post-tenure review in particular point out that they are ineffective and inappropriate in organizations made up of professionals and that operate on the basis of symbolic and intangible rewards such as prestige, status, and peer approval to elicit compliance. Unlike non-professional organizations, colleges and universities have characteristics that make conventional forms of control and coordination, such as incentives, rewards, and threats, highly ineffective. In order to motivate participants, academic organizations rely primarily on symbols rather than coercion (Birnbaum, 1988). Behavior is controlled through group norms (Homans, 1950, 1961), and coordination is obtained through the exercise of professional rather than legal authority (Etzioni, 1964).

A common response to behavioral models of social control is symbolic compliance. Much of what we learned about the implementation and outcomes of post-tenure review at the nine campuses was consistent with symbolic compliance. That is, despite dislike or indifference for post-tenure review, all nine institutions had clearly spelled out post-tenure review guidelines and adhered to them. Tenured faculty who were scheduled to undergo post-tenure review did their part by putting together their dossiers, and chairs did theirs by managing post-tenure review according to the prescribed guidelines and making sure that the associated documents moved through the review process.

The rituals associated with the accountability perspective (e.g., having a structure that delineates the required steps, filing a report on the results, etc.) provide bureaucratic assurance of institutional compliance with post-tenure review policies. Institutions can produce reports (although not always) on the number of faculty who went through post-tenure review, how many were found to be performing satisfactorily (the great majority), how many were found to be performing unsatisfactorily and were required to develop a program for improvement (a very small number), how many completed the improvement program successfully, and in some instances, how many faculty members decided to retire rather than participate in post-tenure review or demonstrate improvement after their performance was judged to be unsatisfactory.

The behavioral model cannot bring about the hoped-for changes in academic culture, such as revitalizing aging faculty, enhancing esprit de corps among faculty, and doing a better job of aligning faculty work with institutional priorities. If the purpose of post-tenure review is to reassure stakeholders outside the institution that faculty are required to undergo periodic reviews then the behavioral model serves this purpose quite well. But if this is the most important goal of post-tenure review then consideration should be given on how to conduct it more economically.

However, if post-tenure review is seen as a means of learning about the performance of faculty individually and collectively in relation to departmental and institutional goals, or if the aim is developmental, to revitalize faculty or help them develop new competences or roles, the behavioral model is inappropriate. Accordingly, the next sections consider two questions:

- What model of post-tenure review might be more suitable to organizational learning?

- What model of post-tenure review might be more suitable for the professional development of individuals?

We believe that systemic change is more likely to be accomplished if post-tenure review incorporated the principles associated with learning organizations as well as the principles associated with the nature of practices in the human realm.

THE LEARNING MODEL OF POST-TENURE REVIEW

The post-tenure review process obtains information about the performance of individuals, the aggregate performance of a department's faculty members, or the aggregate performance of an institution's faculty members. The information gathered through post-tenure review can be useful to institutional leaders who are interested in various aspects of faculty productivity. At the most basic level, post-tenure review reports provide information about the research, teaching, and service activities of tenured faculty members over a specified period of time. If a department chair wanted to have a sense of the five-year trends in the scholarly activities of tenured faculty, he or she could easily extract and synthesize this information from post-tenure review reports. If a provost wanted to have a general sense of how long-time faculty are performing, he or she could develop an answer from a synthesis of the information provided in post-tenure review reports. The information gathered through post-tenure review allows institutional leaders to learn something about the performance of tenured faculty members that they did not know before. The importance of this information is that it can provide a department chair, a faculty committee, or a provost with knowledge about the larger picture. The information can also serve to confirm hunches they may have about someone's work. It is also possible that the information gathered through the post-tenure review process can trigger new ideas or understandings about the work of faculty and provoke new questions. The most likely way in which post-tenure review can serve as a managerial lever for organizational change is if department chairs, deans, and other high-level academic administrators find that the information can be useful and are willing to invest time and effort to interpret it.

Post-tenure review has the potential to function as an organizational learning mechanism, one that enables institutions to systematically collect, analyze, store, disseminate, and use information that is relevant to the performance of the organization (Popper & Lipshitz, 1998). However, none of the chairs, academic administrators, or faculty we interviewed spoke about the uses, processes, or outcomes of post-tenure review in ways that suggest it is being viewed as an organizational learning mechanism.

The considerable amount of information that is gathered about the activities of faculty members undergoing post-tenure review offers numerous possibilities for a department chair, a faculty committee, a strategic planning task force, and an office of institutional research to *learn* about the work of faculty members in relation to departmental goals, patterns of productivity, the quality of teaching, and any number of other topics.

We did not learn whether institutions expected to use the very extensive repositories of post-tenure review information to determine, say, the state of research productivity or the state of teaching quality or to do comparative studies across departments or across schools. In other words, post-tenure review was not used for answering, even if only partially, questions such as how the institution is doing or how a department is doing.

None of the individuals we interviewed mentioned having a structure and/or process to transform the raw information collected through post-tenure review into knowledge about a department, an academic unit, or the institution. Based on our observations, it was clear that most administrative leaders understood post-tenure review as having to do with individuals; that is, whether they are being productive and if they are not, whether there is anything that can be done about it. Post-tenure review provided information about individual performance and was rarely treated as a resource for decision-making, planning, or evaluation.

WHY ISN'T POST-TENURE REVIEW PROMOTING INSTITUTIONAL LEARNING?

Even though post-tenure review provides an ideal structure to promote learning among decision-makers who are in positions to use that learning to bring about institutional change, post-tenure review is not being implemented with that purpose in mind. Why? One reason is that the potential for learning inherent in post-tenure review is contingent on the value of the information that is gathered through the process:

- What questions do the information answer?

- Are these questions important to faculty, department chairs, and other academic leaders?

- What might be learned from the answer to these questions that was not already known?

- In what ways can this learning be useful?

Another reason is that the potential for learning is contingent on whether the information is made available in a manner that is user-friendly:

- Is the raw information (e.g., the individual faculty dossiers) organized in ways that make it easily interpretable?

- Is the information organized in ways that invite discussion?

- Is the raw information organized in a manner that is compatible with the questions it is designed to answer or that may be of particular interest to different stakeholders such as department chairs or members of a governing board?

Our case studies indicate that for the most part these two aspects of the information—value and user-friendliness—were not prominent concerns, mainly because post-tenure review is structured primarily for the purpose of certifying that individual faculty members meet the minimum expectations for satisfactory performance. Most of the participating institutions had not linked the content and process of post-tenure review to other goals such as attaining a better alignment between faculty work and institutional goals or gathering evidence about changes in teaching approaches to be more responsive to new student needs.

We came to this conclusion because none of the institutions' post-tenure review structures had characteristics that we associate with the conditions that support organizational learning. First, faculty undergoing review submitted reports on their activities organized according to the traditional and generic criteria of scholarship, teaching, and service, much in the same way as they would for a tenure or promotion review. Clearly, these generic report formats provided a wealth of descriptive information on basic metrics of productivity that could be useful in a variety of ways, such as determining how hard faculty work, how much teaching is done, how many new courses have been developed, and so on. However, the institutions had not routinely attempted to convert post-tenure review dossiers into databases that could generate reports for internal use or for external stakeholders concerned with productivity and accountability. Typically, once the review process was completed, the faculty activity reports were stored and more than likely not looked at again. Of the institutions we visited, only three shared a retrospective study about the outcomes of post-tenure review. The report described the number of faculty reviewed, the number of faculty found to have a satisfactory performance, the number of faculty found unsatisfactory who completed their development plans, and the number of faculty who chose to retire before going through the review process or after their performance was found to be unsatisfactory. The report documented in a detailed manner the implementation of post-tenure review and the kind of outcomes it had for individuals. But it failed to provide an encompassing picture of changing patterns in productivity or in faculty vitality.

For most of these institutions, post-tenure review was not viewed as an opportunity for learning, thus no provision was made to turn the raw data (i.e., the individual activity reports) into interpretable information for decision-making or planning. It was not structured in a way that might encourage decision-makers to turn to the results of post-tenure review and ask, "What might we learn about faculty vitality from this year's post-tenure reports?" or "What might we learn about the link between faculty work and our strategic plan?"

IMPEDIMENTS TO THE LEARNING MODEL

Institutions of higher education have been identified as an example of organizations that do not learn. According to Garvin (1993), universities are "effective at creating or acquiring new knowledge [but they are] notably less successful in applying that knowledge to their own activities" (p. 80). Similar observations about the underutilization of information by institutions of higher education have been made by scholars and policymakers (see Birnbaum, 1988; Ewell, 1997; Knight Higher Education Collaborative, 2000; Wergin & Swingen, 2000). Institutions of higher education may have difficulties learning because they lack some of the essential structural and cultural facets that are associated with organizational learning. For example, most institutions today have extensive information systems, institutional research offices, and the ability to systematically collect, analyze, store, and disseminate information, but they do not seem to have the structures or practices to engage in the interactive processes that are essential to transform data into knowledge. Institutional processes and resources that are particularly well suited to promote organizational learning, such as accreditation reports, databases of students, finances, and faculty (Birnbaum, 1988; Knight Higher Education Collaborative, 2000), and program reviews (Wergin & Swingen, 2000), are much more likely to be enacted as rituals rather than as a means to detect and correct error (Popper & Lipshitz, 1998).

We did not find much evidence that the information generated by post-tenure review about faculty performance changed the leadership behaviors of academic leaders. Very little was said to suggest that what chairs learned about their faculty as a result of post-tenure review made them reflect on their own practices. It is possible that this did happen but the individuals were not fully aware of the impact of post-tenure review on their own behaviors. For example, a chair describing his views of post-tenure review said:

> *The benefit is that the faculty members start to see what the others are doing. A lot of times they don't know what John, two doors down, is doing because it doesn't come up over a lunch conversation. So you start to see some synergism created, a little bit of joint authorship, discussions of different teaching techniques because they see what the other has done.*

However, even though this chair recognized the benefits of making faculty work more public there was no indication that this realization led to reflecting on ways in which this side effect of post-tenure review could be internalized into the culture of the department or to find ways of promoting this as a departmental norm. The chair in another institution acknowledged:

> *We missed the opportunity of [discovering] how to use this tool at the department level. And so instead of saying, "Well, we'll make this work for us at the department level," we picked it up as "This is something that is imposed upon us from up above, which we know will be toothless up there."*

Argyris and Schon (1971) maintain that organizational learning is contingent upon an institutional culture that values inquiry, openness, and trust.

> Organizational learning has two facets—a tangible "hardware" facet that consists of learning mechanisms and an intangible "software" facet that consists of shared values and beliefs that ensure that the mechanisms produce actual learning (i.e., new insights and behaviors) and not mere rituals of learning. (as qtd. in Popper & Lipshitz, 1998, p. 172)

The processes of post-tenure review require a faculty member to complete the necessary forms, which are reviewed by a department chair, a dean, or a committee of peers. All of these aspects represent the learning system that resides in the structural processes of post-tenure review. A faculty member might indicate in the forms that he or she is aware of X, Y, and Z; the department chair might be surprised to find out about X, Y, and Z as it relates to the work of faculty members, and so on. The intangible facet of post-tenure review has to do with how well it fits into the culture of the academy. It is not a smooth fit. For example, in professional organizations such as colleges and universities, social forms of control prevail, and post-tenure review is frequently viewed as a structural control by faculty.

The potential of post-tenure review as a lever for institutional change is constrained by its image as a form of surveillance. Organizational learning depends on the availability of undistorted and verifiable information (Popper & Lipshitz, 1998). If post-tenure review is seen as a form of structural control used to determine productivity levels, then one would expect that individuals might "withhold, distort, or fabricate information to defend themselves and/or others" (Argyris & Schon, 1971, as qtd. in Popper & Lipshitz, 1998, p. 172). Therefore, there has to be an organizational culture that "values transparency and encourages individuals to open themselves up to inspection in order to receive feedback" (Popper & Lipshitz, 1998, p. 172).

POST-TENURE REVIEW AS A PRACTICE TO ADVANCE THE GOOD OF FACULTY MEMBERS AND INSTITUTIONS

We close this chapter with an alternative way of conceptualizing and conducting post-tenure review. This alternative is based on the overall value model described in Chapter 6 and on what we believe a learning organization should embrace. Rather than framing post-tenure review as a means of oversight to guard against abuses of tenure, we suggest that it may be far more beneficial to frame it as a practice to advance the good of faculty members and institutions.

Post-tenure review is based on the assumption that individuals and organizations change as a consequence of new structures and new mandates. Initiatives of this kind might work well in organizations that manufacture products that conform to specified standards, but change that is directed at people or groups needs to be thought of differently. One promising model can be found in emerging theories about the nature of practice in professional fields such as clinical psychology, where the purpose of the work is to help individuals achieve fulfilling lives. As education turns more and more to business models of management, there is an inclination to seek out programmed approaches or techniques that can be applied to different categories of problems. For example, Total Quality Management was adopted by many institutional leaders who saw it as a program or technique for improving quality and reducing errors. Similarly, post-tenure review has been conceived as a strategy or technique to maintain oversight of faculty productivity. Accordingly, it has turned into standard operating procedure, and as long as institutions can demonstrate that it exists and it is being implemented, then they have met their obligation.

But there is no reason why post-tenure review could not be conceived differently. Polkinghorne (2004) proposes that if we conceive of practices (e.g., teaching, counseling) as having the purpose of advancing the good of an individual, a group of individuals, or an institution, then such practices are more likely to result in self-change. If the intended result of post-tenure review is to help individuals in the latter stages of their career to remain vital and productive and do work that advances the goals of their departments and institutions, the concept of post-tenure review as a helping and caring practice is better suited for these ends than the concept of surveillance or oversight.

From the perspective of post-tenure review as a helping and caring practice, the process of implementation and the roles of those involved, whether chairs, deans, or peer committees, would need to be different. The processes would be more dialectical, more individualized, and more developmental. They would also be more time-consuming, particularly for chairs and deans, who are primarily responsible for managing post-tenure review. The objective of post-tenure review would be for individual faculty in dialogue with others to reflect on their work, to become knowledgeable of their own practices as scholars and teachers, and to consider in what ways they would change these practices. The notion of post-tenure review as a way of revitalizing stuck faculty is consistent with its being framed as a practice to do good for the individual and the community. Conducting post-tenure review from this perspective, however, would require a different mindset, particularly for department chairs and deans. Rather than administering post-tenure review from a compliance stance, more attention would need to focus on ways to structure the process as a reflective dialogue rather than as a bureaucratic requirement. It would also require extensive professional development of chairs and deans to create the appropriate competences to carry out post-tenure review as a helping intervention. Our interviews caught glimpses of department chairs who are trying more dialectical and therapeutic-like approaches, but this is not the norm, nor is this approach being encouraged by upper-level administrators.

Drawing on Aristotle, Polkinghorne (2004) suggests that "The model of practice should be informed by the nature of those conducting it and those served by it" (p. 75). The present model of post-tenure review is informed by assumptions and values that are alien to the culture of the academy and the professoriate. The behavioral/surveillance model of post-tenure review calls for peer review committees to oversee individuals who are their peers, not their subordinates. This situation creates considerable discomfort and uneasiness for the evaluators and those being evaluated. We heard time and again from department chairs and faculty that they were reluctant to make negative judgments of their colleagues. In most instances, it was easier to choose the path that would cause the least conflict. In view of this, one might ask whether the reluctance to pass judgment on one's peers reflects a disregard for academic duty. After all, don't peer-review and self-policing characteristics distinguish the educated professions from other types of occupations? On the other hand, it is possible that turning post-tenure review into a bureaucratic routine is an instinctual response to resist a project that is incompatible with the norms of academic culture and which might cause harm. Indeed, the attitude of many of the individuals we interviewed was one of "If it ain't broke, don't fix it."

Department chairs have used "dampening strategies" to prevent post-tenure review from being disruptive (Bensimon, Polkinghorne, Bauman, & Vallejo, 2004). For some, dampening strategies may be further evidence of the academy's tendency to avoid responsibility. But these strategies may also be viewed as a way of reshaping post-tenure review to make it more compatible with the traditional relationships of chairs and faculty. The concept of post-tenure review as a helping and caring practice is closer to Polkinghorne's (2004) proposition that the model of practice should fit the nature of those conducting it and those being served by it. But for it to be done well and ethically, chairs will need to acquire new competencies and understandings of the nature of human motivation.

In the behavioral perspective, post-tenure review becomes one more administrative task to be completed. The emphasis is on the procedure for both the chair and the faculty member. In the helping or developmental perspective, post-tenure review allows faculty members to accomplish their goals in ways that are consistent with and that support communal values (Polkinghorne, 2004). And, from a developmental perspective, post-tenure review is conceived as a practice that is future-directed, whose aim is to help the individual faculty member move to a different state.

Estela Mara Bensimon is director of the Center for Urban Education and professor of higher education in the Rossier School of Education at the University of Southern California. She was a member of the post-tenure review project research team.

REFERENCES

Bensimon, E. M., Polkinghorne, D. E., Bauman, G. L., & Vallejo. E. (2004). Doing research that makes a difference. *Journal of Higher Education, 75*(1), 104–126.

Birnbaum, R. (1988). *How colleges work: The cybernetics of academic organization and leadership*. San Francisco, CA: Jossey-Bass.

Etzioni, A. (1964). *Modern organizations*. Englewood Cliffs, NJ: Prentice-Hall.

Ewell, P. T. (1997). Organizing for learning: A new imperative. *AAHE Bulletin, 50*(4), 3–6.

Garvin, D. A. (1993). Building a learning organization. *Harvard Business Review, 71*(4), 78–91.

Homans, G. C. (1950). *The human group*. New York, NY: Harcourt, Brace, Jovanovich.

Homans, G. C. (1961). *Social behavior: Its elementary forms*. New York, NY: Harcourt, Brace, Jovanovich.

Knight Higher Education Collaborative. (2000). The data made me do it. *Policy Perspectives, 9*(2), 1–12.

Pfeffer, J. (1997). *New directions for organization theory: Problems and prospects*. New York, NY: Oxford University Press.

Polkinghorne, D. E. (2004). *Practice and the human sciences: The case for a judgment-based practice of care*. New York, NY: State University of New York Press.

Popper, M., & Lipshitz, R. (1998). Organizational learning mechanisms: A structural and cultural approach to organizational learning. *Journal of Applied Behavioral Science, 34*(2), 161–179.

Wergin, J. F., & Swingen, J. N. (2000). *Departmental assessment: How some campuses are effectively evaluating the collective work of faculty*. Washington, DC: American Association for Higher Education.

Pulling It All Together: Considerations for the Future

We should be careful to get out of an experience only the wisdom that is in it—and stop there.

—Mark Twain

We conclude this volume by asking the following question: At the end of the day, how can institutions be future-directed in the formulation, development, and modification of post-tenure faculty review and renewal practices?

We build our response on the research findings and ideas framed in the previous chapters and supplement that wisdom with the lessons learned from our work with 40 other four-year institutions and state systems—all were participants in the American Association for Higher Education's New Pathways II Project.[1] Many of these institutions received challenge grant funding from AAHE that helped them start, maintain, or experiment with novel approaches to tenured faculty review and development. We worked very closely with these campuses over a four-year period. Our experience in these settings further deepened our knowledge about post-tenure review on a very practical level.

It is from this expanded experiential base that we "pull it all together" and ask our readers to consider with us:

- What specific call to action grows from our findings and experiences?

- What will the future hold for post-tenure review?

CALL TO ACTION

Gold Star or Black Hole?

Based on the experiences of the nine early-adopting institutions reported in this book, the scorecard on effectiveness and benefit is mixed—a series of pluses and minuses. On the one hand, many post-tenure review practices we examined did not fit smoothly into the academic campus culture, especially when a behavioral model drove the plan. Frequently, procedures fell short because they were seen as time-consuming busywork established in response to external pressures. These processes did not lead to sustained institutional change and renewal.

On the other hand, some institutional plans did offer the glimmer of a gold star and provided valuable insight into what is necessary for post-tenure review to hold value and worth. The most curious aspect of our data collection with these same nine institutions and with others is that despite policy shortcomings, the majority of faculty were not clamoring to abandon post-tenure evaluation practices and assessment. Instead, we heard repeatedly that the process did not work well and needed a major overhaul. But on the heels of this message came thoughtful solutions and suggestions for improvement.

What is clear to us is that faculty are concerned about career development and growth and are not trying to shy away from demands for accountability and responsibility. Quite the opposite, most faculty seem to understand and appreciate the contemporary accountability context. The notion that tenured faculty actively try to avoid evaluation, view it as a nuisance, or prefer to rest on pre-tenure laurels is not supported by our research or our field work.

We conclude, therefore, that faculty and administrators want an evaluation system that is fair, meaningful, and consequential. In such a system, consequence translates to follow-through, opportunities for improvement, options for career development, reward, and administrative action when all else fails. The confounding challenge for campus leaders is to devise policies and practices that are not redundant with other policies, offer tangible benefits, satisfy external requirements, and help create a learning model.

In meeting this challenge, we suggest that an institution's evaluation and development compass include 10 specific directionals that help set an enlightened destination for tenured faculty review and renewal.

Ten Directionals

1) Make sure you know and understand the overarching goal for tenured faculty review. The objective for review practices cannot be aimed solely at satisfying external regulation or expectation. The risk in doing so is that a simplistic solution is established which results in unnecessary procedures, redundancy with the annual review, or worse—a serious disconnect with existing evaluation practices. The desired end is lost because all attention is directed to one flashpoint.

Do not ask, "How do we set up a post-tenure review process?" Instead, begin with the query, "Do we currently have a performance review culture and specific evaluation procedures that effectively balance and support both sides of the performance equation: summative judgments and formative opportunities?" To know for sure whether this balance exists, careful analysis of current policy and practice is necessary and must include assessment by faculty and administration of current overall practice effectiveness and benefit. This examination is dependent upon accurate information from faculty and academic leaders about the shortcomings of current procedures and how those shortcomings might be ameliorated. This analysis is essential before determining whether new policy provisions are warranted and serves as the platform upon which additional review is built or modifications made to current practices.

Most institutions have annual reviews in place that determine salary increases. Whether pro forma or substantive, these reviews require time and effort. They also represent an important locus on the evaluation continuum. Annual reviews must contribute in some meaningful way to overall evaluation outcomes. If annual review results represent more motion than direction, institutions need to understand why and then figure out what changes are needed.

In some situations, the annual review may be comprehensive enough and already infused with a prospective career planning component appropriate for accountability, development, and career planning. When this happens, the annual review might actually become the post-tenure review. Unfortunately, we did not see this occur frequently enough.

Whichever approach is taken, the model described in Chapter 6 should serve as a starting point because it clearly identifies the factors that are most important to overall policy effectiveness.

2) Ensure that the time required to conduct a performance review is not disproportionate to the time invested in feedback and follow-through. Provosts, deans, and chairs must pay special attention to this point. Faculty feel let down when administrators fail to recognize and follow up on evaluations. Neglect of meaningful follow-through can signal lack of importance.

Peer review bodies must make feedback a top priority as well. When peer review is central to the process (which we believe it should be), the tenured faculty members begin to view the department as a planned community rather than a confederation of free agents. Peer review becomes a way for senior faculty to consider how an individual faculty member contributes to the department's overall mission and productivity. Such a process allows the work of individuals to be understood, appreciated, and assessed. It emphasizes and helps outline what follow-up actions are expected and needed. It invites collegial discussions about career-long growth, development, and contribution. It initiates a conversation in the short term that can extend to longer-term planning and contribution.

3) Direct a reasonable and visible amount of resources to support individual outcomes and career plans, but make sure these plans benefit both the individual and the academic unit. Most of the needed resources may already be in the budget but may not be organized or promoted in a strategic fashion. Resources and support must be seen as enablers for recognizing achievement, redirecting energies, improving productivity, and/or shifting career interests. An institution's teaching and learning center or office of faculty development should be included in this resource equation as should sabbaticals, focused start-up grant monies, innovative teaching awards, and other special funding.

Faculty development resources and how they are allocated should be continually assessed. It is here that administrators must act more strategically and consider where the best allocation of faculty development resources lies to achieve maximum gain for both the individual and the department. Such an approach helps a unit build a collective view of its future and plan for how each member contributes to that future. Continuous learning is critical to any learning organization, but particularly so for higher education. In many institutions there is the prevailing opinion that faculty development is solely the professional responsibility of the faculty member. Such a perspective does not necessarily guarantee the strategic use of resources for faculty development. A comprehensive system of tenured faculty review and development has the benefit of using incentives for faculty development to steer resources strategically, thereby strengthening the department. As part of resource planning, serious consideration must be given to differential faculty workloads. Allocation of time and effort should be related to the strength and interests of the particular faculty member vis-à-vis the department.

We are often asked how much professional development funding is required. This is difficult to answer. One might start by ascertaining the total faculty development budget and how funds are used. We would then recommend one of the following courses of action to decide whether additional funds are necessary:

- Tie a certain dollar figure (say $1,500) to each faculty member for development and then allocate those dollars accordingly across the departments.

- Set aside, say 1%, of the faculty salaries for development and place the fund in the provost's or dean's office to be accessed by chairs based on proposals for specific post-tenure faculty needs. The provost and/or dean should allocate those funds based on the strategic goals of the university and/or college, thus reinforcing the overall strategic direction of the institution.

4) Never forget that engaged leadership matters. The provost, dean, chairs, and peers must accept both formal and informal leadership roles if the evaluation and development system is to work effectively. In those institutions we studied where post-tenure review was positively regarded, leadership was critical. Leadership in those settings emphasized that the review focused on developmental objectives. What is also key is that chairs and peers are adequately prepared to carry out their review roles and understand when and how to exert leadership. A training program for chairs and peers is an important step in this direction. Department chairs can benefit from programs that focus on strategic utilization of resources and identification of faculty development needs. For peers, a clear understanding of the faculty evaluation and development process, faculty career development needs, and what a community view of the department's needs entails should be highlighted. We found that when chairs and peers are uncertain about their influence over the process or unprepared for it, they opt to comply in a way that minimizes the potential for conflicts and in so doing abort the possibility of positive consequence. In effect, they merely go through the motions. Ritualistic compliance is certain to undermine the process.

5) Make sure the range of appropriate institutional actions for substandard performance are identified. This is important for all types of policies but it is particularly salient for institutions with a triggered review. A developmental and career planning focus should steer the evaluation course, but chairs and deans often feel powerless and defenseless when there are not appropriate institutional actions identified and available for them to judiciously employ. At the risk of placing this discussion in a surveillance or behavioral context, we feel it is shortsighted not to acknowledge that within every evaluation context, chairs must understand what recourse they have when performance is judged as consistently below the bar. We heard chairs say time and again, "What can I *really* do when attempts at improvement fail?" We asked this question of faculty in one research institution where the post-tenure review survey was administered. Responses describe what faculty considered to be appropriate actions. Those actions mentioned in order of frequency were:

- Salary freeze or reduction

- Workload modification or reassignment which emphasizes the strengths of the faculty member

- Encouragement to resign/retire

- Probation (first step in progressive discipline leading to dismissal for cause action)

- Demotion in rank

- Removal of resources (lab space, research support, etc.)

Although a behavioral approach will not lead to sustained organizational change, ambiguity about what intervention options are available, when all efforts to remediate fail, leads to frustration and inaction. This cannot be ignored. Chairs and peer committees must push for greater clarity about options and gain assurance of support up the line when difficult decisions are made.

6) Establish regular opportunities for deans and department chairs to discuss evaluation and development issues. From our interactions with chairs and deans we've discovered they are looking for opportunities to discuss with other academic leaders what works and what does not work in evaluation. This interest extends to understanding how chairs can work together to best utilize scarce resources to support development, how to write a negative review, how to manage a difficult conversation about performance, and how to track and report individual and departmental outcomes. Provosts need to set the stage for these conversations and promote this dialogue in a comfortable and risk-free context.

7) Close the loop on results. Institutional leaders must enhance campus awareness about the results of post-tenure review. No matter where we traveled, we found that awareness and information about outcomes were generally lacking. Rarely did we find campus discussions centered on this topic or even a written document summarizing results. If review results were discussed, it was usually with external constituents in mind. The fact of the matter is that both internal and external stakeholders want to know the short-term and long-term outcomes of these reviews, how the university addresses issues of incentive and reward for performance, and how the university addresses performance in need of improvement. Providing this information requires systematic tracking and organized communication. It also powers the post-tenure review process and adds value to it. We draw your attention to the range of different institutional reporting formats described in *Post-Tenure Review and Renewal II: Reporting Results and Shaping Policy* (Licata & Brown, 2004). The book's content and appendices provide excellent examples of the various ways information on results can be organized and how to communicate results to interested stakeholders. We entreat practitioners to consider very carefully when and how to use quantitative, qualitative, comparative, and anecdotal data in their reporting. Remember that reporting is an opportunity to tell a story. The story about faculty performance and productivity is important to internal consumers and external stakeholders. We need to tell the story. If we don't, others will tell it for us.

8) Carefully shape new faculty performance expectations. Our research did not specifically address generational differences of perspective about the need or benefit of tenured faculty review. Although we cannot provide hard evidence, our impression from numerous interactions in the field with junior faculty and academic leaders leaves us with the opinion that early-career faculty members hold different employment expectations and are more in tune with the myriad of accountability reporting than senior faculty. This may be due to training, previous employment experiences, or enculturation in a world where success tends to be measured by results and where one values what one can measure.

Teaching portfolios, peer review of teaching and research, expanded definitions of scholarship, innovative approaches to pedagogy, and integration of technology into courseware are more business as usual than unusual business for this younger generation of academics. Even so, faculty orientation programs need to prepare probationary faculty for post-tenure performance expectations and for the responsibilities associated with peer review.

9) Borrow from promising practices. Do not work in isolation: Build on the growing base of institutional experiences and best practices. As noted in the first directional, before an institution begins to design a faculty review program, an assessment of what already exists should be conducted. This analysis helps campus leaders understand what the task at hand really involves and where the gaps are. Two checklists can assist with this analysis. Checklist A in Appendix 8.1 can be used by deans, chairs, and faculty to assess their current departmental, college, or institutional evaluation culture. The end game here is to determine whether an effective culture is currently in place and where modifications are needed. Checklist B provides a tool to assess the presence and effectiveness of the infrastructure needed to support evaluation and development. Taken together, institutions can use both checklists (even without the scoring guide) to get a general picture of overall strengths and weaknesses of current policies and procedures. This is a useful starting point.

Another way to tackle policy development is to determine what faculty say they need and want in an evaluation system. The University Senate Faculty Affairs Ad Hoc Subcommittee at Purdue University is a good example of this approach. The faculty subcommittee hosted an open forum on post-tenure faculty review and renewal and followed it with a series of focus groups with randomly selected tenured and tenure-track faculty. Faculty in each focus group were asked to discuss five questions:

- *How is your performance at Purdue evaluated at the present time?*

- *How effectively does this evaluation cover all aspects of your contributions to the university?*

- *In the original faculty survey (66% of full professors, 80% of associate professors and 95% of assistant professors) agreed with the statement: "All full professors should undergo performance reviews by their peers." What do you think the respondents were thinking about when they answered "yes"?*

- *Shifting now from performance reviews to professional development, what motivates you, or could motivate you, to continue your professional development?*

- *What can Purdue do to enhance your professional development?*
                                    (Purdue University Faculty Senate, 2003, p. 10)

Responses to these questions served as the basis for a report and recommendations to the university administration titled *Building a Foundation for Career Long Faculty Growth at Purdue University* (Purdue University Faculty Senate, 2003). The report asserts that the faculty's performance goals would not be achieved by ". . . another institutional review process in addition to our already pre-existing but often *pro-forma* and sometimes bogus annual review process" (p. 38). The committee proposed instead that "Purdue University attempt to create a culture in which our faculty are encouraged to plan their future development goals and are assisted in the process of accomplishing these goals" (p. 39).

In order to accomplish this cultural transformation, the committee recommended five major goals and enabling strategies. The five goals and some of the enabling strategies are highlighted in Appendix 8.2. The committee's key recommendations center on ways to:

- Strengthen the annual review process and incorporate short-term (1 year) and long-term (3 years) development goals into it

- Require training in leadership and personnel management skills for department heads

- Create a faculty mentoring system

- Reconceptualize the guidelines for sabbatical leaves

- Expand the way in which the academic career is defined, valued, and rewarded

The ideas and thinking generated by this faculty report are bold, creative, and forward thinking. Other institutions should take note.[2]

If an institution or system already has a post-tenure review program, continuous process improvement is also essential. We offer two approaches for consideration.

Campus-wide faculty and administration satisfaction survey. Institutions wishing to assess the level of satisfaction with current review policies might consider using the Post-Tenure Review Outcomes Survey (see Appendix C) available upon request from the authors. This survey can provide decision-makers with systematic data on the effectiveness, benefit, and value of institutional practices. Results can be reported in aggregate fashion or disaggregated by any number of demographic variables (e.g., by discipline, gender, or rank). The advantage of using a common instrument across all academic units is that differences can be readily seen and areas in need of improvement can be easily identified.

System-wide assessment of policy effectiveness. State systems might also consider a system-wide approach to assessing policy effectiveness. The University of North Carolina System (14 institutions) adopted such a strategy. A system-wide committee comprised of a representative from each campus worked with a program consultant to identify system-wide implementation issues associated with post-tenure review.

An Issue Identification Form (see Appendix 8.3) was used to collect the range of implementation issues that the committee considered important. These issues served as the foundation for developing a comprehensive campus and system-wide review of policies, procedures, outcomes, and benefits (see Appendix 8.4). This approach to continuous improvement is currently underway and received the formal endorsement of the Statewide Faculty Assembly.

10) Use what research tells us about faculty career stages, productivity, vitality, and well-being as the foundation for a system of post-tenure review and development. We found that institutional leaders often ignored an important body of research concerning academic careers and faculty work life. Instead of building policies and expectations on this information, we often noted a one-size-fits-all approach. This is myopic and contributes to many institutions' inability to create positive individual and institutional change. When the only purpose of post-tenure view is to catch nonperforming outliers, the potential of the process to benefit the other 98% of the faculty is lost.

We encourage campus leaders to reconceptualize their evaluation and development processes in light of what research on mid- and late-career faculty reveals. Serious review of this body of work will sensitize policymakers to the fact that faculty attitudes, interests, and goals vary by career stage. Further, such awareness will help advance the following:

- Adult development theory suggests that as individuals change over time, their need for differentiation in interests, abilities, and tasks becomes important (Bland & Bergquist, 1997).

- Pre-tenure faculty strive to establish an academic identity (Baldwin, 1990a; Braskamp, Fowler, & Ory, 1984), achieve tenure (Furniss, 1981), and settle into a career and make a name for themselves (Baldwin, 1990a; Braskamp, Fowler, & Ory, 1984; Furniss, 1981).

- Mid-career tenured faculty temper the drive for autonomy with the drive to create meaning in life (Cohen, 2000), set new goals or accept a mid-career plateau (Baldwin, 1990b), and are ready to assume greater service roles (Terenzio, 2002).

- Mid- to late-career tenured faculty seek greater integration and balance in their personal and professional lives and hold community and colleague relationships on equal footing with a desire to keep one's name in the field; attention is given to activities that nurture the success of others and make a difference (Bland & Bergquist, 1997).

- Mid- and late-career faculty more frequently report feeling less challenged and recognized than early-career faculty (Walker, 2002).

- Scholarly productivity is saddle shaped over a career and is not linear (Pelz & Andrews, 1976).

- There is little relationship between teaching excellence and forms of research productivity (Feldman, 1987; Hattie & Marsh, 1996).

- A small percentage of faculty achieve high levels of output in both teaching and research but, in general, the complete scholar is rare (Fairweather, 2002).

- Faculty, especially in research-oriented institutions, "satisfice" their teaching (reach an acceptable teaching quality threshold and hold there) but put creative time into their research efforts because that is where the rewards are perceived to be (Massy & Wilger, 1995).

- Career inflexibility is a frequently reported source of dissatisfaction among college faculty (Blackburn, 1997).

- Faculty success and renewal depends on the interplay between an individual's satisfaction and interest with academic work (teaching/research) and the level of caring that the individual perceives the institution expends on them (Karpiak, 2000).

THE FUTURE OF POST-TENURE REVIEW: CREATING A FLEXIBLE FACULTY DEVELOPMENT MODEL

The implications of our fieldwork and the findings of the researchers just cited strongly coalesce and call for the creation of a new, flexible development model for post-tenure faculty renewal. A new world order of sorts in which policies and practices intentionally support the following new and not-so-new realities:

- Alternating periods of career ease and difficulty are typical and expected.

- Complete scholar status over the course of an entire career is probably more fiction than fact.

- Career doubt and reassessment are typical for mid-career faculty.

- Faculty role preferences should be expected to evolve gradually. Anticipate that faculty might become more comfortable with teaching and adept with university service later in their careers. Later-career faculty will probably look for ways to leave a legacy. For some, this might mean a deeper involvement with teaching, service, or outreach and a move away from traditional research.

- The relationship between a faculty member and the institution must always be considered fluid and dynamic. High faculty interest in the institution requires high caring by the institution.

- Among other things, intrinsic rewards for senior faculty should include opportunities to pursue efforts that keep them energized.

This new world order uses institutional processes, especially faculty development and associated resources, to create an environment where the fit between the individual's talents and interests matches the institution's needs at different points across one's academic career and at different points in an institution's history.

If designed with prospective career planning as its nexus, post-tenure review can play an important role in this flexible development approach because the review itself and the career planning that accompanies it become the means or the tie that binds both together and leads to cohesion. The Associated New American Colleges (ANAC) characterize this kind of revisioning as a new academic compact (McMillin & Berberet, 2002). ANAC scholars propose a "fundamental shift in thinking about the faculty role, about community work and governance associated with that role, and about the broader role of professional development in all domains of the institution" (Terenzio, 2002, p. 33). ANAC recommends redefining professional development to have "a more far-reaching and strategic impact, one that acknowledges both the developmental nature of faculty careers and the evolution of institutional priorities" (p. 31). At the heart of this proposed paradigm shift is the acceptance of a fundamental shift in expectations:

> There will be more career opportunities but less job guarantees; individual autonomy will be kept constantly in check by institutional mission; traditional faculty productivity metrics will be replaced by reasonable accommodation for career interests, talents, and changing priorities; strategic planning will be a continuous iterative process, not a one-time event; trust between faculty, administration, and boards will be crucial . . . (Licata, 2002, p. 171)

Our findings suggest that in this reengagement, post-tenure review becomes one part of a larger evaluation and development construct. Moving to this construct requires institutions to recognize that faculty careers do not follow a linear trajectory and be willing to infuse flexibility into performance expectations.

This new world order demands that the evaluation and development culture:

- Situate post-tenure within a coherent continuum of review, development, and well-being strategies—consider how it can be a helping and caring practice

- Establish faculty renewal as an institutional priority

- Require peer review to be part of the process in order to make faculty work more public and more appreciated

- Guarantee that feedback and follow-through are always expected and that nothing less is accepted

- Expect high levels of faculty performance and productivity but also give faculty room to grow and change

Conclusion

The initial furor over post-tenure review policies that rocked many campuses and legislative chambers in the mid-1990s has subsided. Current velocity has decreased considerably because most public and many private institutions are now well into the implementation stage. Policies have been nested within normal institutional procedures.

Even so, both the Reauthorization of Higher Education Act and the recently established National Commission on Accountability in Higher Education will keep the pressure on institutions to demonstrate that they have been accountable for quality and performance. We expect that post-tenure review and its results will be part of this larger accountability agenda. Future post-tenure review debate will take aim at whether reported results are credible, impactive, and convincing enough to offset the concerns of tenure's harshest critics.

Institutions about to engage in this dialogue about quality and performance must be armed with well-conceived and effectively executed evaluation programs that reflect shifts in faculty hiring patterns, countervailing external conditions, needs for faculty career transition counseling and, most important, an ongoing emphasis on assessing results.

Hiring Trends and External Conditions

A market-driven environment has wrought differentiation in the roles of faculty and new classifications of nontenure-eligible academic appointments. The number of tenured faculty is declining. This has been referred to as a silent revolution, with the majority (55.4%) of new full-time faculty being hired off the tenure track (The Future of the American Faculty, 2004). These full-time faculty are not necessarily being expected to carry out faculty responsibilities in teaching, research, and service as traditional tenure-track appointees have in the past, resulting in tenure being "circumvented *de facto*" (The Future of the American Faculty, 2004, p. 30).

The implications of these hiring trends are far reaching. First, the meaning of tenure itself is at risk. Second, even though there will be fewer tenured faculty and, therefore, fewer who qualify for post-tenure review, performance evaluation will continue to be critical. Institutions that have developed good pre- and post-tenure evaluation practices will be well equipped to draw from those practices in designing systems to review nontenure-track faculty. Performance accountability will reach much further into the academic rank and file. There will be more evaluation in the future, not less.

Another implication of these hiring trends is that traditional governance and university citizenship responsibilities may be short shrifted, or worse, fall to the weakest or least interested faculty because there will be fewer tenured faculty to pick up these duties. If the academy values shared governance and other long-held traditional academic values, post-tenure review may be an opportunity to ensure that institutional citizenship roles are valued, evaluated, and rewarded.

On this point we draw attention to the medical school in our study. The volatile fiscal conditions faced by medical schools, as a reflection of such conditions in the healthcare industry, have forced considerable rethinking of faculty work, contractual arrangements, and reward systems in that sector. In particular, the rationale underlying tenure for medical school faculty and the relationship of tenure to salary have undergone dramatic modifications. Medical schools have relied much less on traditional tenure and more on term contracts, rolling contracts, and clinical faculty appointments. The rest of higher education may be confronting the same realities because the external conditions that faced the healthcare sector now confront all of higher education including:

- Growing demand for entry into colleges and universities

- Budget reduction by public sector funding

- Budget reduction in funding for research

- Greater competition from profit sector universities

- Rising cost of educating and, therefore, increasing the cost of attendance for students

- Increasing importance of higher education to the health and future of the United States and world economy

In the healthcare sector, rapid cost escalation and excess demand were eventually constrained by applying a more business-oriented model through managed care. So it is possible that the medical model might be applied to the academy in general. Could we envision managed higher education? The question, of course, is do we want to? It is a direction wrought with quagmire and erosion of traditional academic values.

Formal Faculty Career Planning

Conflict between one's professional and personal responsibilities is commonplace, and faculty seek greater balance between the two. Faculty need to be able to discuss career directions, learn about what characterizes the stages of faculty careers, and seek advice on both career and retirement transitioning. Career planning and counseling should be viewed comprehensively and extend from pre-tenure through post-retirement. University administrators and faculty leaders must also consider ways to establish formal and comprehensive faculty career planning services and career counseling opportunities. Career planning is an essential component of future-directed development.

Ongoing Assessment of Evaluation Results

The question of whether post-tenure review is "worth it" will continue to be raised, as well it should. Post-tenure review has reaped some benefits for individuals, but do these outweigh the time, effort, and resource costs required? If career planning, professional renewal, resource availability, and administrative follow-through were strengthened, the benefits would be enhanced. The 10 directionals described earlier can help institutions increase their benefit quotient. However, our results warn that the costs must be kept in check and the administrative burden in terms of time, effort, and paperwork must be kept manageable.

Will post-tenure review be a lever for organizational change? We conclude that it can be, particularly if the process is framed as developmental and placed within a learning organization context as Chapter 7 suggests. Yet even if this happens effectively, an organization must have a clear vision about how it wants or needs to change. In other words, how do you know change when you see it? The researchers who raise this issue usually refer to indicators of organizational change as affecting the status, quality, or quantity of faculty work; revitalizing faculty behavior; or creating a better alignment between the work of faculty and institutional goals. Post-tenure review has not yet dramatically changed faculty outcomes or altered the role of faculty work within universities and colleges. Post-tenure review by itself was never designed to do so. It is an evolutionary process not a revolutionary reform designed to fundamentally impact the work of faculty. It can, however, be one means to this transformation.

The key question—How are we doing?—should be answered by departments and institutions using all of the results collected during a review cycle. In its present stage of development, post-tenure review is not being used to its fullest capacity nor are most institutions well positioned to answer questions about impact and outcomes. However, the potential is there, and in the future post-tenure review can be one lever that helps an organization move in desired directions. As mentioned earlier, this requires leadership and training for deans and chairs in the strategic use of information and in creating a culture of faculty development. Creating a collective sense of both responsibility and development will have to become the norm and replace the more individualized oversight approach.

PARTING THOUGHTS

The information shared and the advice given in this book are meant to help administrators and faculty understand more fully what is required to power an effective program of post-tenure review and renewal. For post-tenure review to carry sustained value, it must do more than require faculty to go through the motions or jump through hoops. It must lead to positive individual outcomes and add value to the department and university. We are strong proponents of a formative and developmental process that blends longer-term strategic needs of the department with individual faculty interests and contributions. The flexible development model that we advance presupposes that there is departmental acceptance and respect for diversified faculty roles and differentiated faculty work effort. It blends a culture of evidence with a culture of reflection. It incorporates faculty career stage theory into performance expectations. It is rooted in an overall organizational culture that values and encourages professional development.

While post-tenure review discussions across the country may be at a dull roar now, the accountability elephant still looms large and near. We encourage readers to use our findings and recommendations to recast, redirect, and reshape practices so they lead to positive results. Post-tenure faculty review and renewal, regardless of purpose, requires considerable energy to implement. Energy is expended whether the process reaps benefits or results in ritualistic compliance.

The faculty and administrators in our study clearly want the scales tipped dramatically in the direction of benefit. We expect the same holds true for most faculty in America. The call to action is clear. Responding to this call, however, requires enlightened leadership and courage to reconceptualize academic career models and recontextualize faculty evaluation and development.

ENDNOTES

1) Christine Licata directed the New Pathways II Post-Tenure Review project. Joseph Morreale served as a senior scholar with this project.

2) For additional information about this report, contact Dr. William Harper at Purdue University: wharper@purdue.edu.

REFERENCES

Baldwin, R. G. (1990a). Faculty career stages and implications for faculty development. In J. H. Schuster & D. W. Wheeler (Eds.), *Enhancing faculty careers: Strategies for development and renewal* (pp. 20–40). San Francisco, CA: Jossey-Bass.

Baldwin, R. G. (1990b). Faculty vitality beyond the research university. *Journal of Higher Education, 61*(2), 160–180.

Blackburn, R. T. (1997). Career phases and their effect on faculty motivation. In J. L. Bess (Ed.), *Teaching well and liking it: Motivating faculty to teach effectively* (pp. 314–336). Baltimore, MD: Johns Hopkins University Press.

Bland, C. J., & Bergquist, W. H. (1997). *The vitality of senior faculty members: Snow on the roof–fire in the furnace* (ASHE-ERIC Higher Education Report, 25[7]). Washington, DC: George Washington University, School of Education and Human Development.

Braskamp, L. A., Fowler, D. L., & Ory, J. C. (1984). Faculty development and achievement: A faculty's view. *Review of Higher Education, 7,* 205–222.

Cohen, G. D. (2000). *The creative age: Awakening human potential in the second half of life.* New York, NY: HarperCollins.

Fairweather, J. S. (2002). The mythologies of faculty productivity: Implications for institutional policy and decision making. *Journal of Higher Education, 73*(1), 26–48.

Feldman, K. A. (1987). Research productivity and scholarly accomplishment of college teachers as related to their instructional effectiveness: A review and exploration. *Research in Higher Education, 26*(3), 227–298.

Furniss, W. T. (1981). *Reshaping faculty careers.* Washington, DC: American Council on Education.

The future of the American faculty: An interview with Martin J. Finklestein and Jack H. Schuster. (2004, March/April). *Change, 36*(2), 26–35.

Hattie, J., & Marsh, H. W. (1996). The relationship between research and teaching: A meta-analysis. *Review of Educational Research, 66*(4), 507–542.

Karpiak, I. E. (2000). The 'second call': Faculty renewal and recommitment at midlife. *Quality in Higher Education, 6*(2), 125–134.

Licata, C. M. (2002). A panel of experts responds. In L. A. McMillin & W. G. Berberet (Eds.), *A new academic compact: Revisioning the relationship between faculty and their institutions* (pp. 167–172). Bolton. MA: Anker.

Licata, C. M., & Brown, B. E. (Eds.). (2004). *Post-tenure faculty review and renewal II: Reporting results and shaping policy.* Bolton, MA: Anker.

Massy, W. F., & Wilger, A. K. (1995, July/August). Improving productivity. *Change, 27*(4), 10–21.

McMillin, L. A., & Berberet, W. G. (Eds.). (2002). *A new academic compact: Revisioning the relationship between faculty and their institutions.* Bolton, MA: Anker.

Pelz, D. C., & Andrews, F. M. (1976). *Scientists in organizations: Productive climates for research and development.* New York, NY: John Wiley & Sons.

Purdue University Faculty Senate, Faculty Affairs Ad Hoc Subcommittee. (2003). *Building a foundation for career long faculty growth at Purdue University.* West Lafayette, IN: Author.

Terenzio, M. (2002). Professional development across the faculty career: An engine for implementing a new faculty-institutional compact. In L. A. McMillin & W. G. Berberet (Eds.), *A new academic compact: Revisioning the relationship between faculty and their institutions* (pp. 29–60). Bolton, MA: Anker.

Walker, C. J. (2002). Faculty well-being review: An alternative to post-tenure review? In C. M. Licata & J. C. Morreale (Eds.), *Post-tenure faculty review and renewal: Experienced voices* (pp. 229–241). Washington, DC: American Association for Higher Education.

APPENDIX 8.1

FACULTY EVALUATION AND DEVELOPMENT CULTURE

Checklist A: Evaluation/Development Culture
Put a check in the appropriate box below.

		Y	N
1)	My institution has a well-defined and understood philosophy toward faculty evaluation and development for faculty.		
2)	The performance of faculty is reviewed on a systematic and comprehensive basis.		
3)	The results of the performance review are shared and discussed regularly with each faculty member.		
4)	Faculty understand the basis upon which evaluation occurs, and the outcomes of the evaluation are shared with faculty.		
5)	Career and professional development goals of faculty are discussed and included in the evaluation process.		
6)	Faculty development opportunities are available within my institution.		
7)	Peers play an important role in helping shape the evaluation and development plans of colleagues.		
8)	Shifting departmental priorities and missions are taken into consideration when faculty work assignments are developed.		
9)	Faculty reward systems are in place and are tied to performance review.		
10)	Current policy and practice effectively and efficiently identify faculty whose performance doesn't meet expectations and provide an appropriate mechanism for improvement and remediation.		
11)	Current policy and practice effectively take care of egregious cases of unproductive or unsatisfactory performance.		
12)	Our campus evaluation and development environment respects and values academic culture and is understood and respected by external stakeholders.		

Scoring
- Give yourself 1 point for each check in the "Yes" column.
- Give yourself 2 additional points if you answered Questions 10 and 11 in the affirmative.

[A] Total Score _____

Checklist B: Evaluation/Development Infrastructure
Put a check in the appropriate box below to indicate how well each component is defined and whether the component is effectively administered.

	Is This Well Defined?		Administered Effectively?	
	Y	N	Y	N
1) Workload policy				
2) Salary/compensation policy				
3) Academic program review policy that meshes with faculty plans of work and priorities				
4) Student rating of teaching policy				
5) Peer review of teaching/research/scholarship				
6) Criteria and standards for satisfactory performance at associate professor level				
7) Criteria and standards for satisfactory performance at full professor level				
8) Faculty development policies, practices, and resources				
9) Formal chairperson training and development				
10) Faculty grievance and appeal process				
11) Dismissal-for-cause policy that details what constitutes adequate cause				

Scoring

- Give yourself 1 point for each check in the "Yes" column.
- Give yourself 1 point for each check in the "No" column.
- Subtract "No" points from "Yes" points to get your total. (Total can be a negative number.)

[B] Total Score _____

Index A

Score: 16–12	Effective evaluation/development culture—no dramatic action needed
Score: 11–6	Moderately comprehensive culture—refinement may be necessary
Score: 5 and below	Effectiveness of current culture in question—further analysis suggested to identify improvement needed

Index B

Score: 22–15	Highly effective infrastructure
Score: 14–8	Moderately effective infrastructure—refinement may be needed
Score: 7 and below	Infrastructure effectiveness in need of improvement

APPENDIX 8.2
BUILDING A FOUNDATION FOR CAREER-LONG FACULTY GROWTH AT PURDUE UNIVERSITY
(NOVEMBER 2003)

Goal 1: Standardize the procedures for the annual performance review across all academic units; fold longer-term faculty development goals into a deliberate expansion of the existing review process

- At the outset of this standardized review process, all faculty members will be encouraged to develop both short- (one year) and long-range (three year) goals and strategies. These goals should reflect activity in discovery, learning, and engagement with the understanding that there could be differentiation between the amount of activity/time given to any particular area of contribution.

- . . . it would be the prerogative of the departmental faculty whether to include an internal peer review body for assessing all three-year plans. This might be especially useful in large departments, but the option should be made available to the faculty notwithstanding the size of the department. If departmental faculty prefer not to create the peer review, the three-year review would become the department head's responsibility.

- It is the responsibility of the faculty member to include in his or her one-year and three-year goals and strategies reasonable justifications for the activities stipulated that describe both the ways in which the activities will impact individual faculty development *and* the ways in which this development is consistent with the department's strategic plan.

- In each successive year, the faculty member will create new annual goals and strategies and prepare a short report on the progress toward achieving the longer-term goals.

- If at the conclusion of the three-year period the faculty member has indeed accomplished what he or she set out to accomplish, the faculty member will receive a non-recurring salary bonus (we recommend either a flat dollar amount or a percent of base—the literature indicates the 8% of base is the point at which salary incentives are considered meaningful).

Goal 2: Condition the appointment to position of department head on the candidate successfully completing a defined training experience in leadership and personnel management skills

- In addition to department heads, for those faculty members who are carrying out internal periodic peer review assessment, training or workshop sessions should also be provided. Reasonable release time or other compensation should accompany this responsibility.

Goal 3: Improve the quality and range of what until now has been a laissez-faire mentoring system

- This goal must be a mutually accepted responsibility between the university and its faculty; in a true community we help one another.

- The decision to be mentored should be voluntary, but it should also be available for any and all faculty at any stage in their career and in any appointment category defined in this report.

- Mentoring should include possible matches designed to improve successes in the entire range of categories, including but not limited to the areas of discovery, learning, and/or engagement, and/or to special circumstances or characteristics where support might be desired such as gender, age, rank, or ethnic background.

Goal 4: Reconsider and reconfigure the concept of sabbatical leave in order to recreate what sabbaticals were originally intended to make possible: disengaging from one's day-to-day responsibilities in order to experience unfettered time to think, to create, to explore, to discover, to study, to learn, and to renew

- We encourage adopting more expansive definitions of what we mean by sabbatical leaves, namely, flexible time blocks or responsibility release times creatively dispensed irregularly as career stages unfold.

- A short yet focused mini-sabbatical time period could be useful for future career planning, for seeking further development opportunities, or for finding networking contacts.

- Some other ideas for less traditional sabbaticals include creating a time-bank for every faculty member to spend in pursuit of periodic growth and development; creating quasi-sabbaticals with the ebb and flow of any given semester by semester-long release from all committee assignments; creating periodic lighter teaching loads; creating more opportunities for study in a second discipline; creating semester-long forays into administrative interning made possible by appropriate release time.

Goal 5: Expand conception of the typical individual academic career from the traditional, linear transition through the ranks based on a personal identity established at the earliest career point, to a conception of a career that also can evolve in often unanticipated but significant and important ways and where one's contribution to the whole is still recognized, valued, and rewarded

- As a precursor to achieving this goal, we believe that every reasonable effort must be made within each and every academic unit to create regular mechanisms to share and make visible the entire range of any single faculty member's contribution to the entire enterprise, whether via newsletters, colloquia, retreats, bag lunch seminars, or electronic postings—we are still haunted by the comment of one faculty member quoted earlier in this report: ". . . if I don't see it, I think it must not be going on. There's no shared visibility for what we're doing." This must change.

- If faculty productivity is viewed as a university-wide collective, then it is defensible to accommodate shifts and changes in faculty career goals over time, and especially where a particular member's strengths, talents, and motivations are recognized, facilitated, and rewarded, not turned against them as evidence of failure when held up against a static norm of conventional productivity.

- This fifth and last goal, and admittedly the fuzziest of them all, will require the efforts of the entire university to redefine what counts as a productive faculty member career-long; incorporating multiple faculty career models could have direct and therapeutic effects on any and all of our existing and future faculty review systems.

Text extracted from Purdue University Senate Faculty Affairs Ad Hoc Subcommittee Report, pages 40–46. Only selected portions of the report are printed here.

APPENDIX 8.3
UNIVERSITY OF NORTH CAROLINA
EVALUATION OF POST-TENURE REVIEW POLICY

Issue Identification

Please take a few minutes to reflect on the post-tenure review process on your campus.

How have you personally experienced the process and what have your colleagues shared with you about their impressions of the process?

These recollections can be helpful in signaling important issues that have arisen and in identifying particular aspects of the evaluation that should be addressed in the assessment plan.

To get us started and to make issue identification easier, I have listed some basic questions below. Please forward your responses to_____

I will summarize all responses received into a group summary, and we will use the summary at our meeting in October. Thanks for helping get us off to a good beginning. I look forward to working with you on this project.

---

1) Purpose of Post-Tenure Review Policy as Stated in Policy

    a) Clear purpose?   ___yes   ___no

    b) Reasonably easy to implement?   ___yes   ___no

    c) Other:

    Comment:

2) Procedures

    a) Review timeline:

        Understood by faculty?   ___yes   ___no

        Followed by administrators?   ___yes   ___no

        Comment:

    b) Required documentation:

        Manageable for faculty?   ___yes   ___no

        Manageable for reviewers?   ___yes   ___no

        Comment:

    c) Review procedures:

        Clear?   ___yes   ___no

        Followed fairly?   ___yes   ___no

Followed consistently? ___yes ___no

Comment:

d) Review criteria:

Clear? ___yes ___no

Applied fairly? ___yes ___no

Applied consistently? ___yes ___no

Comment:

e) Peer review:

Process understood? ___yes ___no

Followed consistently? ___yes ___no

Comment:

f) Department chair:

Role in process understood? ___yes ___no

Role taken seriously? ___yes ___no

Comment:

g) Dean:

Role in process understood? ___yes ___no

Role taken seriously? ___yes ___no

Comment:

3) Results

a) Results of review:

Expected? ___yes ___no

Adequate range of actions? ___yes ___no

Actions actually taken? ___yes ___no

Comment:

b) Follow-up after review:

Expected? ___yes ___no

Occurs in timely way? ___yes ___no

Occurs consistently? ___yes ___no

Comment:

4) Administrative Support

    a) Support for process visible?   ___yes   ___no

    b) Support adequate?   ___yes   ___no

    c) Resources sufficient?   ___yes   ___no

    Comment:

5) Faculty Development and Post-Tenure Review

    a) Review supports development?   ___yes   ___no

    b) Review assists in career planning?   ___yes   ___no

    c) Review supports meeting departmental priorities?   ___yes   ___no

    d) Review helps with retirement transition?   ___yes   ___no

    e) Review helps remediate poor performance?   ___yes   ___no

    Comment:

6) Overall Judgments

    Post-Tenure Review:

    a) Is effective in achieving purpose?   ___yes   ___no   too soon___

    b) Is beneficial for faculty?   ___yes   ___no   too soon___

    c) Is beneficial for departments?   ___yes   ___no   too soon___

    d) Is beneficial for university?   ___yes   ___no   too soon___

    e) Is worth keeping as is?   ___yes   ___no   too soon___

    f) Needs improvement?   ___yes   ___no   too soon___

7) In my opinion, the two greatest benefits from post-tenure review are:

    1)

    2)

8) In my opinion, the two greatest weaknesses of the current post-tenure policy are:

    1)

    2)

9) Anything else you want to share?

APPENDIX 8.4

UNIVERSITY OF NORTH CAROLINA

MEETING WITH EXPANDED COMMITTEE ON INNOVATION IN FACULTY
WORK LIFE

OCTOBER 6, 2003

FACILITATOR/CONSULTANT: DR. CHRISTINE M. LICATA

Key Questions, Discussion Points, and Action Steps

Topic: Comprehensive Evaluation of UNC's System of Performance Evaluation of
Tenured Faculty (aka Post-Tenure Review)

Question 1: Should UNC conduct an assessment of policy implementation?

What Is Known About Policy Results and Effectiveness?

UNC's Performance Review of Tenured Faculty Policy was adopted by the Board in
May 1997 based on the recommendations of the University of North Carolina
Committee to Study Post-Tenure Review.

The UNC system of post-tenure review is built on the principle that its purpose is to
"support and encourage excellence among tenured faculty by:

1) Recognizing and rewarding exemplary faculty performance,

2) Providing for a clear plan and timetable for improvement of performance of
faculty found deficient, and

3) For those whose performance remains deficient, providing for the imposition of
appropriate sanctions, which may, in the most serious cases, include a recom-
mendation for discharge."

(UNC Policy Manual, 400.3.3 and 400.3.3.1{6})

Board policy also recognizes that each institution's specific policies and procedures
for conducting a review will reflect the unique mission of each institution while
incorporating the six board-mandated components: 1) cumulative review that
acknowledges the annual review; 2) to occur at least every five years for each tenured
faculty member; 3) involvement of peers as reviewers; 4) written feedback following
review; 5) required career development plan for faculty receiving unsatisfactory rating; (6) consideration of resources necessary to promote meaningful review.

Campus efforts (since 1998) have focused primarily on the development of specific
campus procedures that translate board policy into approved campus implementation.

Given the differing missions of the 15 campuses, approved practices vary across institutions with respect to

- How faculty are selected for review
- Composition and selection of peer review committees
- Materials submitted for review
- Available rating categories: deficient or satisfactory versus categories that allow greater discrimination and meritorious judgment
- Process to monitor *required* performance improvement plans
- Available recognition or reward linked to review

Reported results (after one complete 5-year cycle of over 5,000 reviews) show that the 5-year overall average for faculty judged to be performing at a satisfactory or above level is 97%. This is not out of line with reported results from other state systems and institutions with similar missions and policy objectives.

Results and outcomes are inconsistent, however, across the 15 campuses. Some institutions are decidedly more satisfied with their post-tenure review outcomes than others. For example:

- Over the past five years, four institutions have accounted for most of the deficient ratings given.
- Only a handful of institutions have either chosen or been able to grant any special monetary or supplemental reward to faculty judged to be meritorious.

Administrative personnel (chief academic officers, deans, and department chairs), who provided requested feedback on the effects of the policy to the Office of the President identified examples of problems and positive results. Again, these vary considerably by institution and include a range of both problems and benefits.

Reported problems include:

- Lack of rewards
- Duplicative of other processes
- Unclear review criteria

Reported positive results include:

- Increased faculty accountability
- Enhanced understanding about performance expectations
- Increased interest in career planning and career development
- Increased retirements (difficult to document and directly attribute to post-tenure review)

What Perspective Does the Innovation in Faculty Work Life Committee Bring to the Issue?

Innovation in Faculty Work Life Committee Members unanimously concur that the UNC post-tenure review practices need improvement. The group is divided, however, in its opinion about whether the process as it currently is implemented is worth keeping.

Committee members noted certain benefits and weaknesses experienced on their own campus. These benefits and weaknesses vary according to campus. What is a benefit for one campus can be a weakness for another:

Benefits

- Opportunity to improve tenure review system
- Encourages productivity
- Affirms contributions of strong faculty
- Identifies performance problems and remediates
- Tool to determine merit
- Opportunity for career planning
- Overview of long-term contributions

Weaknesses

- Inconsistency in application
- Peer reviewers not invested in process
- Performance weaknesses not always remediated
- Process seen as punitive
- Lack of adequate funding for reward and development
- No rewards for exemplary performance

Members of the Innovation in Faculty Work Life Committee expanded on their opinions about how well the post-tenure review process is working. Key themes and issues articulated by this group included the following:

- *Need for Continued Accountability*

  Past and current political and economic climate demand that higher education demonstrate accountability in the area of faculty productivity and quality. This mandate is not diminishing and, if anything, continues to be the mantra of external stakeholders.

- *Tenure Under Suspicion*

  Tenure can never be seen as untouchable. Post-tenure review was developed, in part, because threats to tenure were bubbling up in the North Carolina legislature. The policy, although intentionally driven by the Office of President, was designed to head off external pressure to do so.

- *Dichotomy in Purpose*

  To some, the main objectives of the post-tenure review policy seem dichoto-mous. Stated plainly, is the purpose to provide a rigorous review of productivity and remediation, if needed, or is the review supposed to be part of the standard reward system?

- *Tension Between Career Development and Performance Improvement*

  There is some confusion in implementation about whether the post-tenure review process *should* or *could* focus on the career development of *all* faculty or whether it should focus primarily on those who are judged deficient. Some say faculty see the process as a positive opportunity to help better understand the individual themes associated with a colleague's career and where they might fit into the larger departmental picture in the future. Post-tenure review can help pull together the talents and interests of faculty in determining future direc-tions. Others, however, see the process as principally punitive with the emphasis on remediation of deficiencies.

- *Ritualistic Not Substantive*

  For some, the process up until now has appeared to be more ritualistic than substantive. Some units apparently do not provide any meaningful follow-through and faculty are left with the impression that the process is a useless exercise that serves no real purpose. Even follow-through for faculty judged to need improvement is not happening in a consistent or effective way on some campuses or within some units.

- *Unit Analysis Missing*

  One interesting perspective offered was the notion of conducting an analysis of how unit post-tenure review procedures affect the overall outcome. Using departmental/unit planning priorities as the commonweal around which career development conversations occur seems to work on some campuses. There is a perceived need to make public what works in the implementation of post-tenure review.

- *Inflated Peer Reviews*

  By board policy, peer review is a required aspect of the review process. However, in many instances the results from peer review have not been rigorous, critical, or constructive. In some cases, the reviews are inflated. One person character-ized peer review as "a joke" because cronyism and favoritism become the opera-tive principle. This calls into question the ways in which peers are selected or elected to serve as peer reviewers and the context in which peer review is seen.

- *Powerless Department Chairs*

  The role of the department chair in the process varies by institution. In many cases, the chair is an ex-officio member of the peer review committee. This role, especially when the peer reviewers do not take their roles seriously, makes a review of substance and follow-through extremely difficult.

- *Comparing and Contrasting Conversations*

  Tied to the opinion that post-tenure review is invisible on campuses is the associated view that discussions among campus stakeholders and across campuses need to be enlarged and expanded so that best practices are shared and replicated when appropriate. This apparently seldom occurs.

- *Do Not Underplay Political Benefit*

  A pervasive perspective among committee members is the need to demonstrate a shared valuing between external publics (e.g., legislature, board) and internal bodies (e.g., administration, faculty) of the need for sufficient checks and balances to ensure that the objectives of evaluation and development are realized. Further, assessment of current practices with a view toward improvement should drive ongoing efforts and carry communication to all constituents.

Action

Expanded Innovation in Faculty Work Life Committee Members agreed that:

- Given the previous issues identified, a need exists at this moment in time, to step back and assess how well the post-tenure review process is achieving its intended purpose within the University of North Carolina system. It is important to note that at least three institutions had already decided (prior to the 10/6/03 meeting) to assess their policy with an eye toward strengthening their results. These institutions are Appalachian State University, UNC–Chapel Hill, and North Carolina State University.

- Some would like this assessment to clarify whether the process as practiced *can* or *should* lead to both reward and remediation, as the formulating principles suggest.

- The assessment plan must focus on policy improvement and refinement.

- Nonnegotiables must be stated at the outset. These include recognition that abolishing the post-tenure review policy is not an option nor is changing the policy from a periodic to a triggered approach.

- The assessment plan should be designed to include a core of common questions that every institution will answer. In addition, it was strongly felt that each of the 15 participating institutions should be given the opportunity to add campus-specific questions which probe more deeply certain aspects or components of campus policy and implementation of local interest.

Question 2: Recommended assessment methodology—How should information
be gathered? From whom? On what schedule?

After considerable discussion with respect to the benefits and shortcomings of various approaches to data collection and the need for reasonableness to drive the assessment, committee members recommended the following process and timeframe:

Instrumentation

- An online survey will be used to solicit the opinions and perspectives of various stakeholders in the process.

- The online survey will focus on questions related to the effectiveness, benefit, and value of the purpose, procedures, and results.

- The American Association for Higher Education's (AAHE) Post-Tenure Review Outcomes survey (Licata & Morreale, 1999) will be used as a starting point from which to build the specific UNC survey. The AAHE survey has been used nationally with systems and individual institutions to collect information on the outcomes associated with tenured faculty review practices.

Informants

- Tenured faculty and department chairs will receive the same survey. Questions will be imbedded in the survey in such a way that tenured faculty who have also served as peer reviewers will be asked to comment on both their reactions to the process as a faculty member under review and in a separate section as a peer reviewer. Likewise, specific questions will be included for department chairs.

- Deans will receive a separate online survey with questions specifically tailored to their role in the process and their judgment of process effectiveness and usefulness.

- Chief academic officers will participate in a focus group. The line of inquiry for this team of academic administrators will focus on policy purpose, implementation, and results.

Timeframe

- If possible, at least one institution (and ideally three institutions—one representing the baccalaureate, comprehensive, and research missions) will pilot the tenured faculty and department chair survey in spring 2004. Based on this pilot, the survey will be refined as needed based on campus experience.

- The majority of UNC institutions will administer the system-wide survey in fall 2004.

- Results will be summarized and a report of findings and recommendations will be completed in winter/early spring 2005.

Distribution and Endorsement

- The success of this survey will depend, in large part, on the way in which the survey is described and marketed. Endorsement and partnership between the UNC faculty assembly and the Office of the President is extremely critical and must be established from the outset.

  Faculty need to clearly understand:
  - The purpose of the overall assessment
  - Why a survey is being used
  - How results will be used
  - How the faculty assembly is involved
  - How confidentiality will be protected
  - Why it is important for each faculty member to share his or her candid views about how post-tenure review is working on his or her campus

---

Question 3: Next steps—What questions/information need to be answered and gathered?

- Peter Petschauer and Judy Peel will confer with their chief academic officer to determine campus readiness and willingness to pilot the survey.
- Betsy Brown will affirm or disaffirm with Gretchen Bataille the aforementioned nonnegotiables.
- Chris Licata will send an electronic version of the AAHE survey to Betsy and Peter. Betsy will distribute to committee members for suggestions on how to make the survey more relevant and useful to the UNC context.
- Betsy will meet with chief academic officers in November 2003 to review overall recommendations and discuss specific logistical issues including:
  - Whether there are any drawbacks to having the survey come from the Office of President
  - Whether there is any downside to having results sent to a non-university entity who will tally results by campus and by system
  - Whether the recommended timeline is reasonable and practical from a campus and demand on faculty time perspective

APPENDIX A

Research Design, Methodology,
and Data Collection

APPENDIX A
RESEARCH DESIGN, METHODOLOGY, AND DATA COLLECTION

This appendix outlines the research design and methodology used in the American Association for Higher Education's (AAHE) New Pathways II Study on post-tenure review. It discusses the qualitative and quantitative methodologies used, data collection methods and analysis, and the strengths and limitations of the methods and the study.

CASE STUDY METHOD

Case study methodology drove the data collection for this research project. Yin (1984) defines the case study research method as "an empirical inquiry that investigates a contemporary phenomenon within its real-life context . . . in which multiple sources of evidence are used" (p. 23). This type of approach is widely utilized when qualitative inquiry is desired in order to understand people's level of experience, their perceptions, and the meaning they place on certain processes and events. It is particularly useful in situations where researchers have access to previously unexamined situations (Yin, 1994).

The strength of case study research is that it helps us understand a complex issue. Selecting this approach for our research seemed essential because we wanted to conduct empirical inquiry which could be carried out within the context of an institution, its faculty, and its administrators. Further, we considered it critical that we gather multiple sources of evidence. No research has yet explored the results and impact of post-tenure review on various institutional stakeholders within one setting and across differing institutional settings. Therefore, this represented a unique opportunity for us to access information not yet examined and to understand the meanings that key institutional players placed on the post-tenure review process and on the ways it affected individual and institutional performance.

INSTITUTIONAL PARTICIPANTS: INVITATION AND SELECTION

The research design called for qualitative and quantitative data to be collected through a series of site visits to nine specifically chosen institutions. The invitation to participate was based on a set of pre-established requirements. The overarching requirement was that every participating institution come from the four-year public sector and have at least five years of implementation experience with post-tenure review. Because the majority of policies were established in the mid- to late-1990s, this five-year requirement significantly limited the number of eligible institutions.

Further, certain contextual considerations were also applied when inviting institutions to participate. These considerations included:

- *Diversity of mission.* Public four-year institutions representing a focus on research (doctoral/research universities—extensive) and teaching (doctoral/research—intensive universities and master's I and II) were desired.

- *Differing size and geographic location.* A cross-section of small, medium, and large institutions from differing geographic regions of the country were sought.

- *Ease of access.* Willingness to grant access to the campus and pertinent institutional records and information was crucial. Only institutions that were able to designate an internal institutional liaison to assist with all aspects of the site visit, participant selection, document retrieval, and survey dissemination were considered. This designated liaison did not participate in analysis of data or preparation of findings but was instrumental in ensuring that the research design was followed.

- *Type of policy.* Three types of post-tenure policies were solicited: 1) periodic, comprehensive review for all faculty, 2) triggered, consequential review for poorly performing faculty, and 3) enhanced annual reviews. Nationally, periodic review policies far outweigh triggered polices by about 8:1. This same proportion was sought in the study.

Invitations were extended to 11 potential institutional partners who fit the criteria. From this pool we were able to successfully recruit eight public institutions, as well as a medical school, for a total of nine case study institutions. Interest in a medical school environment grew from preliminary research conducted by scholars working with the AAHE's New Pathways project. Their work suggested that professional schools, and in particular medical schools, had significant experience working with accountability and market-based challenges facing the academy (Chait & Trower, 1997; Gappa, 1996; Trower, 1998). By using different approaches to faculty employment and evaluation, the experience of a medical school could expand and possibly inform findings related to the effects of post-tenure review programs on performance and productivity. (See Appendix B for a profile of the nine institutions included in the study.)

The final mix of institutions provided us with a range of institutional settings with differing missions (4 research/doctoral and 4 teaching/comprehensive), size of student body (<5,000 students to >25,000), numbers of full-time tenure eligible faculty (<200 faculty to >2,000), and type of post-tenure review policy practiced (6 periodic, 1 triggered, and 1 periodic and triggered). The medical school was situated within a private research university and had a 25-year history with a tenure review system. Of all the institutions, the medical school had the most experience in reviewing tenured professors (see Chapter 5).

INSTRUMENTATION AND DATA COLLECTION

A case study approach was used in each institution studied. A key strength of the case study method is the use of multiple sources and techniques in data gathering.

Data gathering is normally largely qualitative, but it may also include quantitative approaches. For this study, we collected descriptive data and individual narratives about what faculty, chairs, deans, and other academic administrators experienced in the post-tenure review process and how they assessed its effectiveness and value. Both quantitative and qualitative data-collection methodologies were used in an effort to be as inclusive of differing perspectives as possible and as a way to bolster reliability by expanding and verifying recurring themes that developed. (A two-day retreat was held in November 1998 with each institutional liaison and the full research team. The research design, interview protocols, and survey questions were drafted in a collaborative way during this convening.)

The majority of information and data on each campus came from: 1) institutional documents and records, 2) on-site interviews with faculty and administrators, and 3) a university-wide survey.

Institutional Documents

All relevant institutional background information was collected, including archival documents on the development of post-tenure review, institutional mission and strategic plans, institutional policies/statements on faculty evaluation and faculty development, and all institutional records on the specific results of post-tenure review.

Interviews

Individual interviews and focus group interviews were the main sources of data gathering during each three-day on-site campus visit. The opinions of tenured faculty were critical because faculty are directly affected by the reviews. The views of chairs, deans, and other administrators were also important because each had different roles and oversight responsibilities in the process. Thus, in order to make sense of the review process, it was important to understand the experiences of both faculty and administrators. The interview plan included:

- One-on-one interviews with tenured faculty who had undergone a post-tenure review
- Focus group interviews with department chairs
- Focus group interviews with deans
- Focus group interviews with peer review committee members (if applicable to policy)
- One-on-one interviews with senior-level academic officers and others with a role in the review process

Sampling

The number of interviews and focus groups within each of the nine institutional settings was in part pre-established and in part determined by the numbers comprising each particular category of interest (e.g., tenured faculty, chairs, deans, and senior administrators). Regardless of the number of tenured faculty or size of the institution, we established 18 as the minimum number of individual tenured faculty interviews per institution. In the larger institutions we often exceeded that number, and in the two largest universities, we conducted 31 individual interviews at one and 23 at the other. By starting with 18, we were also able to add additional interviews if we uncovered a particularly interesting line of inquiry that we wished to probe further or if we felt we needed additional narrative on a particular aspect of the post-tenure review experience.

With the assistance of the institutional liaison, a call to participate in the study was sent out by the AAHE research team to all tenured faculty who had been reviewed within each institution's post-tenure review policy. Interested individuals were then randomly selected to participate. Random selection was guided by consideration of the sample representativeness desired with respect to gender, ethnicity, rank, and disciplinary affiliation. Every effort was made to ensure representativeness to the university population in general.

In addition to the individual faculty interviews, chairs, deans, peer review committee members, and other academic leaders were invited to participate in focus groups. The sampling plan within each setting included a broad representation of deans, department chairs, and peer reviewers from differing disciplines. Individual interviews with senior-level academic administrators were also arranged. The interview protocols were submitted and approved by the Institutional Review Board for Human Subjects at each institution.

The one-on-one interviews and focus groups, which lasted an hour on average, were audiotaped and transcribed. The research team also took field notes during the interviews and site visits. Numbers were assigned to each interview in order to protect the confidentiality of each participant. Every participant completed a release form at the time of the interview.

Because each of the informant groups had differently defined roles in the post-tenure review process, it was expected that each group might share different experiences and opinions about the process. Based on this, three semi-structured interview protocols were used: one for faculty interviews, one for department chairs, and one for deans and other senior-level academic officers. The interview protocols explored participants' views and experiences with respect to the purpose and effectiveness of the policy, outcomes and tangible results of the review related to individual performance and development, procedural aspects including amount of time and preparation involved, impact of the review on the department, the benefits and problems associated with the process, and suggested improvements. (See Appendix C for each interview protocol.)

Interview transcripts and field notes were read, coded, and analyzed in order to draw out patterns and themes. Clustering was used as appropriate.

Survey

In an effort to corroborate further the information collected through the interviews, a post-tenure review outcomes survey was administered. Similar to the topical areas probed through the interview protocol, the survey contained a core of questions designed to elicit individual opinions and experiences about the post-tenure review process, including its purpose, effectiveness, impact on performance and career development, benefits, problems, clarity/fairness/consistency of procedural aspects, and suggestions for improvement. The survey contained both forced-choice, Likert-type questions and open-ended questions. (See Appendix C for survey.)

The core survey questions were developed and reviewed by an eight-member national panel of experts and then field tested. Following each site visit the survey was examined to ensure that the questions were relevant to the particular institutional context and policy. Questions were deleted if needed or added as appropriate. The survey was then administered to all tenured faculty, including academic administrators, and returned directly to the AAHE national office. The survey required no self-identification, and respondents were advised that results would be reported only in an aggregate format.

Use of a survey enabled the research team to further group the interview results within a larger context of experiences. Most important, it aided us in our attempts to use multiple sources of evidence—to triangulate in order to bring increased validity and reliability to our findings. Combining quantitative and qualitative approaches "leads to high quality studies and has gained increasing value in the literature" (Miles & Huberman, 1994, p. 29).

DATA ANALYSIS

Information from one-on-one faculty interviews and from focus groups with department chairs, deans, and peer reviewers were analyzed along with the responses from faculty and administrators to survey questions. For the interviews and focus groups, appropriate qualitative techniques—coding, identifying emerging themes and ideas based on language and quotes, collecting additional data, and constructing categories—were used. For the surveys, quantitative methods—frequency distributions, measures of central tendency, cross tabs, tests of statistical significance, analysis of variance, and structural equation modeling—were used.

Through repeated review of all transcripts and survey responses, response patterns were identified and categories developed. Themes were generated from the grouping of categories and conclusions drawn.

To maintain confidentiality, each institution was assigned a fictitious name, such as University A, B, or C. Following each site visit, a comprehensive case study report was prepared for each institution, which contained in-depth discussion of findings, implications, and recommendations. Each case study was written so that institutional leaders could better understand how their post-tenure review process was perceived to be working. The information presented also furnished useful insights about how to improve the process and, in some cases, suggested ways to lessen the burden.

Following the completion of the nine case studies, a cross-case analysis was performed in order to derive common themes and provide answers to the key research questions that initially drove the study. Through structural equation modeling, factors were identified that strongly influenced whether faculty and administrators considered post-tenure review to be effective, valuable, and worthwhile.

Research Team

The core research team was comprised of nationally recognized and greatly skilled higher education scholars. A team of two investigators conducted each site visit and prepared the associated case study report. Members of the research team included:

- Christine M. Licata, AAHE senior associate and associate vice president for academic affairs at the Rochester Institute of Technology/National Technical Institute for the Deaf
- Joseph C. Morreale, AAHE senior scholar and provost at Pace University

Dr. Licata and Dr. Morreale were the co-principal investigators for the study. Together or paired with another member of the AAHE project team, they visited eight of the nine institutions. In addition, analysis of survey results for each of the nine institutions was completed by:

- R. Eugene Rice, AAHE senior scholar and director of the New Pathways II Project
- Estela Mara Bensimon, AAHE senior scholar and director of the Center for Urban Education and professor of higher education in the Rossier School of Education at the University of Southern California
- Susan B. Foster, consultant and research professor at the Rochester Institute of Technology/National Technical Institute for the Deaf

Survey results were compiled and analysis completed by Dr. Jeffrey Jolton of Genesee Survey Services, an independent organization specializing in data analysis and survey research. Two graduate students from the Rossier School of Education at the University of Southern California, Georgia Bauman and Lisa Patriquin, assisted with transcript analysis for two of the case studies.

Limitations

A word of caution about the study: It was limited first by the finite number of institutions studied. Further, it looked primarily at public institutions so applicability to private institutions is questionable.

In any study that uses volunteers, it is difficult to know what motivates people to participate. In fact, studies of this nature can suffer from dependence on the local elite as informants—those who are interested, articulate, and available. In this particular circumstance, it might be that individuals who carry a particularly positive or negative opinion about post-tenure review were inspired to participate. One always hopes for diverse perspectives, but this cannot be assured in a study of this nature. The fact that selection was done randomly helps assuage some of the pitfalls of representativeness, but it does not remove the limitation completely.

Both qualitative and quantitative techniques were used to help provide a more complete picture and to compensate for the limitations inherent in each individual approach. The interviews offer an insider's view of experiences and meanings but may not be representative of all faculty at the particular university. The survey results also offer an insider's view but provide data and observable indicators in addition to perspectives and experiences. Again, the survey respondents may not be representative of all tenured faculty, so our results should be interpreted accordingly. But this limitation is blunted somewhat by the fact that all tenured professors and administrators were provided an opportunity to participate in the survey.

One criticism of the case study method is that the study of a small number of cases does not offer sufficient grounds for generalizations, nor does it guarantee reliability of results. Because our study is based on a large number of participants from diverse institutions, we feel comfortable that our analysis and findings provide important insights into the post-tenure review process and can serve as a touchstone for further work in this area.

Our study provides the most comprehensive picture currently available on the outcomes of post-tenure review within public senior-level institutions. Although these new data have many strengths, they also have limitations. We realize that while we did our best to use multiple sources of data and to be as objective as possible in the process, the conclusions we have drawn from survey data and interview transcripts may differ from what other researchers may find when pursuing the same topic in different settings. Analyzing findings across settings and deriving conclusions from multiple case studies is a very complex process and requires considerable interpretation. We made every attempt to be evenhanded in our work and to approach the data in a neutral fashion. However, we also realize that total objectivity in research of this sort may not be possible.

Given these considerations, we ask that the reader be mindful of the scope and boundaries associated with making reasonable generalizations from this study.

REFERENCES

Chait, R., & Trower, C. A. (1997). *Where tenure does not reign: Colleges with contract systems* (New Pathways Working Paper Series No. 3). Washington, DC: American Association for Higher Education.

Gappa, J. M. (1996). *Off the tenure track: Six models for full-time, nontenurable appointments* (New Pathways Working Paper Series No. 10). Washington, DC: American Association for Higher Education.

Miles, M. B., & Huberman, A. M. (1994). *Qualitative data analyses: An expanded sourcebook.* Thousand Oaks, CA: Sage.

Trower, C. A. (1998). *Employment practices in the professions: Fresh ideas from inside and outside the academy* (New Pathways Working Paper Series No. 13). Washington, DC: American Association for Higher Education.

Yin, R. K. (1984). *Case study research: Design and methods.* Beverly Hills, CA: Sage.

Yin, R. K. (1994). *Case study research: Design and methods* (2nd ed.). Thousand Oaks, CA: Sage.

APPENDIX B

Institutional Profiles of Nine Universities

APPENDIX B
PROFILE OF NINE UNIVERSITIES

This study was carried out in eight diverse, four-year public universities across the United States and in one private medical school. This appendix contains summaries of key institutional and contextual characteristics and an individual profile of each institution.

Figure 1
Summary
Institutional Profiles:
Contextual Characteristics

# of Institutions	4 Institutions	4 Institutions	Medical School
Principal Mission	Public/Research-Oriented (Doctoral/Research–Extensive)	Public/Teaching-Oriented (Either Doctoral/Research–Intensive or Masters I or II)	Private/Medical School and Academic Health Center
Control/Governance Structure	Public: System Board of Regents	Public: System Board of Regents	Private: Board of Trustees
Impetus for Establishment of Post-Tenure Review	External (3) Internal (1)	External (3) Internal (1)	Internal
Unionized Faculty	1 Campus	1 Campus	None
Location	West (1) Midwest (1) South (2)	West (2) Midwest (2)	South
Purpose of Policy	Formative and Summative (4)	Formative (2) Formative and Summative (2)	Summative
Approach	Periodic (3) Triggered (1)	Periodic (3) Periodic and Triggered (1)	Periodic Retenuring Process
Range of Experience With Post-Tenure Review	6–13 years	7–19 years	25 years

Figure 2
Institutional Size

Size of Student Body	# of Institutions
Over 20,000	2
10,000–20,000	4
Under 10,000	3

Number of Full-Time Tenure-Eligible Faculty	# of Institutions
2,000 or more	2
700–1,000	2
400–600	3
Under 200	2

Figure 3
Profile of Participants:
Interviews and Focus Groups

Individuals Interviewed Across Nine Institutions	# of Individuals	%
Tenured Faculty	176	40.7%
Department Chair	134	31.0%
Peer Reviewers (Tenured)	45	10.4%
Union/Faculty Association Representatives	18	4.2%
Deans	41	9.5%
Senior-Level Academic Administrators	18	4.2%
Total	432	100%

Figure 4
Profile of Survey Respondents

Individuals Interviewed Across Nine Institutions	# of Individuals	%
Tenured Faculty	1,230	73.3%
Department Chairs	225	13.4%
Deans/Associate Deans	90	5.4%
Other	132	7.9%
Total	1,677	100%

Gender	%
Male	72%
Female	28%

Rank	%
Professor	70%
Associate Professor	24%
Assistant Professor	3%
Instructor	.1%
Other	2.9%

Tenure Status	%
Tenured	98%
Non-Tenured	2%

Survey Response Rates by Institution

University	Response Rate
University A	35%
University B	46%
University C	52%
University D	66%
University E	32%
University F	30%
University G	30%
University H	46%
University I	28%

Appendix B
Individual Institutional Profiles

University A

Description

University A is a public, doctoral/research–extensive institution in the southern region of the United States. It is the second largest institution within the state system and has evolved over the last 80 years from an evening school of commerce to an urban university. It has an enrollment of about 24,000 students. University A has approximately 475 tenured faculty comprising five colleges, one school, a counseling center, and the library. There is no collective bargaining, and the fiscal climate can be described as stable.

Purpose

The initial impetus for post-tenure review came from the campus provost who framed the need in developmental terms and emphasized formative benefits. University A became the first institution in the state system to develop a policy. The other 33 state institutions followed suit due to a state mandate. University A commenced its Cumulative Review and Development policy in spring 1995, following academic senate approval while other institutions in the system were expected to have their plans in place by September 1998.

During the phase-in period, the policy underwent minor revisions. The review objectives remained the same and were characterized as an opportunity to assess faculty development goals and achievements, to provide assistance to faculty in ensuring continuous intellectual and professional growth, and to provide assistance to the unit in ensuring that all faculty members are contributing to the unit's goals and responsibilities.

Assessment

After six years of implementation, the provost's office tracked results. After 359 reviews, the findings showed that about 37% of faculty were assessed to be performing satisfactorily with traditional expectations in teaching and research. The numbers of faculty who were judged to be marginal decreased by almost half from the first three years of implementation to the next three years from 7.4% to 3.4%. Likewise, the number of faculty assessed to have limited research productivity but effective teaching and service were asked to modify their workload profile to one of teaching and service. Altered expectations usually meant taking on more teaching in exchange for lowered research expectations. In the first three years, 40% of the reviews resulted in this process; in the next three years, only 17% did. The number of retirements also declined from 24 in the first three years to 3 in the next. Other results noted the increase in the number of faculty in the promotion potential category. The group included many longtime associate professors hired when the university placed less emphasis on research. The numbers increased from 38 to 45.

After six years, approximately 94% of the faculty were judged to be performing at levels commensurate with the traditional profile or with a modified profile.

Outcomes

No faculty were terminated and development plans were developed in the case of those assessed to be marginal—about 7% retired.

Policy Purpose

* Formative
* Opportunity to assess faculty development goals and achievements over a longer term and potentially at differing levels.

Review Cycle

* Five-year cycle

Review Criteria

* Unit based

Documentation

* Annual reports, student/peer evaluations of teaching, curriculum vitae, publications
* Candidates provide a two-page statement of effectiveness in teaching/research/service over previous five years
* Candidates provide one page outlining five-year goals

Role of Peers

* Peer reviews conducted either by the elected promotion and tenure committee of the college/unit or by an independently elected committee consisting of at least three tenured faculty

Role of Chair/Deans

* Cumulative review reviewed and commented on by department chair, dean, and provost

Results/Actions

* Faculty receive a written report of results
* Conference is held between chair and faculty member to produce a plan which focuses on professional goals and/or workload profile for subsequent approval by dean

- Dean confers with faculty member and monitors progress on plan through annual evaluation
- Unsatisfactory reviews require improvement plan
- Faculty who have unacceptable research productivity but effective teaching can modify workload expectations to be more teaching/service oriented

UNIVERSITY B

Description

University B is a public, doctoral/research–extensive university located in the western region of the United States. It is the flagship campus of a 10-campus state system and has evolved from a land-grant college of agriculture and mechanic arts to one of the top 50 public universities in the nation. Eight colleges, 10 professional schools, and 4 specialized academic centers offer degrees to more than 18,000 students. University B has about 2,000 full-time faculty, 1,100 of whom are tenured. Collective bargaining has existed for 29 years. The university has been in a state of fiscal constraint for the last 10 years.

Purpose

The post-tenure review policy was established by the board of regents in 1981 principally as an accountability measure. After a long legal battle between the regents and the union over whether evaluation was a negotiable item, the court affirmed in 1986 that the regents had the unilateral right to establish an evaluation system. Subsequently, a joint committee of faculty, chairs, deans, and union representatives developed implementation guidelines, and the first reviews were conducted in 1987.

Assessment

After 10 years of implementation, University B conducted its own internal assessment of how well the process was meeting its stated objectives. The report concluded that the process appeared to have reduced the number of underperforming faculty and was successful in helping underperformers either revitalize their careers or consider retirement. The report also noted that the process seemed to have lost sight of the professional development objective and had become focused instead on identification of deficiencies and remediation. The greatest reported impediment to the system was the lack of rewards/incentives and the disincentives that existed.

Outcomes

After 10 years, about 93% of the faculty were judged to be performing their duties in adequate fashion. When faculty were found to be deficient, more than 80% of the cases were either due to unsatisfactory research productivity alone or in combination with other areas of performance.

Policy Purpose

- Accountability
- Recognition and incentives for superior performance (No merit monies have been available since 1986, but this objective remains intact should funds be initiated again.)
- Performance improvement

Review Cycle

- Five-year cycle for all tenured faculty

Review Criteria

- Departmentally established

Documentation

- Academic profile, including curriculum vitae and other evidence

Role of Peers

- No direct role as reviewer
- Department chair is part of bargaining unit and is considered a peer

Role of Chair

- Chair conducts review

Results/Actions

- Satisfactory reviews are communicated in writing to faculty member; meetings and/or constructive feedback are rare
- Unsatisfactory reviews trigger a required professional development plan (PDP)
- PDP is mutually agreed upon among faculty member, chair, and dean

University C

Description

University C is a public master's I institution in the Midwest. It is a regional campus of the state flagship university in the state university system. It has an enrollment of 8,200 students and 225 full-time faculty. The university has evolved from a center for cooperative education to a metropolitan regional university of choice. The university offers undergraduate and master's-level programs. The campus is comprised of one college and three professional schools. There is no collective bargaining. The

College of Arts, Sciences, and Letters is the only unit with a post-tenure review policy.

At its own initiative, the college established procedures for the periodic evaluation of tenured full professors in 1977. The policy was developed by a group of faculty within the college as a means to ensure that quality standards were maintained into the senior rank. The fiscal environment can be labeled stable.

Purpose

The main purpose of the policy is to improve faculty performance. While primarily formative in focus, there is a summative component. If performance does not improve after an improvement plan is developed, a salary freeze or decrement is possible.

Assessment

University C does not conduct routine assessment or tracking of specific results from the reviews. The dean was able to provide anecdotal commentary on specific results.

Outcomes

After more than 20 years, no faculty member has been fired. About 10% of those reviewed have either retired or have corrected unacceptable performance. The rest have used the process to enhance their productivity, contributions, or their professional development.

Policy Purpose

- Continued professional development
- Along with annual assessment, it is used to determine salary increments and other benefits based on merit

Review Cycle

- Four- to six-year cycle for tenured full professors

Review Criteria

- College-based criteria

Documentation

- Dean collects curriculum vitae, publications, annual activity reports, and student evaluations
- Faculty member provides self-assessment in teaching, scholarship, and service

Role of Peers

- Ad hoc college committee of four to six peers conduct review

- Committee members are chosen and appointed by the dean; at least one tenured associate professor serves on the committee

Role of Chair

- No direct role in review

Results/Actions

- The committee develops final letter of evaluation
- Dean acts as facilitator and is responsible for the format, preparation, and mailing of the final letters of evaluation
- Committee's letter should contain comments on strengths and weaknesses of professor's performance; as to weaknesses, evaluation should be specific, suggest remedies, and in extreme cases may recommend a special evaluation for the following year
- Professor may respond to the committee in writing regarding the evaluation and may discuss with dean
- An objection may lead to a review by the committee with a possible revised letter, committee standing by the original letter, or an appeal
- Professor has the right to appeal to the provost and vice chancellor for academic affairs

UNIVERSITY D

Description

University D is a private, doctoral/research–intensive university in the southern region of the United States. More than 150 years old, it is one of the oldest institutions of higher learning in the state and has evolved from religious roots as a college of liberal arts to what today includes two campuses. The university serves 5,000 students and is comprised of an undergraduate college (offering a baccalaureate in 40 fields), a graduate school, a school of medicine, a school of law, and a graduate school of management.

The school of medicine—the unit studied by AAHE—was founded in 1902. Over the past 25 years, the medical center has expanded and is one of 125 academic medical centers in the United States. Nearly 2,400 students receive training annually through the center's teaching programs.

The work of the school of medicine is divided among 29 academic departments. Clinical departments also utilize the services of volunteer faculty drawn from the state's privately practicing physicians and surgeons. The control of the school of medicine is vested in the board of trustees of University D.

The medical school has about 700 full-time faculty, of whom 94 are currently tenured. Tenured faculty fall primarily into two appointment classifications: clinical faculty and basic science faculty. Tenure can be granted in either category. Tenure is not a condition, however, for continued employment. Only about one-third of the tenure-eligible faculty (at rank of associate or full professor) currently hold tenure. They can be promoted in rank without tenure.

Purpose

At the initiation of a former dean, the five-year tenure review policy was established in 1975. This policy is referred to as post-tenure review, but it is defined in policy as a retenuring process. Continuation of employment is implied provided the faculty member continues to demonstrate productivity. Every five years, the department chair makes a written report to the dean on the performance of each tenured faculty member. If the performance is judged by the dean or the chair to be inadequate, the dean, after consultation with the chair, must formally notify the faculty member of the specific inadequacies and inform the faculty member that there is a two-year probationary period in which he or she must correct deficiencies in performance or resign the appointment.

Assessment

University D has not formally kept records of the results of five-year reviews.

Outcomes

Anecdotally, the belief is that 95% of the reviews have been positive. Phased retirement has occurred in a few cases and individuals have chosen to voluntarily leave. Large-scale tenure revocation has not resulted.

Policy Purpose

- Summative
- Accountability
- Assure continued productivity as compared to peers in same department or section

Review Cycle

- Five-year cycle

Review Criteria

- Departmentally (unit) established, plus school funding profile
- Must demonstrate productivity in the appropriate areas of patient care, research, teaching, service, and other school functions at a level comparable to that demonstrated by peers within the same department or section

Documentation

- Report written by chair and sent to dean
- Curriculum vitae and activity reports used
- Review of productivity is essential

Role of Peers

- No defined role

Role of Chair

- Major role in preparing review

Results/Actions

- If performance is judged inadequate, the dean, in consultation with the chair, notifies the faculty member of specific inadequacies and informs the faculty member that there is a two-year probationary period in which to correct deficiencies in performance or resign appointment

UNIVERSITY E

Description

University E is a comprehensive, doctoral/research–intensive university in the western region of the United Sates. It is the urban campus of a four-campus state system. As the urban campus within the state system, it has evolved over the past 25 years from its original mission as an extension center of the flagship campus of the system. University E has an enrollment of about 10,800 students. Through 8 colleges and schools, it offers undergraduate degrees in 48 different fields, master's degrees in 45 fields, and the doctoral degree in 6 areas of study.

The university has about 400 full-time faculty, of whom approximately 213, or 54%, are tenured. Faculty fall into several different classifications: tenured, tenure-track, and nontenured. All faculty on a tenure track are required to meet university criteria for tenure and promotion. According to university policy, approved criteria and guidelines for tenure and promotion include duties, responsibilities, and minimum qualifications.

Purpose

Post-tenure review at University E has a long history with two distinct phases. The first phase began in the early 1980s and was motivated by the regents of the state university system. During this period a system of comprehensive periodic peer-based post-tenure review was established. The second phase began in the late 1990s, this time sparked by legislative concerns about tenure. A new dimension incorporating a triggered consequential administrative-based post-tenure review was added to the regular comprehensive review. All tenured faculty were required to undergo post-tenure review every five years. This policy was formed in accordance with the state system-wide policy. The system policy was first adopted in 1984 and then revised in 1997.

Post-tenure review is intended to facilitate continuing faculty development consistent with the academic needs and goals of the university and the most effective use of institutional resources, and ensure professional accountability by a regular, comprehensive evaluation of every tenured faculty member's performance.

Assessment

After two complete years of implementation of the second phase policy, the vice president for academic affairs is required to report to the board and faculty council on the effectiveness of the revised post-tenure review process. If serious problems are identified, they should be remedied at this time. Thereafter, assessments of the effectiveness of the post-tenure review process are to be made at the discretion of the regents.

Outcomes

In the first full year of implementation (1998–1999), 35 faculty were reviewed. Twenty-six were positively reviewed, two retired or resigned, three were negatively reviewed, and six reviews were incomplete and needed further consultation.

Policy Purpose

- Developmental
- Accountability

Review Cycle

- Five-year cycle with triggered administrative review possible

Review Criteria

- Primary department unit

Documentation

- Examine previous five annual performance reviews
- Peer review of technology, faculty member's professional plan

Role of Peers

- Peer review of faculty member by unit committee

Role of Chair/Deans

- Primary unit writes a brief report summarizing unit's findings
- Report forwarded to the dean

Results/Actions

- There are three possible outcomes of the annual merit evaluation: above meeting expectations, meeting expectations, and below meeting expectations
- Faculty who receive two "below expectations" ratings within the previous five years must undergo extensive review (triggered post-tenure review)

University F

Description

University F is a comprehensive, master's I state institution in the western region of the United States. It is one of 23 campuses of a public university system and has an enrollment of 18,113 students: 14,768 undergraduates and 3,345 graduates.

The university is under the oversight of a single board of trustees that is responsible for the system-wide management of the 23 campuses and is overseen by the chancellor's office. A collective bargaining unit represents the faculty in all employment-related negotiations. The collective bargaining unit has been in existence since 1983.

The university has 1,096 faculty. The university has eight instructional colleges/schools, a graduate division and Division of Extended Education, a library, a faculty mentoring program, a counseling center, and academic support offices.

Purpose

University F's academic senate, as well as the president, approved the policy on Periodic Evaluation of Tenured Faculty in 1981. The policy was revised in 1995.

Assessment

None to date

Outcomes

None available

Policy Purpose

- Developmental
- Enhancement of instructional performance

Review Cycle

- Five-year cycle for all tenured faculty

Review Criteria

- Unit based

Documentation

- Curriculum vitae, statement of accomplishments, statement of self-evaluation, five-year report of professional development, and university/community service activities

Role of Peers

- Peer review committee conducts review

Role of Chair/Deans

- Chair may concur with peer review committee report or may submit a separate written report

Results/Actions

- Satisfactory reviews are communicated in writing to the faculty member; dean may inform the professor and chair in the form of a letter; faculty member rarely receives feedback
- Unsatisfactory reviews are communicated in writing to the faculty member; faculty member has opportunity to make a 30-minute presentation to the committee and the chair and/or submit his or her comments about the assessment in writing; interim evaluations the following year with possible developmental plan required
- All reports are submitted to the dean

UNIVERSITY G

Description

University G is a public, doctoral/research–extensive university in the Midwestern region of the United States. Established in 1848, it is the oldest institution of higher learning in the state and the flagship campus within the state's system of higher education. It is one of the world's preeminent public research universities and ranks among the top echelon of universities in the number of doctorates produced and the amount of research and development funds it receives.

The University offers undergraduate programs of study in 147 fields, master's degrees in 161 areas, and doctoral programs in more than 100 fields. Approximately 40,000 students are currently enrolled in these programs.

A board of regents oversees the higher education system in the state. The system consists of 13 four-year campuses and 13 two-year campuses. University G has about 2,100 full-time faculty, of whom approximately 80% have tenure.

Purpose

The impetus for post-tenure review at University G came in the form of external pressure from the board of regents. In 1992, the university received a mandate from its regents to develop through the normal governance process a plan for tenured faculty review and development to be presented to the university system administration for acceptance.

The purpose of the policy, as articulated in the regents' mandate, was primarily developmental in nature and intended to ensure continuing growth and development in faculty professional skills, encouraging faculty to explore new ways to promote academic excellence and to identify areas for improvement and provide solutions for problem areas.

The chancellor of University G worked with the executive committee of the faculty senate to comply with the regents' mandate. A subcommittee of the university committee prepared a report which included recommendations for how the campus should respond to the regents' mandate. This document helped guide the drafting of a policy statement that was used to guide implementation. This process took about eight months and was approved in April 1993. Policy implementation began in the 1993–1994 academic year.

Assessment

The policy has been in effect for seven years and all tenured faculty have been reviewed at least once. University G has not undertaken any formal study of results from post-tenure review. An internal audit was conducted by the system administration office in 1995–1996 to determine that implementation of the policy was in place and that campus plans complied with the regents' guidelines. The audit examined seven institutions within the system, including the university studied in this report.

The audit report indicated that there tends to be a common set of factors that are present in some of the more effective review plans: 1) the active involvement of an institution's administration, 2) written criteria, 3) faculty taking the process seriously, 4) use of a review committee, and 5) positive assistance provided when improvement is needed.

Outcomes

The vice chancellor reported to the regents during one of their meetings about the outcome of the first review cycle. He emphasized that the process was being implemented as the regents had intended. Several tenured faculty who had been reviewed also provided testimony about their experiences and results. The vice chancellor believes that the regents were satisfied with how the policy had been implemented.

Policy Purpose

- Developmental
- Performance improvement

Review Cycle

- Five-year cycle for all tenured faculty

Review Criteria

- Departmentally established

Documentation

- Current curriculum vitae, annual activity reports, teaching evaluations, other evidence, and brief summary of career plans

Role of Peers

- Review run by colleagues in department

Role of Chair/Deans

- Department executive committee conducts review
- Chair does follow-up of action required

Results/Actions

- Written report to faculty member and copy to chair
- Recommendations for action are forwarded to chair

UNIVERSITY H

Description

University H is a public master's II regional comprehensive institution located in the Midwestern region of the United States. Established in 1965, it is one of 13 degree-granting, four-year institutions in the state university system. It is defined as a metropolitan university that offers undergraduate programs in 17 interdisciplinary and 20 disciplinary fields and master's degrees in two areas. Approximately 5,000 students are enrolled. There are 141 full-time faculty. There is no collective bargaining and the fiscal environment is constrained.

Purpose

The impetus for post-tenure review was mandated by the board of regents in 1992. The regents established broad components that were to be included in each institution's plan but gave each campus considerable latitude in determining specific procedures. The chancellor of University H worked with a subcommittee of the faculty senate to develop a campus policy. As a result, units were empowered to establish specific procedures as long as they recognized that the review was a formative process with a goal of continuing to support to the fullest extent possible the talents and aspirations of each faculty member. Reviews were conducted at least once every five years and were based in part on a professional development proposal prepared by the faculty member which was to be consistent with the mission and goals of the institution and the unit. The reviews included a discussion with the faculty member. A peer committee from the unit's executive committee conducts the review. Policy implementation began in 1994.

Assessment

University H has not conducted a formal assessment of the policy, but an internal audit was conducted by the system to determine whether the campus plan complied with the regents' mandate. University H tracked specific results from the review during the first five-year cycle.

Outcomes

After one cycle, 36 retirements and resignations occurred, although none can be directly attributed to an unsatisfactory appraisal from a post-tenure review. Of the remaining reviews, 98% were satisfactory.

Policy Purpose

- Growth and development
- Exploration and innovation
- Performance improvement

Review Cycle

- Five-year cycle for all tenured faculty

Review Criteria

- Departmentally (unit) established

Documentation

- Peer and student evaluations
- Professional development plan

Role of Peers

- Peer review
- Unit executive committee

Role of Chair/Deans

- Chair is part of executive committee

Results/Actions

- Summary of review sent to faculty member and dean
- Satisfactory reviews are placed in faculty members' official files
- Unsatisfactory reviews include identified needs for improvement and a plan for improvement is developed by faculty member and the unit executive committee

UNIVERSITY I

Description

University I is a comprehensive, doctoral/research–extensive university in the southern region of the United States. It is an urban university and is part of the state university system of 15 public four-year institutions. It has been a university since 1962 and currently has an enrollment of 19,000 students. Through its seven colleges and schools, it offers undergraduate degrees in 65 different fields, master's degrees in 68 fields, and 22 doctoral degrees.

University I has about 607 full-time faculty, of whom approximately 60% are tenured. The state university system is governed by a state board of visitors and the state council on higher education. There is no collective bargaining agreement for the faculty.

Purpose

University I has always had an annual review of all tenured faculty, with merit raises as the outcome. In October 1992, due to pressure from the board of visitors, the president began a process of revising the formal review of tenured faculty. There was much delay in the development of an agreement between the faculty senate and the administration on a new post-tenure review proposal. The board of visitors desired a mandatory five-year comprehensive review for all faculty, but the faculty opposed this idea. The state council on higher education mandated that University I adopt a new and more comprehensive policy. Once the faculty saw that the consequences of inaction could be much worse, the provost began to make headway in getting agreement on a new policy. It took 18 months to obtain agreement of a policy statement, then 9 additional months to implement the policy. The new policy of triggered comprehensive post-tenure review was implemented in fall 1994. The specifics of the post-tenure review policy were developed through negotiations of the faculty senate, the council of deans, and the provost.

Assessment

The provost and vice president for academic affairs present an annual report to the deans and the faculty senate on the number of new and continuing post-tenure review cases and their general outcomes. The provost monitors the use of the policy by the deans with the goal to improve teaching and research. The deans have indicated that, for the most part, there are very few poor performers on the faculty. The trigger device also keeps down the potentially high cost and burdensome nature of the process.

Outcomes

Since 1993, five faculty have undergone an in-depth review and nineteen have chosen to retire or take an unpaid leave rather than be reviewed.

Policy Purpose

- Begins as formative but is also summative
- Performance improvement

Review Cycle

- Annual review of all tenured faculty
- Two years of poor performance leads to in-depth post-tenure review

Review Criteria

- Departmentally established

Documentation

- Full review of teaching, research, and service
- Evaluation of student questionnaires
- Based on annual reviews

Role of Peers

None

Role of Chair/Deans

- Chair or dean conducts intensive review
- Annual review conducted by chair

Results/Actions

- Summary review
- Unsatisfactory reviews trigger a required strategic development plan—faculty mentor in consultation with chair and/or dean

Appendix C

Interview Protocols and Survey Instrument

Appendix C
American Association for Higher Education
New Pathways II Project
Post-Tenure Review Outcomes Survey

This survey has been developed by the American Association for Higher Education as part of its work to assess the outcome and impact of post-tenure review of faculty, departments, and institutions. Your careful response to these questions will help us reflect the opinions of faculty and administrators on this topic. We ask that you respond to these questions based on your own understanding and experience with post-tenure review at your institution. Please feel free to briefly elaborate on any of your responses.

We value your perspectives and are most grateful for your participation.

Instructions

Please circle the number that best reflects your opinion.

1) How familiar are you with your institution's policy for the performance review of tenured faculty *(post-tenure review)?*

   1 Very familiar with policy

   2 Somewhat familiar with policy

   3 Not very familiar with policy

   4 Not at all familiar with policy

   5 Other *(please elaborate)*_____

2a) As you understand it, what is the primary purpose for post-tenure review at your institution? *(circle all that apply)*

   1 Review performance in order to assess if performance expectations are being met

   2 Assess individual performance in order to reward excellence

   3 Assess individual performance in order to remedy deficiencies

   4 Assess career development goals and establish plans for continued growth or redirection

   5 Increase institutional effectiveness and responsiveness

   6 Increase accountability to outside constituencies

   7 Other *(please specify)*_____

2b) In your opinion, what should the primary purpose for post tenure review be at your institution? *(circle all that apply)*

   1 Review performance in order to assess if performance expectations are being met

   2 Assess individual performance in order to reward excellence

   3 Assess individual performance in order to remedy deficiencies

   4 Assess career development goals and establish plans for continued growth or redirection

   5 Increase institutional effectiveness and responsiveness

   6 Increase accountability to outside constituencies

   7 Other *(please specify)* _____

3) In your opinion, how effective has the post-tenure review process been in achieving its primary purpose at your institution? *(circle one)*

1	2	3	4	5
Effective				Not Effective

4) If you circled 4 or 5 in Question 3 above, what is the major reason for this response? *(circle all that apply)*

1 Post-tenure review has shown little evidence of positive outcomes so far

2 Post-tenure review is not taken seriously because peers are unable or unwilling to constructively criticize each other—so no one knows if performance improvement is needed

3 Post-tenure review is not taken seriously because there is no significant follow-up action to the reviews

4 Post-tenure review is not taken seriously because there are no resources for faculty development or improvement

5 Post-tenure review is not taken seriously because there are no consequences for poor performance

5) In your opinion, how beneficial has post-tenure review been for the performance and/or development of faculty members within your immediate department? *(circle one)*

1	2	3	4	5
Beneficial				Not Beneficial

6) If you circled 4 or 5 in Question 5 above, what is the major reason for your response?

7) Have you been reviewed according to your institution's post-tenure procedures?

1 Yes. How many times?

2 No *(please skip to Question 13)*

8) If you have been reviewed, what was the overall result of your review? *(circle one)*

1 My work was assessed as meeting or exceeding expectations—no other outcome

2 My work was assessed as meeting or exceeding expectations and a professional career plan was developed as a normal part of the review process

3 My work was assessed as meeting or exceeding expectations and I was rewarded accordingly

4 My work was assessed to be in need of improvement and a professional plan was required and developed

5 Other *(please elaborate)*

9) How beneficial has the post-tenure review process been to your work as a faculty member? *(circle one)*

1	2	3	4	5
Beneficial				Not Beneficial

10a) If you circled 1 or 2 in Question 9 above, what is the major reason for your response?

10b) If you circled 4 or 5 in Question 9 above, what is the major reason for your response?

11) How beneficial has the post-tenure review process been to your professional/personal career development and planning *(circle one)*

1	2	3	4	5
Beneficial				Not Beneficial

12a) If you circled 1 or 2 in Question 11 above, what is the major reason for your response?

12b) If you circled 4 or 5 in Question 11 above, what is the major reason for your response?

	Yes	Somewhat	No	Insufficient experience to know
13) From your direct experience with post tenure review within your academic department/unit, please respond to the following questions regarding different components of the review:				
Is the process widely known and well understood?	1	2	3	4
Are the procedures clear?	1	2	3	4
Are the procedures followed in a fair fashion?	1	2	3	4
Are the procedures followed in a consistent fashion?	1	2	3	4
Are the review criteria clear?	1	2	3	4
Are the review criteria applied fairly?	1	2	3	4
Are the review criteria applied in a consistent fashion?	1	2	3	4
Is the documentation prepared by the faculty member manageable?	1	2	3	4
Are the peer review committee members selected appropriately?	1	2	3	4
Are the peer review committee members prepared and trained appropriately?	1	2	3	4
Is the peer review committee's role in the process clearly understood?	1	2	3	4
Is the department chairperson's role in the process clearly understood?	1	2	3	4
Is the dean's role in the process clearly understood?	1	2	3	4
Are the faculty appeal procedures adequate?	1	2	3	4
Are the possible outcomes from the review clear?	1	2	3	4
Are the possible outcomes from the review applied in a fair manner?	1	2	3	4
Is there an adequate range of rewards and development opportunities available following the review?	1	2	3	4
Does the review help with faculty reflection on past/present/future accomplishments and directions?	1	2	3	4
Do feedback and follow-up on the review occur?	1	2	3	4
Is there an adequate range of sanctions available following the review, if called for?	1	2	3	4

14) Do you think the composition of the peer review committee leads to a fair and rigorous review?

   1 Yes

   2 No

   Please elaborate: _____

15) Have you served on a post-tenure review committee?

   1 Yes

   2 No *(please skip to Question 18)*

	No opinion
	No
	Somewhat
	Yes

16) If you have served on a post-tenure committee, please respond to the following questions:

	Yes	Somewhat	No	No opinion
1 Did you feel appropriately prepared for this peer review role?	1	2	3	4
2 Were the peer review procedures clear?	1	2	3	4
3 In your view, was the peer review performed in a fair and objective manner?	1	2	3	4
4 Did the outcomes of the review result in a positive impact for the person under review?	1	2	3	4
5 Did your participation increase your knowledge of your colleagues' work?	1	2	3	4
6 Did your participation increase your appreciation of your colleagues' work?	1	2	3	4

17) In your opinion, are peer committees capable of rendering fair and objective recommendations regarding the evaluation and development of tenured faculty?

1	2	3	4	5
Capable				Not Capable

18) To what extent has post-tenure review affected annual review practices within your department/academic unit? *(circle one)*

   1 It has increased the rigor of annual review practices.

   2 It has prompted the department to reexamine its policies and procedures for annual review.

   3 It has diminished the rigor of annual review practices.

   4 It has not affected the rigor of annual review practices.

   5 Uncertain about the effect of post-tenure review on annual review practices.

   6 Too soon to assess.

   7 Other *(please elaborate)*_____

		Too little experience/too soon to know	No benefit	Minor benefit	Major benefit

19) Based on your direct experience with post-tenure review, have any of the following benefits been associated with the post-tenure review process within your department/academic unit?

	Too little/No benefit/Minor/Major			
1 Stimulates greater efforts in teaching	1	2	3	4
2 Stimulates greater efforts in research /scholarship/creative activity	1	2	3	4
3 Stimulates greater efforts in professional service and outreach	1	2	3	4
4 Stimulates greater efforts in university citizenship	1	2	3	4
5 Increases faculty accountability	1	2	3	4
6 Helps sustain senior faculty vitality	1	2	3	4
7 Increases opportunities for mid- and late-career transition planning	1	2	3	4
8 Establishes a culture and expectation for continuous growth and development	1	2	3	4
9 Provides opportunities for additional support for new professional directions	1	2	3	4
10 Facilitates exchange of information which leads to professional collaboration	1	2	3	4
11 Encourages departments to consider different workloads for members	1	2	3	4
12 Allows for comparison of standards for judging work across unit lines	1	2	3	4
13 Improves collegiality	1	2	3	4
14 Links departmental planning objectives with personal professional plans	1	2	3	4
15 Focuses attention on improvement of annual review procedures	1	2	3	4
16 Increases public confidence in higher education	1	2	3	4
17 Forestalls further external interference	1	2	3	4
18 Acts as a safeguard to tenure	1	2	3	4

19 Other benefits *(please specify)* _____

	Too little experience/too soon to know			
		No benefit		
			Minor benefit	
				Major benefit

20) Based on your direct experience with post-tenure review, have any of the following problems been associated with the implementation of post-tenure review within your department/academic unit?

1 Invasion of professional autonomy	1	2	3	4
2 Erosion of confidence in tenure	1	2	3	4
3 Excessive paperwork	1	2	3	4
4 Excessive time	1	2	3	4
5 Erosion of collegiality	1	2	3	4
6 Negative effect on risk-taking and scholarly pursuit of controversial areas of inquiry	1	2	3	4
7 Unevenness in application of criteria and standards within unit and/or across units	1	2	3	4
8 Unreasonable demands placed on university to support faculty improvement plans	1	2	3	4
9 No positive change in performance of individuals over the long term	1	2	3	4
10 Insufficient funds to support self-initiated faculty development plans	1	2	3	4
11 Insufficient funds to support required faculty development plans	1	2	3	4
12 Insufficient training for peers	1	2	3	4
13 Insufficient training for chairs/ department heads	1	2	3	4
14 Erosion of faculty professionalism	1	2	3	4
15 Hampers faculty recruitment efforts	1	2	3	4
16 Prompts effective senior faculty to feel devalued	1	2	3	4

17 Other problems *(please specify)*_____

_____

21) Based on your direct experience with post-tenure review, do you think that post-tenure review is worth the time and effort required? *(circle one)*

1 Yes, the benefits outweigh the costs.

2 No, the costs outweigh the benefits.

3 Not sure. Please elaborate on your response _____

_____

22) Do you think there are improvements that could be made to your institution's procedures that would make the post-tenure review process more beneficial, effective, and/or constructive? *(circle one)*

1 Yes

2 No

If yes, please suggest one or more major improvement: _____

_____

23) Is there anything else about the impact and outcomes associated with the post-tenure review process that you would like to share with us? (Please feel free to attach an extra page if you have extended comments.) _____

_____

_____

Background Information

We ask for the following demographic information so that we can determine if specific groups of respondents have unique experiences and/or ideas about post-tenure review. Data will be reported in aggregated form. In no instance will tabulated results be broken down in such a way that might lead to identification of a particular respondent.

Please circle the response that applies to you.

A) What is your gender?

Female 1

Male 2

B) What is your age?

Less than 30 years 1

31–45 years..................... 2

46–59 years..................... 3

60 years or older 4

C) What is your current rank?

Professor 1

Associate professor 2

Assistant professor............... 3

Instructor 4

No rank........................ 5

Other 6

D) If you hold rank, how many years have you held your current rank?

_____ years

E) Are you tenured at your institution?

Yes........................... 1

No 2

If yes, how long have you held tenure?

_____ years

F) How many years have you been employed at your current institution?

G) Do you hold an administrative appointment?

No 1

Yes........................... 2

Please circle appropriate administrative title:

Dept./division chair or head 1

Dean.......................... 2

Associate dean................... 3

Director 4

Other (please specify) 5

_____

H) At what campus are you employed?

_____

_____

I) Do you currently hold any of the following positions?

Chairperson 1

Dean/Director................... 2

Associate/Assistant Dean........... 3

Other 4

If yes, how many years have you held this position?

_____ years

J) Which of the following best describes your discipline?

1 Agriculture

2 Architecture & Environmental Design

3 Arts (including music & visual & performing arts)

4 Business, Marketing, & Management

5 Communications & Media

6 Computer & Information Science

7 Education

8 Teacher Education

9 Engineering

10 English and Literature

11 Foreign Languages

12 Health Sciences

13 Veterinary Medicine

14 Home Economics

15 Industrial Arts

16 Law

17 Library & Archival Sciences

18 Mathematics/Statistics

19 Natural Sciences: Biological Sciences

20 Natural Sciences: Physical Sciences

21 Parks & Recreation

22 Philosophy, Religion, & Theology

23 Physical Education

24 Protective Services (e.g., Criminal Justice, Fire Protection)

25 Psychology

26 Public Affairs

27 Science Technologies

28 Social Sciences & History

APPENDIX C

PROTOCOL

AMERICAN ASSOCIATION FOR HIGHER EDUCATION

NEW PATHWAYS II

POST-TENURE REVIEW OUTCOMES STUDY PROTOCOL

INDIVIDUAL INTERVIEW QUESTIONS

For All Interviewees: Faculty, Union Leaders

1) Please describe the purpose and goals of post-tenure review as you understand them at your university. Has post-tenure review achieved its goals? Why or why not?

2) Describe the outcomes of your own review. How effective was the process in satisfying the purposes and goals as you understand them? Please explain. Use specific examples whenever possible (without names).

3) Please describe the activities and amount of preparation you have invested in your own post-tenure review.

   • How much time (in terms of total hours) do you estimate is required in preparation?

   • Do you consider these activities time well spent? Please explain using specific examples to illustrate your experience.

4) Some faculty report that post-tenure review has changed behavior while others report it has not. What is your perception about this in terms of faculty within your department? If possible, please explain providing specific examples.

5) Some faculty report problems with post-tenure review while others do not. Where do you fall along this continuum? Please explain.

6) Likewise, some faculty see benefits while others do not. Where do you fall along this continuum? To whom and in what ways is post-tenure review most and least beneficial to faculty, administration, and external constituencies?

7) In your opinion, does the post-tenure review process fit (or not fit) within the larger institutional system of reward, professional development, and improvement? With which other campus practices is it connected?

8) From your experience, how, if at all, has the nature of faculty work (including collaborative work and work to advance departmental and institutional goals) changed as a function of post-tenure review?

9) What improvements do you think could be made in the process at your institution to enhance its effectiveness and benefit to the individual and the institution?

10) What is your reaction to the substance of the review, such as the criteria or standards used and the documentation required for the review? Are they clear? Too

quantitative? Too qualitative? Are faculty appropriately involved in shaping the criteria and setting standards?

11) If a professional improvement plan has been required:

- How was the plan developed? What was (is) helpful about it? What was (is) problematic about it?

- Do you think the professional development plan process accomplished what it was supposed to do?

- How did you feel when it was resolved/completed?

12) Deans only: What is your role as a dean in the process?

- What do you do to ensure that the post-tenure review process is consistently followed across departments and divisions?

- Is the dean's role in the process clear and appropriate?

APPENDIX C

PROTOCOL

AMERICAN ASSOCIATION FOR HIGHER EDUCATION
NEW PATHWAYS II
POST-TENURE REVIEW OUTCOMES STUDY PROTOCOL
FOCUS GROUP QUESTIONS

Questions for Chairs, Deans, and Chief Academic Officers

1) Please describe the purpose and goals of post-tenure review as you understand them at your university. Has post-tenure review achieved its goals? Why or why not?

2) Does the post-tenure review process fit (or not fit) within the larger institutional system of reward, professional development, and improvement? With which other campus practices is it connected?

3) Have you noted any changes in faculty performance because of the post-tenure review process? If so, please describe. If not, why do you think there has been little or no impact?

4) How would you characterize your time involvement in the process?

5) In your opinion and from your experience is post-tenure review worth the effort? Why or why not?

6) If university policy has a peer review component, is it effective? Why or why not?

7) What kinds of resources and types of tangible opportunities for development and improvement are most frequently provided (list examples)?

8) Have resources been sufficient?

9) Some report problems with post-tenure review while others do not. Where do you fall along this continuum? Please explain.

10) Likewise, some see benefits and others do not. To whom and in what ways is post-tenure review most and least beneficial? From your experience, how, if at all, has the nature of faculty work (including collaborative work and work to advance departmental and institutional goals) changed as a function of post-tenure review?

11) What improvements do you think could be made in the process to enhance its effectiveness and benefit to the individual and the institution?

12) As a chair (dean) is there any kind of support, guidance, skill building, or help that would enable you to deal more effectively with the post-tenure review process?

13) Are there other perspectives or points you'd like to make before we conclude?

APPENDIX D

Factor Analysis and
Structural Equation Modeling

Appendix D
Factor Analysis and Structural Equation Modeling

Factor Analysis

Items from the American Association for Higher Education (AAHE) survey were categorized using factor analysis. By using this type of analysis we grouped together items that were more highly related to one another than they were to other items in the survey and organized them into a smaller number of meaningful categories. When using this technique, it is expected that the higher interrelationship among items within factors (a group of related items) is due to some common underlying construct. By looking at the items that comprise a factor, it is possible to derive what the construct is and use that to name the factor.

A varimax rotation was used and the analysis produced 16 initial factors (those factors with eigenvalues greater than one). Some factors were combined with others or broken into smaller groups, resulting in 13 final factors or categories for statistical and reporting use.

1) Overall Value of the Post-Tenure Review Process
2) Peer Review Procedure
3) Public Nature of Faculty Work
4) Fairness of Procedures
5) Outcomes of Review
6) Understanding of Roles and Process
7) Benefit of Accountability
8) Culture of Professional Development
9) Stimulating Faculty Efforts
10) Preserving Tenure
11) Erosion of Faculty Values
12) Insufficient Resources
13) Administrative Burden

Table 1 contains a list of the final factors and the survey items that correspond to each factor.

Table 1
List of 13 Factors and Corresponding Items

Factor 1: Overall Value of the Post-Tenure Review Process

Item 10   How beneficial is the process to work as a faculty member?

Item 13   How beneficial is the process to professional/personal career development/planning?

Item 3   How effective is post-review process in achieving its primary purpose?

Item 6   Impact of review on performance/development of faculty members within department.

Item 25   Is post-tenure review worth the time and effort required?

Factor 2: Peer Review Procedure

Item 20   Are peer committees capable of rendering objective/helpful recommendations?

Item 19_A   Were the peer-review procedures clear?

Item 19_B   Did you feel prepared for the peer-review role?

Item 19_C   Was the peer review performed in a fair and objective manner?

Item 10_D   Did the outcome of the review result in positive faculty actions?

Factor 3: Public Nature of Faculty Work

Item 19_E   Did your participation increase your knowledge of your colleagues' work?

Item 19_F   Did your participation increase appreciation of your colleagues' work?

Factor 4: Fairness of Procedures

Item 16_C   Are the procedures followed in a fair fashion?

Item 16_F   Are the review criteria applied fairly?

Item 16_G   Are the review criteria followed in a consistent fashion?

Item 16_D   Are the procedures followed in a consistent fashion?

Item 16_N   Are possible outcomes applied in a fair manner?

Item 16_L   Are faculty appeal procedures adequate?

Item 24_G   Unevenness in application of criteria and standards within unit and/or across units.

Factor 5: Outcomes of Review

Item 16_O   Is there an adequate range of rewards and development opportunities available?

Item 16_R   Is there an adequate range of sanctions available if called for?

Item 16_P   Does the review help with faculty reflection on past/present/future accomplishments/directions?

Item 16_Q   Does follow-up occur based on the review?

Item 16_M   Are possible outcomes from the review clear?

Factor 6: Understanding of Roles and Process

Item 16_J   Is the department chair's role in the process understood?

Item 16_A   Is the process widely known and well understood?

Item 16_K   Is the dean's role in the process understood?

Item 16_B   Are the procedures clear?

Item 16_E   Are the review criteria clear?

Item 16_I   Are peer review committee members prepared and trained appropriately?

Item 1   How familiar with institution's policy for review/development of tenured faculty?

Factor 7: Benefit of Accountability

Item 23_K   Encourages departments to consider different workloads for members.

Item 23_L   Allows for comparison of standards for judging work across unit lines.

Item 23_N   Links departmental planning objectives with personal professional plans.

Item 23_J   Facilitates exchange of information which leads to professional collaboration.

Item 23_I   Provides opportunities for additional support for new professional directions.

Item 23_G   Increases opportunities for mid- and late-career transition planning.

Item 23_O   Focuses attention on improvement of annual review procedures.

Item 23_M   Improves collegiality.

Item 23_H   Establishes a culture and expectation for continuous growth and development.

Factor 8: Culture of Professional Development

Item 23_I   Provides opportunities for additional support for new professional directions.

Item 23_G   Increases opportunities for mid- and late-career transition planning.

Item 23_H   Establishes a culture and expectation for continuous growth and development.

Factor 9: Stimulating Faculty Efforts

Item 23_A   Stimulates greater efforts in teaching.

Item 23_C   Stimulates greater efforts in professional service and outreach.

Item 23_D   Stimulates greater efforts in university citizenship.

Item 23_B   Stimulates greater efforts in research.

Item 23_F   Helps sustain senior faculty vitality.

Factor 10: Preserving Tenure

Item 23_R   Acts as a safeguard to tenure.

Item 23_E   Increases faculty accountability.

Item 23_Q   Forestalls further external interference.

Item 23_P   Increases public confidence in higher education.

Factor 11: Erosion of Faculty Values

Item 24_N   Erosion of faculty professionalism.

Item 24_B   Erosion of confidence in tenure.

Item 24_F   Negative effect on risk-taking and scholarly pursuit of controversial areas of inquiry (academic freedom).

Item 24_A   Invasion of professional autonomy.

Item 24_E   Erosion of collegiality.

Item 14_P   Prompts effective senior faculty to feel devalued.

Factor 12: Insufficient Resources

Item 24_K   Insufficient funds to support required faculty development plans.

Item 24_J   Insufficient funds to support self-initiated faculty development plans.

Item 24_L   Insufficient training for peers.

Item 24_M   Insufficient training for chairs/department heads.

Factor 13: Administrative Burden

Item 24_D   Excessive time.

Item 24_C   Excessive paperwork.

Item 16_H   Is the documentation prepared by the faculty member manageable?

Category scores were then created for each factor by averaging the scores for the items within the category. The category scores were scaled and coded so that a lower score was typically more positive and ranged from 1 to 3 points. This scale was chosen because it was congruent with most of the items on the AAHE survey and afforded the least amount of recoding. Table 2 contains the list of items recoded for category creation and how they were rescored.

Table 2

Item Recoding for Category Scores

Item Recoding for Category Scores

Item 25. Raw score is on 3-point scale: (Yes; Yes, on Balance; No): recoded for the category calculation as Yes = 1; Yes on Balance = 1; No = 3.

Items 3, 6, 10, 13, 20 – Recode 7-point scale into 3-point scale: 1 = 1, 2 = 1, 3 = 2, 4 = 3, 5 = 3, 6 = Missing, 7 = Missing.

Item 16_H and 24_G are reverse scored for the category score (to be consistent with the direction of other items in the category): 1 = 3, 2 = 2, 3 = 1.

Structural Equation Model

To more fully understand what makes the post-tenure review process valuable in the minds of faculty, department chairs, and deans, the categories derived from the factor analysis were used in a structural equation model designed to predict the outcome: "Overall Value of the Post-Tenure Review Process" (Factor 1). Using AMOS 3.2 (a common statistical package designed to perform this type of analysis), the categories were entered into a measurement model as direct drivers (predictors) of Overall Value of the Post-Tenure Review Process using the Maximum Likelihood Estimate approach and the covariance matrix of the items. Nonsignificant drivers were removed, until the initial model was generated. Figure 1 presents the initial model and the standardized values relating to it.

Figure 1
Initial Model of Overall Value

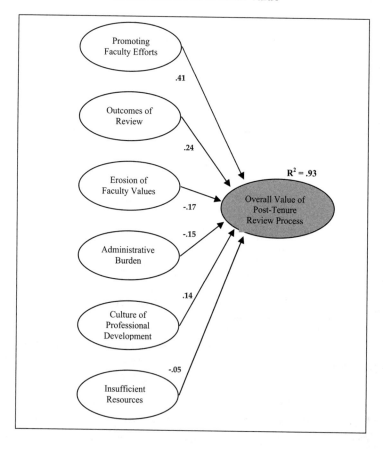

Although the category "Culture of Professional Development" fits the model at the first level, it appears to have a relationship or influence on the other categories in the model as well. This was proposed by the modification indices suggested by the analysis of the initial model. Given this, and the expectation that Culture of Professional Development would serve as an actor that influenced the other drivers in the model, an expanded model was tested with Culture of Professional Development acting as a secondary driver in the model. The fit of this expanded model was reasonable and corresponded to the authors' understanding and expectations. Thus, this expanded model was adopted as the final model of what creates or drives overall value in the post-tenure review process. Figure 2 presents the final expanded model.

Figure 2
Extended Model of Overall Value

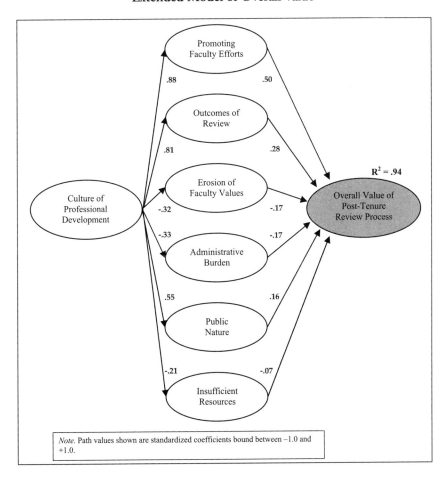

Note. Path values shown are standardized coefficients bound between −1.0 and +1.0.

Explanation of the Expanded Model

The path values presented in the model are standardized coefficients; therefore, we are able to use them to show the magnitude of the category's influence on the outcomes of "Overall Value of the Post-Tenure Review Process" and make relative comparisons to the influence of other categories. What is compelling about the model is the strength of the prediction. The model predicts at .94, which is considered to be a very powerful prediction coefficient. Perfect prediction would carry the value of 1.00.

These relative comparisons result in the identification of a category's influence on the overall prediction. A category that has a strong predictive influence is referred to a major driver, one with considerable influence is identified as a moderate driver, and a category with weak influence is known as a minor driver.